CW01335905

How to Read People Like a Book

Uncover Hidden Body Language Cues and Unlock People's Psychology so You Can Predict Human Behavior

© Copyright 2023 - All rights reserved.

The content contained within this book may not be reproduced, duplicated, or transmitted without direct written permission from the author or the publisher.

Under no circumstances will any blame or legal responsibility be held against the publisher, or author, for any damages, reparation, or monetary loss due to the information contained within this book, either directly or indirectly.

Legal Notice:

This book is copyright protected. It is only for personal use. You cannot amend, distribute, sell, use, quote, or paraphrase any part, or the content within this book, without the consent of the author or publisher.

Disclaimer Notice:

Please note the information contained within this document is for educational and entertainment purposes only. All effort has been executed to present accurate, up-to-date, reliable, and complete information. No warranties of any kind are declared or implied. Readers acknowledge that the author is not engaging in the rendering of legal, financial, medical, or professional advice. The content within this book has been derived from various sources. Please consult a licensed professional before attempting any techniques outlined in this book.

By reading this document, the reader agrees that under no circumstances is the author responsible for any losses, direct or indirect, that are incurred as a result of the use of the information contained within this document, including, but not limited to, errors, omissions, or inaccuracies.

Free Bonus from Andy Gardner

Hi!

My name is Andy Gardner, and first off, I want to THANK YOU for reading my book.

Now you have a chance to join my exclusive email list related to human psychology and self-development so you can get the ebook below for free as well as the potential to get more ebooks for free! Simply click the link below to join.

P.S. Remember that it's 100% free to join the list.

Access your free bonuses here:
https://livetolearn.lpages.co/andy-gardner-how-to-read-people-like-a-book-paperback/

Table of Contents

INTRODUCTION 1
CHAPTER 1: THE ART OF OBSERVATION 3
CHAPTER 2: 10 TIPS FOR DECODING FACIAL EXPRESSIONS 13
CHAPTER 3: ANALYZING GESTURES AND POSTURES 24
CHAPTER 4: LYING EYES: DETECTING LIES AND DECEIT 38
CHAPTER 5: UNDERSTANDING PROXIMITY 48
CHAPTER 6: TONE OF VOICE AND HOW TO UNDERSTAND IT 59
CHAPTER 7: CULTURAL CONTEXT AND NON-VERBAL CUES 68
CHAPTER 8: INTUITION: TRUSTING YOUR GUT 79
CHAPTER 9: APPLYING YOUR KNOWLEDGE 89
CONCLUSION 102
HERE'S ANOTHER BOOK BY ANDY GARDNER THAT YOU MIGHT LIKE 104
FREE BONUS FROM ANDY GARDNER 105
REFERENCES 106

Introduction

Have you ever been in a situation where you wished you could read minds? Knowing what people think and feel can make you a better communicator, and you can anticipate and protect yourself against harm by gaining insight into their intentions. Unfortunately, mind-reading is impossible, but there are other powerful tools to help you read people like a book. Learning to read body language, uncover hidden body language cues, and unlock a person's psychology can allow you to predict human behavior.

Many people don't know that most communication occurs through non-verbal cues. It is key to how people express themselves, show their emotions, and reveal their attitudes and intentions. Non-verbal cues complement verbal interactions and support communications that words can't. Hence, mastering the art of body language is essential.

Looking for non-verbal cues allows you to confirm your suspicions. A person's body language can either verify or falsify their claims. If a person says one thing, but their body language says another, you can tell they're lying. Paying attention to non-verbal cues also teaches you to be more empathetic. You learn to spot signs that someone is anxious or uncomfortable and respond accordingly.

Learning to read non-verbal cues is a skill that can be acquired and practiced. However, it requires honing your attention to detail, observation, and interpretation skills. You must pick up on subtle cues like posture, tone of voice, facial expressions, and other body gestures to read people like a book. This book is the ultimate guide to reading humans and becoming an excellent communicator.

This book has crucial skills and tips for becoming an effective communicator. You learn to lean into your instincts when observing gestures and know when others are lying. You'll understand how to read a person's emotions and level of honesty by observing their body language.

This book will show what can be learned about a person's body posture in communications and discover the different postures. You'll know what it means when someone holds an open or closed posture and what this reveals about their personality or engagement level. Chapter four teaches you how to protect yourself against deception. Many people rely on deception when communicating with others, so learning to detect it helps you easily tell when others are lying and when they have ill intentions.

Another essential factor you learn is the need for proximity when deciphering peoples' non-verbal cues and how different tones of voice convey different emotions and meanings. You'll learn the importance of context in interpreting messages, such as cultural norms, values, and social influences. You'll understand how each person's background influences their communication efforts and body language.

The final chapter provides in-depth information on applying the knowledge and skills you've obtained throughout the book in numerous contexts, such as in the workplace, social situations, and personal relationships. Tips and strategies for using body language to improve communication, build stronger relationships, and gain insight into human behavior are included.

When you have read the book, you should have a deeper understanding of non-verbal cues using them to understand and communicate with others effectively. With dedication, patience, and practice, you can incorporate these skills into your daily life in different situations and read people like a book.

Chapter 1: The Art of Observation

People don't only communicate with their words. In fact, 65% of communication is through body language. However, many only pay attention to the spoken part of a conversation, forgetting that many thoughts and emotions are often non-verbal. For instance, a person can joke or laugh during a conversation, but if you pay attention to their facial expressions, certain cues can reflect whether they are sad or irritated. The same applies to lying. You might assume someone is telling the truth, but one look in their eyes can reveal they aren't being straightforward. Body language is a strong tool. By learning to interpret certain cues, you will better understand what the other person is communicating.

Observing those around you can allow you to interpret body language.
https://www.pexels.com/photo/woman-facing-the-ocean-during-day-169908/

You can only have successful professional and personal relationships by learning communication skills, and understanding body language is one of the most significant keys to communication. Sometimes a person can express how they truly feel without saying a word. Some of the loudest messages are through body language. For instance, you argue with your partner and say hurtful things, and they don't respond but sit with their arms crossed instead. This indicates that they feel attacked and are protecting themselves from you. When you understand the meaning behind this cue, you will realize how your words hurt, *so sit back down and apologize!*

Body language is the non-verbal cues people emit to express their feelings and thoughts. Usually, it includes facial expressions, body movements, tone and volume of your voice, and various other signals. A person's body language can express their true and real emotions since these gestures are often made unconsciously. Hence, it reveals a person's truest nature which they can't hide. You can read others by paying attention to the signals their bodies give through the art of observation.

What Is the Art of Observation?

Observation is a mental process using thoughts and vision. However, it is different from seeing. When you see something, you only look at what is on the surface, but observing is a more complex and deeper process. The art of observation involves creating an unconscious or conscious link to the information you already have. For instance, you will link what you consciously or unconsciously perceive from the speaker to the information which you already have about body language and be able to interpret what they are communicating.

Developing the skill of observation means always watching people with an inquisitive mind to understand what they want to say but can't or don't.

The Significance of Observation in Body Language

Although you aren't aware of it, you pick up various non-verbal cues daily. You only interpret these signals when you truly observe others' body language. However, nowadays, people barely listen to each other, let alone notice someone else's physical or facial expressions. They are either waiting for their turn to speak, so they aren't fully engaged in the conversation and are more likely preoccupied with what they will say. Or they are looking at their phones and distracted, so they don't even pay attention to the speaker.

Observation requires letting go of distractions and personal bias and only paying attention to what someone is communicating, verbally and non-verbally. Since body language often involves subtle cues, you will miss many signals if you aren't completely observant. For instance, a person usually smiles with their mouth and eyes. However, most people only pay attention to the lips. A genuine smile involves crinkles at the corner of the eyes you will only notice through proper observation. The person's smile isn't genuine if these crinkles aren't there. Depending on the context, this observation can tell you a lot about the person. For instance, you share your good news with a friend, and they congratulate you with a big smile, but on further observation, you notice their smile isn't genuine, indicating they you are faking their reaction. By learning this information, you will be careful with future interactions because they don't have your best interest at heart.

Or you are with friends, and one is smiling, but their eyes tell another story. They could be upset but hide their feelings with a fake smile. Once you notice your friend might not be OK, inquire and try to cheer them up or wait for the appropriate moment to check on them. These, and many more, are examples of why observation is significant in body language. It shows things that you won't notice with other methods.

However, one cue can have more than one interpretation. For instance, in the example above about the good news, it is possible that your friend received bad news, so they couldn't truly celebrate your accomplishment. Don't hesitate to ask questions to understand the person's intentions better. The following chapters include the meanings behind various signals and cues like the nose, teeth, posture, etc., revealing more information.

Skills to Become an Effective Observer

Some people are more observant than others but fret not. You can improve this ability by learning essential skills. Observation skills are specific qualities allowing you to use some or all of your senses to acknowledge the received information, analyze, and understand it.

These skills are simple, and you can easily implement them to become an effective observer.

Know the Person

Knowing the person you are observing gives you a better perspective on their communication. You can still read a stranger, but understanding the person will make your interpretation of their body language more accurate, especially since one gesture can have various meanings. For instance, your co-worker is in a meeting sitting with her hand on her chin. This gesture usually indicates someone is either defiant or in deep thought. You know, she only sits this way when she is thinking really hard. Hence, you can interpret her body language based on your knowledge of her.

Increase Interactions

Interact more with others so you can learn the different body language signals, broaden your perspective, and improve your observation skills. Try to read everyone you meet, even if it isn't necessary. Consider it practice. Force yourself to focus on others. Eventually, observation will come naturally to you.

Watch Strangers

It doesn't mean staring at others and making them uncomfortable. Go to a coffee shop, a quiet restaurant, or just wherever you are, and watch people. Observe their body language and how they interact in different situations. For instance, notice the difference between someone focused on their work with a serious facial expression and another sitting in a relaxed posture reading a book. You might encounter a couple arguing or on a date. Notice the difference in the tone of voice, gesture, body language, etc. It is a great way to practice observation skills and interpret people's signals.

Journaling

Write down your encounters with other people and your observations from watching strangers. You can do this while watching them. For instance, you can write, "Angry people often clench their fists" or "The couple on a date often mirror each other's gestures."

Be Focused

Observation requires patience and focus. If you are stressed, distracted, or rushing around, you cannot read and comprehend what the other person is signaling. Reading body language involves simultaneously noticing every detail about the person's facial expression, tone of voice, eyes, posture, etc. If you aren't present in the moment and are preoccupied with past regrets, future concerns, or other distractions, you will miss many messages that the other person is sending.

Teach yourself to slow down, pause, and quiet your mind to silence all the noises in your head so you can focus outward instead of inward. Mindfulness techniques like yoga, meditation, and breathing exercises effectively keep you focused and living in the moment.

Remove Distractions

It is always polite to put your cell phone down and pay attention to the people around you. Looking at your phone each time you receive a message will not only distract you from the conversation, but you will also miss certain quick or subtle signals like a non-genuine smile. According to American author Tom DeMarco, it usually takes about fifteen minutes to refocus once you are distracted. Therefore, it is recommended to remove all distractions when talking to others.

Employ Your Memory

Observation requires a strong memory. Sometimes, you will need to recall specific aspects of a person to get a better read of their feelings or thoughts. For instance, does your co-worker often cross their arms during meetings, or is this the first time? If this is the first time, this could require further observation.

Think Critically

Thinking critically is an essential skill in observation. You can question what you observe, use reason, and analyze the observation.

Now that you understand the necessary skills in the art of observation, you should apply specific techniques in every conversation for better interactions.

Active Listening

Active listening is a communication and observation skill. You aren't only hearing what the other person is saying but also trying to understand what is beyond their words to learn their intention and show that you are engaged using your body language or by asking questions. When you use active listening, you become fully attentive and empathetic to what the other person says.

American psychologist Carl Rogers developed a technique called "reflective listening," mostly intended for psychologists. This method summarizes what the speaker says using their words instead of paraphrasing and using yours. Using this technique makes the other person feel understood, and you can retain much of the information.

Active listening techniques are:

- Listening without judgment or criticism. Keep an open mind and understand things from their perspective, not yours.
- Exerting effort to understand what the other person says, not merely waiting for your turn to speak or respond.
- Ask open-ended questions to further the conversation and show interest in the other person encouraging them to talk more, like, "How do you think you could have handled the situation differently?" Also, ask follow-up questions to understand better what the person says and collect more information. For instance, "Let me see if I get this correct. You are saying you have had it with your job and want to quit, right?" This way prevents miscommunication and allows you to respond accurately.
- Use non-verbal signals like nodding or smiling when appropriate. Notice their non-verbal cues, too. Use verbal cues to show you are paying attention, like, "I see" or "I understand how you feel."
- Maintain eye contact to show the other person they have your full attention. Consider removing distractions, like setting your phone on silent so you won't constantly look away during the conversation.
- Be fully present, attentive, and engaged in the conversation.
- Avoid interruptions as it shows you aren't interested in what they say and just want to give your opinion or change the subject.
- When asked for your opinion or advice, give it to show you have fully grasped what the other person has conveyed.
- Reflect and paraphrase their words like "I understand what you mean by feeling suffocated in your relationship, and sometimes you wish you could run away." It shows the other person that you are paying attention to everything they say.
- Notice the silence. When they pause and look at you, they expect your response. Respond immediately, or they might

think you aren't paying attention.

- Be Patient. Some people struggle to express their thoughts or feelings. Avoid finishing their sentences since this makes them uncomfortable, and they might think you are frustrated. Give them time, and don't fill the silence.

Types of Active Listening

Therapeutic Listening

Therapeutic listening lets someone, such as a family member or a friend, vent about whatever has upset them. Your role is to play the therapist by only listening to what they say, refraining from judgment, or giving advice unless they ask for it. Sympathize with what they are going through while maintaining eye contact and sending them supportive and understanding signals like nodding your head.

Critical Listening

This is listening while applying reason to analyze the other person's words without personal bias or opinions. Critical listening is beneficial when interacting with people who have a certain goal. For instance, a salesperson will say anything to sell you their product. If you take what they say at face value or are impressed by their charm, you might buy something you don't need. When applying critical listening, you use logic to interpret their information so you can make the right decision.

Full Listening

Full listening means giving your undivided attention to the speaker to comprehend what they say. Usually, this requires one of the active listening techniques like asking follow-up questions or paraphrasing the speaker's words.

Deep Listening

This technique is understanding the other person's perspective. In this case, you observe non-verbal and verbal signals, encouraging the speaker to trust you and express their emotions and thoughts.

Empathetic Observation

Empathy is understanding what someone says emotionally and seeing things from their perspective. It is a rare ability that involves putting yourself in another person's shoes and experiencing their emotions. For instance, your friend tells you about their pain after losing their father. Even though both your parents are alive, you can envision yourself in your friend's situation and experience their feelings.

Empathetic observation is paying attention to the other person's verbal and non-verbal cues and applying empathy to connect with them emotionally. Some people struggle to express their feelings, and half of what they aren't actually saying is revealed in their body language. Using empathetic observation, you can read their physical cues and listen to their tone of voice to understand and experience their feelings as your own. In other words, this technique moves you from the role of the spectator or listener to someone involved in their story, giving you a deeper understanding of their experience.

Situational Awareness

Situation awareness (SA) results from a mental process of observation to collect and understand specific information. You respond by predicting the situation's possible outcome. Although these predictions are not always correct, they can provide a better insight into future events. In other words, it is being aware of your surroundings, collecting the information from various sources, decoding it to assess any risk, and planning your next steps accordingly.

The purpose of this technique is to be aware of the things that don't make sense or don't belong in your environment. When applied correctly, situational awareness can save your life.

The three levels of situational awareness are:
1. **Perception.** Observing and collecting data by focusing on the significant and relevant information around you while ignoring the unimportant ones.
2. **Representation.** Linking your current observations with your previous experience.
3. **Projection.** Using your comprehension of the situation to anticipate what will happen.

Situational awareness can be applied in every aspect of your life. For instance, during a conversation, a person should be aware of every word that is said, like peoples' names, the tenses used, how they convey their message, etc. They should observe peoples' verbal and non-verbal cues to process and analyze the information and prepare the proper response.

Even when watching a TV show, you apply situational awareness by remembering the characters' names, stories, their relationships with one another, the dialogue, and the story's location.

Intuition in Observation

Intuition is the gut feeling that often tells you when something doesn't feel right and you shouldn't go through with it. For instance, a co-worker tells you to invest in a side project with them but deep down, you feel this isn't going to work out. This is your intuition warning you that it isn't a safe endeavor. More often than not, your gut feeling is correct. It isn't like a sixth sense. Your brain employs cues and signals from others or your surroundings and uses past experiences to make an informed decision - this is intuition.

Intuition is significant in observation because it gives you a sensation of the signals others send. For instance, you meet someone and sense they are kind. You don't know why, but you feel comfortable around them. Your brain has unconsciously collected certain cues about the person, like a warm and genuine smile, resulting in the gut feeling.

While observing others, you will often feel their emotions like fear, joy, sadness, or even if they are good or bad people. You have reached this conclusion based on similar patterns encountered in the past. For instance, you know this person is sad because you've seen sad facial expressions before, so the brain quickly makes the association. This process usually occurs unconsciously. You know this person isn't happy, or your co-worker isn't trustworthy, but you don't know how you know.

Intuition is a powerful tool. Never ignore it when interpreting other peoples' body language and how you feel about them.

Tips to Trust Your Instincts When Reading Body Language

Often, people don't trust their intuition. However, collecting this information will make you confident with your decisions.

- Notice the non-verbal cues others communicate and whether they match their words or not.
- If they don't, consider what their intentions or feelings are and if there is a possibility that they aren't aware of being untruthful.
- Ask yourself what they aren't revealing and if their responses are unusual.
- Notice if they are hesitant or confident with their information and what their answers tell you about them and the topic of

discussion.
- Reflect on your relationship with them. Ask yourself whether this change in their personality is because they have a hidden agenda or merely want to bond with you.
- If their words don't match their actions, what does that say about them and their intentions? For instance, they could be confused or pretending to be someone they are not.
- Is their body language more of a habit and doesn't reflect their feelings or true intentions? For instance, some people have a habit of slouching. It is how they carry themselves, so you can't interpret it as a sign of boredom.

Treat the art of observation like real art or poetry. You can only develop by living in the moment and engaging with the world around you. Rather than only listening to or communicating with people on the surface, dig deep and analyze what they aren't saying out loud.

People's facial expressions and body language will reveal their true identity and what they hide. Notice the sadness behind their eyes, the anger behind their smile, or the discomfort in their shoulders. You will develop strong communication skills since you understand the people in your life just by looking at them.

Observing others can also protect you against people lying or keeping things from you. Rather than taking the information given to you at face value, you will notice if someone is tricking you.

Observation is a necessary skill to understand others during interactions. Train yourself to observe rather than look, actively listen, ask follow-up questions, remove distractions, fully engage in the conversation, summarize what others tell you, and always be present in the here and now.

No one is born with strong observation skills. You can develop these skills by using all the tips mentioned in this chapter. Even though it takes time, it is worth it when you realize its impact on your relationships. Don't be in a rush. Learning any new skill isn't easy, but eventually, you will get there, and it will become second nature.

Chapter 2: 10 Tips for Decoding Facial Expressions

Nothing is more expressive than the human face. You don't need to speak to convey your emotions since your eyes, lips, eyebrows, nose, and cheeks reveal your feelings. Although body language is open to many interpretations and some gestures vary from one country to another, facial expressions are the same worldwide. For instance, everyone smiles when they are happy, frowns when sad, raises their eyebrows when surprised, and opens their eyes wide when scared.

Facial expressions are significant in communication.
https://unsplash.com/photos/_VkwiVNCNfo?utm_source=unsplash&utm_medium=referral&utm_content=creditShareLink

You can't talk about facial expressions without mentioning Dr. Paul Ekman, a researcher in the field of body language and facial expressions, and most of the information the world has today is credited to him. He developed the theory that facial expressions are universal, especially those related to basic human emotions, contempt, disgust, anger, sadness, happiness, surprise, and fear.

This chapter covers the significance of facial expressions in communication and provides tips on decoding various cues.

The Significance of Facial Expression in Communication

Facial expressions significantly impact communication and social interactions. When someone keeps something from you, or you feel that their words don't match their actions, their facial expressions can reveal their true intentions. Most people struggle with expressing their emotions. They pretend to be happy when their heart breaks or act as if they are OK when something bothers them. However, no matter how hard they hold in their emotions, their face will always give them away. Look closely at a person's facial cues instead of listening to their words to ascertain if they are hiding something.

Expressing Emotions

People often use various facial cues to express their emotions during social interactions. When both parties are aware of what the other person is feeling, it creates trust and the opportunity for a genuine connection. Facial expressions can convey many emotions so that you can uncover the person's true feelings.

When you experience emotions like happiness, sadness, or fear, they are unconsciously conveyed on your face. For instance, someone receives good news, and they can't stop smiling no matter how hard they try. When you look at their face, you immediately notice they are happy. You can decode people's feelings by paying attention to their facial expressions.

Expressing Needs

When people's needs aren't met, they convey their disappointment with negative facial expressions like pain or anger. People often express themselves with these cues because they want others to recognize and respect their needs. More often than not, people hesitate to ask for what

Chapter 3: Analyzing Gestures and Postures

Non-verbal signs, including gestures and postures in communication, aid in interpreting hidden signals. These signs can convey a lot of information, feelings, and intentions.

This chapter will introduce you to the value and methods for understanding these gestures and postures.

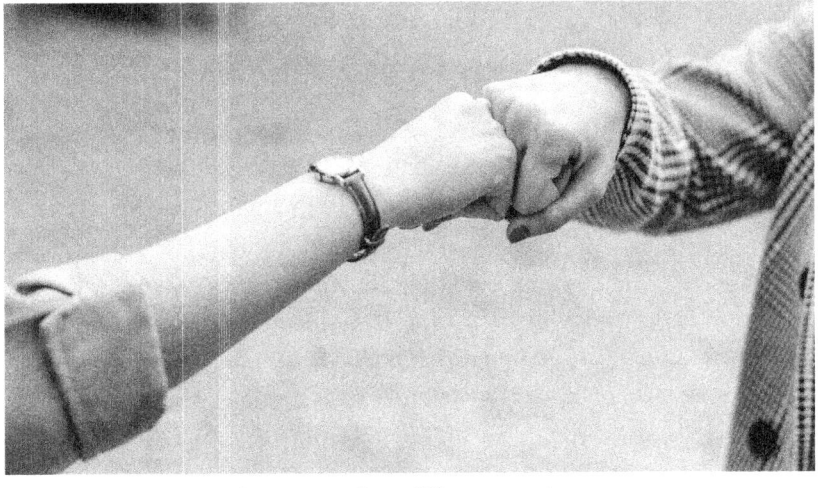

Gestures can have different meanings.
https://unsplash.com/photos/vlPweKlWOmg?utm_source=unsplash&utm_medium=referral&utm_content=creditShareLink

experience and often causes relationship issues. Unlike the other facial expressions, it is displayed on one side of the face.

Facial cues that convey hate and contempt are:

- Raising one side of the mouth

A sad person doesn't only frown, an angry person doesn't only yell, and a happy person doesn't only smile. Human emotions are complicated, and people don't often say how they feel out loud. Nothing emotes more than the human face. American poet Sara Teasdale wrote a poem called "Faces." She discussed that people reveal their secrets when you look them in the eyes. She mentioned feeling guilty about piercing peoples' disguises through their facial expressions. Using her poetic genius, Sara wrote that people hide many secrets deep inside, and they often reveal them without making a sound. She ended the poem by wondering if people could also know so much about her just by looking at her.

As Sarah revealed in her poem, the ability to read facial expressions is a powerful skill. People can ask for help with one look or express grief with a few expressions without using words. People can even scream in pain with their eyes. Like Sara, you can pierce peoples' disguises by decoding facial expressions.

Every feature of the human face can reflect how a person feels. During social interactions, keep your eyes on people's faces. Notice their blinking, eyes, lips, nostrils, cheeks, and teeth, as they can tell you how the person genuinely feels. Since many people maintain eye contact, they don't usually focus on other parts of the face. However, you can always do a quick scan to observe the other features. It won't be easy at first but keep practicing, and eventually, decoding these signals will come naturally.

Never ignore the context. Before you decode the facial expressions, take a moment to consider the context. Is this a happy or sad occasion? What factors contribute to these feelings? Set the scene so you can read the other person's facial cues accurately.

Facial expressions are essential for communication. Without them, it will feel like communicating with others in the dark. These cues give you an idea of how the person feels, even if they fabricate their emotions or fake a smile. You will react once you learn to decode these signals accordingly.

Facial cues that convey fear are:
- The mouth is wide open
- Stretched and drawn back or tensed lips
- The upper white part of the eye shows
- The lower eyelid is drawn up and tensed, and the upper eyelid is raised
- Wrinkles in the center of the forehead
- The eyebrows are drawn together and raised in a flat line

Surprise

One of the most common signs of surprise is the eyebrow flash, lowering and raising your eyebrow in less than a second. It also conveys that the other person is attracted to you.

Facial cues that convey surprise are:
- The jaws drop open, the teeth are parted but not tensed, and the mouth isn't stretched
- The eyelids are open, showing the top and bottom white of the eyes
- Wrinkles show across the forehead
- The skin under the eyebrows is stretched
- Curved and raised eyebrows

Disgust

People squint their eyes when they are disgusted to increase their visual acuity to find the source of the emotion.

Facial cues that convey disgust are:
- Raised cheeks
- Wrinkled nose
- Exposing the upper teeth
- Raising the upper lips
- Narrowing of the eyes

Hate and Contempt

Hate and contempt reflect negative emotions of offense, disrespect, and dislike. Contempt is one of the worst feelings a person can

Anger

According to a study published in Psychological Science, one of the most recognizable signs of anger is lowered eyebrows. The study determined that the participants found angry people untrustworthy because of their lowered eyebrows and squinted eyes. You can tell so much about a person by looking at their eyes. When you can't see the windows to someone's soul, it can be hard to trust them.

Most people conceal their anger in public and hide social cues revealing their emotions because it goes against social norms. They convey their emotions by lowering their eyebrows, which sends the message without causing a scene. For instance, a child misbehaves, and his mother gets mad but doesn't want to raise her voice in public. Instead, she stares at him, lowering her eyebrows to signal her anger.

You can always identify these facial expressions because it is easy to tell when someone is angry. Angry people can be dangerous and harm you or themselves. Once you notice someone is angry, walk away until they calm down.

Facial cues that convey anger are:

- The lower jaw sticks out
- Dilated nostrils
- Lips are pressed firmly against one another with the corners pointing down, or they can take a square shape as if the person is shouting
- An intense stare
- Tensing the lower lip
- Lines form between the eyebrows
- The eyebrows are lowered and drawn together

Fear

The facial expressions of fear are very beneficial. The eyes open wide to improve peripheral vision to help you become more aware of your surroundings. The mouth opens wide so the person can inhale more oxygen, in case they must fight or run away, and to prepare if you need to scream for help. When you recognize someone is afraid, you naturally experience the same emotion and convey it on your face because you sense a present danger.

the French neurologist Guillaume Duchenne, who studied facial expressions to determine the cues behind a genuine smile. A real or Duchenne smile is authentic and reflects real happiness, joy, and enjoyment. It usually occurs by contracting the cheekbone and lip muscles. The cheeks lift, the mouth turns up, and eye sockets crinkle, creating wrinkles on the side of the eyes called "crow's feet." This usually happens involuntarily, but it is the biggest sign of true happiness.

A Duchenne smile is infectious and can't be faked. When someone smiles genuinely at you, you usually can't help smiling back and experiencing positive and warm feelings towards them. According to Western University in London research, peoples' brains can differentiate between genuine and fake smiles. If you don't notice the Duchenne smile signals, the smile is either polite or non-genuine.

Facial cues that convey happiness are:
- Tension or wrinkles in the lower part of the eyelids
- A wrinkle that starts at the nose and extends to the lip
- Sometimes the mouth will be parted, and the teeth exposed

Sadness

It is possible to fake sadness, and recognizing this emotion isn't easy. Unlike happiness, sadness doesn't have strong tell-tale signs like smiling. Some people prefer to hide this emotion for various reasons, like the misconception that it makes them look weak or don't want to make others uncomfortable. Therefore, it is hard to identify when someone is sad. The sad facial expression usually lasts longer because it is a powerful emotion that doesn't go away easily. Some people can convey sad facial expressions when another person is angry to calm them down and diffuse the situation.

Facial cues that convey sadness are:
- The lower lip is pouting
- The jaw draws upward
- The lip corners are drawn down
- The inner corners under the eyebrows' skin rise
- The eyebrows' inner corners are drawn in and upward

- Blinking too little reflects when someone tries to control their eyes
- Quick blinking signifies discomfort and distress

Eyebrows

Often people don't pay attention to the eyebrows, but they are no less significant than the eyes in revealing someone's true feelings.

Common meanings behind the eyebrows:

- The inner corners of the eyebrows drawn up reflect sadness
- Lowering both your eyebrows conveys fear, sadness, or anger
- Arched and raised eyebrows emphasize fear or surprise

Mouth and Lips

People express other emotions with their mouths besides happiness. The mouth is a prominent feature since it can mask true feelings conveyed in other facial features. For instance, if you are angry and staring intensely but don't want others to notice, you can conceal it with a fake smile.

Common meanings behind the mouth and lips are:

- Covering the mouth indicates the person is hiding a secret
- Pursing the lips reflects displeasure
- Biting the lips conveys anxiety
- The mouth corners drawn down reflect sadness
- Raising the mouth corners to show happiness
- Raising one side of the mouth signifies contempt or hate
- An open mouth indicates fear
- A jaw drop conveys surprise

Interpreting Different Emotions

Now that you understand the most common meanings behind facial features, you can learn to interpret various emotions.

Happiness

Smiling is often the first sign that someone is happy. However, it is also the easiest facial expression to fake. There is a difference between a non-genuine and a real smile, called the Duchenne smile. Named after

The Context in Facial Expressions

Almost all facial expressions require context. People rarely convey emotions without something involving another person or object prompting them. For instance, you're at a wedding and notice one of the bride's maids tearing up and emotional. Based on the context, she is obviously crying happy tears and excited her friend is getting married. If this scene takes place at a funeral, the interpretation will be different since this person is clearly crying out of grief.

The same facial expressions have different meanings depending on the situation. For instance, raising eyebrows can mean fear and surprise, and you can only decode it based on the context.

Example #1
You are in a restaurant and see a guy kneeling, taking a ring out of his pocket, and proposing to his girlfriend. She raises her eyebrows and puts her hands over her mouth. Clearly, she is surprised and happy by the proposal.

Example #2
You are watching a scary movie with friends, and one friend who doesn't like this genre has their eyebrows raised during the whole movie. In this context, they are afraid.

How to Decode Facial Expressions

Most people associate lips with smiling and happiness and eyes with lying and sadness. However, every facial feature reflects different emotions you should know so that you can decode facial cues easily.

Eyes
"The eyes are the windows to the soul." This is true, especially in the context of body language, since it reveals a person's genuine emotions. Remember, the eyes don't lie.

Common meanings behind the eyes:

- Intense staring can either mean a person is angry or attentive
- Looking away or averting eye contact reflects distraction or discomfort
- Dilated eyes show arousal or interest

Fabricated Facial Expressions

As the name suggests, fabricated facial expressions aren't genuine but are false and masked expressions.

False Facial Expressions

When someone fakes their emotions and pretends they feel something that isn't genuine, they do this deliberately, but it doesn't always reflect bad intentions. For instance, you overhear your friends planning a surprise party for you. You pretend you don't know anything so you don't spoil things for them. On your birthday, you walk into a restaurant to all your friends yelling surprise, so you raise your eyebrows, open your jaw, and raise your eyelids, pretending you are surprised.

Most people convey false expressions daily, like fake smiles when posing for a picture or when someone makes an unfunny joke. It is necessary for social interactions because sometimes you have to fake certain emotions to avoid hurting peoples' feelings, like feigning excitement when listening to someone's boring story or being polite, faking a smile when you see someone you don't like.

Masked Facial Expressions

Masked expressions are when you voluntarily hide your true feelings and convey non-genuine emotions. For instance, you've saved for years to buy an expensive car but still cannot afford it. One day, you have dinner with a friend, and they tell you they bought the same car last week. You couldn't help but feel jealous, so you masked your emotions with a smile and pretended to be happy for them.

Subtle Facial Expressions

Subtle expressions only occur on one facial feature like your lips, nose, cheeks, eyes, or brows. People resort to them when they want to hide a strong emotion. However, some emotions are powerful and can't be concealed, so they reveal themselves in subtle expressions exposing real feelings.

Adaptive Facial Expressions

Adaptive expressions occur when a person wants to fulfill their physical needs, like adjusting their glasses or scratching their nose. These cues can have psychological meaning; for instance, touching your ear can indicate that you are nervous. These gestures are often involuntary, but most people try to control them in public to avoid judgment from others. They usually indicate that the person is feeling hostile or anxious.

Micro expressions are usually driven by unconscious repression, defined as preventing negative thoughts and emotions from reaching the conscious mind, and conscious suppression, deliberately avoiding painful memories or thoughts.

Micro expressions occur when someone expresses an emotion they never intended to reveal. In some cases, this can take the person by surprise as they aren't even aware that they are experiencing these feelings in the first place.

For instance, you and your co-worker are up for the same promotion. Your co-worker tells you they don't care if they get it or not, and there is no competition. You feel relieved because you consider them a friend. When the promotion day arrives, your boss chooses you. All your co-workers look genuinely happy for you except for the one up against you. You sense something is off with them even though they are smiling like everyone else. Your gut feeling is right. What you don't notice is that the person raised one side of their mouth, signaling their contempt toward you. Clearly, they aren't happy for you and unconsciously show their true emotions. Your co-worker might not be aware they harbor these feelings, and their face betrays them in less than a second.

On the other hand, macro expressions last longer, between one to four seconds. They are normal signals and more common. Unlike micro expressions, you can notice these cues easily since they usually match the speaker's body language and tone of voice, so it is impossible to miss them if you pay attention.

For instance, you are having dinner with your brother and his girlfriend. Everyone is chatting and having fun, and suddenly, the girlfriend tells a funny story involving her ex-boyfriend. You look at your brother, who is smiling, appearing amused, but his jaw is tense, and his nostrils are flared. When he speaks, his voice is lower pitched than usual. All signs point that he is angry. You can notice them because they last longer than micro-expressions and match his tone of voice.

Macro expressions can happen naturally when you feel emotions, like smiling genuinely when you see an old friend or frowning when you are sad. You can purposefully convey these signals, like feigning a smile or raising your eyebrows, pretending you are surprised. This facial expression is referred to as a fabricated expression.

they want out of embarrassment or pride, so they resort to facial expressions instead. When you observe peoples' faces, you will understand their needs before they even say a word, developing strong interpersonal relationships.

Expressing Attitude

People use facial cues to express their attitudes. Understanding others' attitudes can be beneficial, especially during conversations when they keep certain thoughts to themselves. For instance, you and your friends are having an intense political discussion. Everyone is voicing their opinion except one person who is silent. On further observation, you notice they have a disapproving expression on their face. You quickly signal your other friends to change the subject because you notice this conversation makes your friend uncomfortable.

Collecting Information

The purpose of observing facial expressions is to collect information about the people around you and understand their feelings so you can interact with them accordingly. For instance, you are talking to a friend but notice they look uninterested or bored, so you quickly change the subject.

Types of Facial Expressions

Facial expressions include micro, macro, fabricated, subtle, and adaptive expressions. Understanding the meaning behind each is necessary before you can learn to decode facial cues.

Micro and Macro Facial Expressions

Micro expressions were discovered by Dr. Paul Ekman. They are facial cues that only last half a second, revealing what a person is truly feeling. Missing these expressions is easy because a person's gestures, tone of voice, and words can distract you from these subtle cues. Most people don't pay attention to body language because they are too focused on other things, like listening to what is said or thinking of their response.

People with ADHD are more sensitive to these signals than others since their brains don't process information the same way. Hence, they make judgments immediately and are prone to angry reactions. However, you can unconsciously pick up on these cues and react quickly during social interactions.

Types of Gestures

Every gesture has a unique purpose and helps communicate thoughts and emotions effectively.

1. Emblems

Emblems are the most common gesture as they are unique and have a special meaning. These gestures can replace spoken words without changing their meanings.

Examples of emblems include:

- Thumbs up: A sign of approval or agreement
- OK sign: A sign indicating everything is alright or satisfactory
- Peace sign: A symbol of peace and goodwill
- V sign: A victory or peace sign in some cultures

Emblems are commonly used to convey a message or highlight a point where verbal communication is impossible. The same emblem can have various meanings in different cultures, so you must be conscious of these variations. For instance, the OK sign is regarded as disrespectful in some cultures.

2. Illustrators

Gestures that accompany speech and deepen its meaning are called illustrators. These gestures add depth and richness to communication, helping communicate ideas and feelings more effectively.

Examples of illustrators include:

- Pointing: To direct attention or highlight something
- Gesturing while speaking: Can help convey enthusiasm, urgency, or excitement
- Facial expressions: Can indicate emotions like joy, sadness, or anger

Illustrators can emphasize ideas, define concepts, or add to the content. For instance, you might use your hands to show the size of an object.

3. Regulators

Regulators are motion signals controlling how a discussion is going. These gestures indicate when it's your moment to talk, when another person should speak, or when a conversation should end.

Examples of regulators include:
- Head nods: Can indicate agreement or interest
- Eye contact: Shows engagement and attention
- Verbal cues like "uh-huh": Indicate active listening

Regulators are crucial in conversation because they harmonize the speakers and avoid misunderstandings. For instance, you might nod to show you're listening while simultaneously offering the speaker a signal to finish their thought.

4. Adaptors

Adaptors are gestures to relieve sensations felt within the body, and these actions could be used to ease discomfort, stress, or anxiety.

Adaptor examples include:
- Touching the face or hair: Indicates nervousness or anxiety
- Fidgeting or tapping: Indicates restlessness or boredom
- Crossing the arms: Indicates defensiveness or discomfort

Adaptors can consciously or unconsciously show a person's emotional state or comfort level.

5. Proxemic Gestures

Non-verbal signs called proxemic gestures refer to the physical separation of people during a discussion. These actions consist of the following:
- Body posture
- Eye contact
- Personal space

These gestures have different meanings based on cultural conventions and personal preferences.

Proxemic gestures are widely used in human communication because they convey power dynamics and assist in building connections. For instance, approaching someone too closely could be interpreted as hostility or a threat to their personal space, yet maintaining eye contact can be interpreted as confidence and assertiveness.

6. Gesticulations

Gesticulations (non-verbal hand/arm gestures) often accompany speech and help emphasize points or express ideas. Culture-specific gestures often have different meanings in different contexts.

Gestures are crucial to human communication, improving how messages are conveyed. For example, raising a hand signifies a greeting, while pointing a finger can indicate blame or accusation.

7. Affect Displays

Body language, facial expressions, and vocal signals called "affect displays" often reveal non-verbal emotions that are unplanned responses to a feeling. These displays frequently appear in communication and help us understand how others feel about a circumstance or engagement. For example, if someone smiles while chatting, it suggests they are content or happy with the conversation. Conversely, a frown implies depression or anger.

The Importance of Context in Interpreting Gestures and Postures

Context refers to the circumstances, environment, and background information surrounding a particular situation. It can be the key to understanding why someone uses a specific gesture or posture.

Here are some reasons why context should be understood while interpreting gestures and posture:

1. Cultural Differences

Different cultures have different meanings for signs and body language. In the West, if people put their thumbs in the air, they support and motivate someone. But for some countries in the Middle East, it is disrespectful. Also, looking directly into someone's eyes might be considered unfriendly or aggressive, depending on where you are. Hence, you must understand the culture to understand the hidden messages behind non-verbal communication.

2. Personal History and Experiences

Individuals have unique ways of moving and holding themselves based on personal occurrences and accounts. For instance, when a person raises their hand with good intentions, it could alarm someone or lead them to retreat if they have experienced physical trauma. A full comprehension of the individual's past can prevent misunderstandings and enhance communication.

3. Dynamics of Relationships

The speaker-listener relationship affects how well people interpret non-verbal cues. For instance, an amusing and friendly gesture between friends can be perceived as hostile and menacing between strangers. Therefore, correctly interpreting gestures and postures requires understanding the relationship dynamics between the parties.

4. Contextual Cues

By looking at the situation, you can determine what someone means by their gestures and posture. For instance, if someone sits with their arms crossed and their head down during a lecture, you might think they're uninterested. But during therapy, you might perceive them as thoughtful. So, understanding context can help you understand what non-verbal cues mean.

5. Emotional Setting

Understanding what someone says without speaking makes their emotions significant. For example, if someone is excited, they show it with their body language as– they will be animated and lively. On the other hand, if someone is anxious or nervous, they might act differently than they normally would.

To read their non-verbal cues accurately, you must observe a person's emotional state during the interaction. Are they happy, sad, angry, or something else entirely? What could be making them feel this way? Considering all these factors, you can better understand what they communicate.

6. The Dynamics of Power

If you're determining what someone's non-verbal cues mean with power dynamics, consider how the dynamics can affect those cues.

For instance, if someone's in charge, they might use non-verbal cues to show they're in control. Meanwhile, someone lower down the hierarchy might use non-verbal cues to signal submission or respect. You must consider who is in power and how they use it to make sense of everything.

Are they trying to assert themselves, show deference, or indicate they're ceding power? The better you factor in these nuances, the more you'll understand what's happening.

Posture

Your posture refers to how your body is positioned in space. Consider your head, neck, spine, and limb placement and how your weight is distributed between your feet. Maintaining good posture is crucial to keeping yourself balanced and steady and ensuring your muscles and bones function properly.

The Importance of Posture in Body Language

How you hold yourself says a lot about you and shapes how others perceive you. Whether standing tall with your shoulders back or slouching with your arms crossed, your posture communicates everything from self-assuredness to unease.

Posture is so essential that it can make or break your ability to connect and communicate effectively. So, it's worth thinking about how you're standing, sitting, or walking and using your body to convey the right message.

- **Posture Reflects Mood and Emotions**

Your posture can reveal much about what you feel inside. Slouching or hunching forward can signify sadness, low self-worth, or nervousness. On the other hand, standing straight with your shoulders and chest open shows pride, confidence, and assertiveness.

- **Posture Affects Perception**

How you hold yourself could potentially alter how others perceive you. A person who exhibits good posture, instead of someone who slouches or leans excessively, is more apt to be viewed as competent, reliable, and attractive.

- **Posture Influences Behavior**

Your posture could influence your conduct and attitude. For instance, sitting properly improves mood, focus, and concentration, while slouching can lead to negativity, stress, and fatigue.

- **Posture Reflects Culture and Social Norms**

Different societies and situations have different views on body positions. In some cultures, it is respectful to incline or crouch. In others, how someone stands and meets their gaze can indicate assertiveness and self-assurance.

The Elements of Good Posture

Good posture involves several elements, including:

- **Alignment**

Straighten your head, neck, and spine with the chin tucked in and shoulders relaxed.

- **Balance**

The weight should be evenly spread between both feet.

- **Core Stability**

Your core muscles (abdominals and lower back) should be engaged to stabilize the spine and avoid excessive arching or rounding.

- **Mobility**

Your joints should move freely and smoothly without stiffness or pain.

- **Breathing**

Your breathing should be deep and relaxed, with your diaphragm and rib cage expanding and contracting naturally.

Types of Posture

The following are different postures:

1. Open Posture

Standing up straight, not crossing your arms or legs, and having a relaxed and open body position is called open posture. This posture makes you appear more confident, open, and friendly to others. When you show an open posture, people will think you're easy to approach, trustworthy, and willing to talk.

Examples of open posture include:

- Standing up straight with shoulders back
- Keeping arms uncrossed
- Facing the person with an open stance

In social situations, an open posture indicates interest and engagement while conveying confidence and competence in professional settings.

2. Closed Posture

When someone stands with their arms and legs crossed and slumps their shoulders, avoiding eye contact, it is a "closed posture." This pose typically indicates defensiveness, insecurity, or discomfort. Those who stand like this appear unfriendly, distant, or even unreliable.

Examples of closed posture include:
- Crossed arms and legs
- Slouching
- Avoiding eye contact

In social situations, a closed posture indicates disinterest or discomfort, while it conveys a lack of confidence or competence in professional settings.

3. Neutral Posture

When someone hangs loose and stands up straight with relaxed shoulders, it sends a chill and calm vibe. It might look like they're paying attention, but they're not giving away specific emotions or motives; this is a neutral posture.

Examples of neutral posture include:
- Standing up straight
- Relaxing the arms and legs
- Holding the head high

In social and professional settings, a neutral posture can indicate a calm and confident demeanor and be perceived as reassuring and trustworthy.

4. Forward Head Posture

Many people hold their heads forward as a habit, which happens when they sit for a long time, use their phones a lot, or don't sit right. It makes their head lean forward, straining their neck and upper back muscles. People with this posture are usually stressed, tense, and uncomfortable.

Forward head posture includes:
- Hunching over a computer
- Tilting the head to read a mobile device
- Slouching in a chair

Forward head posture can indicate a lack of confidence in social and professional settings.

5. Power Posture

When someone takes a power posture, they seem tough and in control. This posture makes them look bigger than they really are. It sends the message that they're strong and confident.

Some examples of power postures include:

- Standing with your feet wider than hip-width
- Placing your hands on your hips
- Taking up more space than necessary
- Holding your head high

Power posture is useful for asserting yourself or gaining respect but can also be intimidating or aggressive. So, you must learn to use it sparingly and appropriately.

6. Submissive Posture

A submissive posture conveys deference and surrender. People appear smaller and less threatening when assuming a subservient posture. It conveys a message of respect or humility.

Examples of submissive postures include:

- Standing with feet close together
- Looking down at the ground
- Crossing legs at the ankle

When you want to be respectful or show you recognize someone's authority, it could be wise to adopt a more submissive posture. On the other hand, if you employ this approach at the wrong time or incorrectly, it might give the impression you lack confidence or assertiveness.

How Posture Communicates Emotions and Intentions

Postures are very effective communication methods. Different postures express different feelings and intentions, influencing how others see and react to you.

The following are examples of how posture reveals feelings and intentions:

- **Confidence:** Open posture with relaxed arms and legs, an upright stance, and direct eye contact conveys confidence and self-assuredness
- **Insecurity:** Closed posture with crossed arms and legs, a hunched back, and a lack of eye contact communicates insecurity and discomfort
- **Approachability:** Open posture with a relaxed stance and open arms and legs conveys approachability and friendliness
- **Hostility:** Closed posture with crossed arms and legs, a tense stance, and a lack of eye contact communicates hostility and defensiveness
- **Stress:** Forward head posture with a hunched back and tense shoulders communicates stress and tension

By recognizing the various body positions and what they signal, people effectively express their goals and feelings by sitting, standing, or moving. This knowledge enables you to read non-verbal cues better and adapt your communication approach accordingly.

Popular Gestures and Their Meanings

The following are some of the most popular gestures and their meaning:
- **The Thumbs Up**

A thumbs-up gesture expresses agreement or approval. It could mean something is going well or everything is OK.
- **Nodding**

Nodding is an unobtrusive way to show your assent or comprehension during conversations. It is a widely used method to indicate that you are attentive and actively participating in the discussion. A rapid nod conveys your agreement or affirmation. A slow, measured nod is indicative of deep thought or contemplation. This subtle gesture can effectively engage with others, display your attentiveness, and demonstrate your understanding.
- **Hand Shaking**

Shaking hands is customary during introductions or business meetings since it conveys respect and suggests a readiness to collaborate or work as a team. A strong handshake is frequently interpreted as an indication of assurance and skill.

- **Crossing Arms**

When the arms are folded, it can mean different things depending on the situation. It could indicate feeling defensive or uneasy or that someone wants to maintain their personal space. Sometimes, it could signal feeling self-assured or in charge. To fully understand the posture, you must observe other elements like the face and body position.

- **The Eye Roll**

Eye rolling is a sign of frustration or displeasure frequently employed to express disdain or mistrust. Use this gesture judiciously and suitably, as it can be interpreted as condescending or dismissive.

- **The Head Tilt**

A slight head tilt can subtly express various emotions, including interest, curiosity, or confusion. It frequently indicates openness or vulnerability and is used when listening or observing.

- **Finger Gesture**

You know the finger point, right? It's when you stretch out your pointing finger to show someone or something. But, be careful before doing it because it might be seen as blaming or forceful. In different situations, it can show you're in charge or guiding others.

- **Shrugged Shoulders**

A shoulder shrug is when your shoulders are raised and lowered. It is frequently used to indicate uncertainty or ignorance. Another meaning of a shrug is "I don't care" or "It's not my problem." When interpreting this gesture, you must consider additional indications, like voice inflection and facial emotions.

- **Hand Motions**

You can use many different hand movements, like waving, calling someone over, or punching the air. These motions help show emotions like happiness, being upset, or being very excited. They help draw attention to what is being said or to clarify a certain point.

- **Facial Expressions**

One of the most revealing non-verbal cues is a person's look on their face. For instance, a smile can express joy, pleasure, or agreement.

- **Touch**

Touch can be a powerful non-verbal cue. A pat on the back can signal support or encouragement, while a hug indicates affection or comfort.

However, touching can violate personal space, so using it appropriately and with consent is important.

Tips for Interpreting Gestures and Postures Accurately

1. Observe Body Language in Context

Examining the context is among the most important things to remember when interpreting gestures and posture. Body language conveys various meanings depending on the situation, culture, and individual. For instance, crossing your arms is a sign of defensiveness or unease, but also boredom or coldness.

To decipher body language correctly, you must examine the person's conduct in its overall context. Pay attention to the dialogue, the setting, and the person's attitude. Observe further non-verbal clues that confirm or refute the gesture or posture you're interpreting. A person might not be defensive if they are grinning and crossing their arms, but rather relaxed and confident.

2. Look for Clusters of Gestures and Postures

Body language is a collection of indicators that form clusters rather than a single gesture or posture. To correctly decipher body language, you must seek groups of gestures and postures representing a specific mood or attitude. A stressed person might touch their face, avoid eye contact, and fidget.

You can read someone's emotions and intentions more accurately by watching for groups of gestures and postures. However, refrain from drawing conclusions about people solely from their body language. Always consider the situation and the person.

3. Consider the Timing and Duration of Gestures and Postures

The timing and duration of gestures and postures are crucial factors in body language interpretation. While some postures and gestures are brief without much meaning, others are more protracted and important. For instance, a polite smile might be quick, but a happy or seductive smile is longer.

You must pay close attention to the timing and duration of gestures and postures to correctly decipher body language. Consider the alterations in behavior over time and contrast them with the setting and context. Consider someone initially anxious in a conversation – but who later becomes relaxed. They might have been apprehensive at first, but now they have become more at ease as the conversation continues.

4. Recognize Cultural Differences in Gestures and Postures

Body language is culturally specific, not universal. Inappropriate or perplexing gestures and postures in one culture might be accepted in another. For instance, making eye contact with someone is a sign of respect and sincerity in certain cultures. Others might view it as rude or combative.

You must understand cultural variations and refrain from making assumptions or stereotyping to read body language effectively. Ask the person politely or research their culture to determine if a particular gesture or stance will offend them.

5. Pay Attention to Your Body Language

Awareness of your own body language is as important as the interpretation of the body language of others. Your physical cues affect how others see you and the conversation. For instance, crossing your arms can convey defensiveness, yet leaning forward can convey involvement and attention.

Pay close attention to your gestures and posture to communicate more effectively and correctly read body language. Be mindful of your posture, gait, and other movements. Keep your body language open and friendly by facing the person, making eye contact, and nodding. By sending positive cues, you can persuade the other person to follow suit and foster a more fruitful dialogue.

6. Practice Active Listening and Empathy

Decoding signals and comprehending the person's emotions and intentions are necessary for body language interpretation. Active listening and empathy are necessary for accomplishing this since they require paying attention to the other person's needs, feelings, and words.

Focus on the person's perspective and use open-ended inquiries to demonstrate active listening and empathy. Show real interest and concern and refrain from interrupting or criticizing them. You can show you understand how they feel by nodding, grinning, or mimicking their actions. This makes a conversation more meaningful and develops trust and connection.

7. Be Mindful of Your Biases and Assumptions

Accurate body language interpretation necessitates awareness of your prejudices and presumptions. Unconscious biases exist and can influence how you perceive and interpret body language. For instance, you might conclude that someone wearing casual clothing is less capable or that someone quiet is insecure.

You must be mindful of how your brain thinks and challenge emerging biases or assumptions. When examining someone's body language or posture, ask yourself if your interpretation is based on reason or preconceived notions.

Deciphering the meaning behind someone's non-verbal communication is key to truly understanding what they convey. You can improve your skills by studying different gestures and attitudes.

Remember, these gestures and postures are not always reliable indicators, so you must communicate verbally. Becoming more adept at interpreting non-verbal cues enhances your connection with others and fosters stronger relationships.

Chapter 4: Lying Eyes: Detecting Lies and Deceit

In a world where competition and individualism are stressed, deception is one expression many people exhibit, with or without the initial mindset. For some, the bargain is so enticing they can't resist the urge. Others feel no guilt and want the fastest and surest way of getting things done.

Eyes can help you identify lies.
https://unsplash.com/photos/splQbzTnaW0

There are ways to practice deception without being caught to avoid confrontation and losing the game. But do you know there are several ways to detect lies and outsmart deceptive behavior? This chapter takes you through the world of deception, its logic, how it is carried out, how to identify lies, and what to do about deceit.

The Psychology behind Lies

Has it always been this way?

One definite thing is that lying often happens in many places and different situations, making it almost inevitable. You might have wondered what the actual psychology is behind lies, the vague, unjustifiable, or cruel reasons for them, and what is established by lying.

Lying involves two people: the cunning deceiver and the gullible deceived. According to the research of psychologist Bella DePaulo, Ph.D., 30 percent of one-on-one human interaction is given to deceit in a week.

The deceiver has to communicate false information, add impressive incorrect details like made-up evidence and witnesses to make it more believable, and apply heavy emotions to increase the deceived gullibility. Generally, men tell more self-oriented lies to impress the second party than lies concerning others. In contrast, women use lies altruistically, not to hurt others' feelings. The deceived are mostly trapped by trust. They believe the deceiver, not thinking of a reason for the lie, might not detect evidence of untruth, or sometimes, the lie is what they want to hear, so they believe it anyway. It can also be a lack of interest in arguing since the lie doesn't affect them in any way. The deceiver ensures the deceived is irrationally overwhelmed and cognitively convinced by emotional displays and arguments.

Reasons People Deceive Others

People lie for various reasons, whether necessary at that moment or not. Lies can be viewed as a defense mechanism hiding the person's vulnerability who tells them. It is the gateway to manipulating a situation to gain control over it. Lies can also be constructed to benefit others or for selfish reasons. Most times, telling the truth won't hurt, but people lie because they are scared and do not want to take chances.

Below are some reasons prompting people to tell a lie or indulge in deceit:

1. To Save Face

You might feel that the only way to get out of a situation is to tell a lie. Like some pressurized situation where you can't tell everyone how badly you performed when they expected so much from you. For example, you would say, "I only came second because the person who got the prize is the judge's relative," to save face when you have no idea of their family relationship.

Also, the lie that you don't want others to learn about is something embarrassing you did, so you blame it on someone else. People can deceive their coworkers to receive praise, feel on top, and advance their status to open more opportunities. Since the deceiver's coworkers already know what motivates them, they have to lie about their features or exaggerate their achievements, telling them what they want to hear to get what they want from them. Even though the person knows they are not what they claim to be, they are better off lying to themselves.

2. To Impress Others

Everybody, if it dares be said, likes to seek the approval and acceptance of the people around them. Some feel intimidated, inferior, and less of themselves without their peers' validation. Hence, they tell lies. You might claim to be more talented or successful than you are or exaggerate your life, pretending it's more interesting than anyone would believe.

You go on to support your claims with many made-up stories or even go as far as involving people in this lie without being aware you're doing so. For example, most of your friends own cars, and you want to fit in but can't afford one. You make claims like, "My boyfriend just bought me a car, but his mother said it's not yet time to gift big things." But in reality, nobody asked or cared if you owned a car, making the lie unnecessary.

This lie begets other lies to keep things smooth and avoid exposure. Once this has started, there's no going back. You have to look for all means possible to keep up with the false notion you created about yourself to others.

For example, a person earns an average monthly salary, with no side jobs or extra income, and lies about living in an extravagant house. Their colleagues would place them in that regard on every occasion and have expectations of them in situations such as making a huge donation. In these cases, the deceiver is forced to borrow to keep up with their forged standard, making them prey to loan sharks and developing medical issues like anxiety, hypertension, and high blood pressure.

3. To Avoid Hurting People

Some people lie out of good intentions. These lies are called "white lies." It happens when the truth comes at the price of a relationship or as far as posing a life risk. Hence, some lies are told to avoid this. Women, especially mothers, commonly tell this lie because they have a greater emotional attachment to others, especially their children. It is a harmless white lie sparing hurting peoples' feelings at that moment or in the future, as long as they don't discover the truth.

For example, telling your children that Santa Claus or the tooth fairy has died when you are financially down. They will feel sad rather than angry when you tell them no. Or laughing at a joke that wasn't funny so as not to hurt the other person's feelings, or saying many imaginary things to avoid a conversation.

Generally, the white lie is solely in the interest of the deceived to avoid the offensiveness or unpleasantness that could develop if these lies are not told. However, when the truth later comes out, it worsens the situation more than if the truth had been told initially.

4. To Avoid Responsibility

These lies are told to avoid taking responsibility or protecting peoples' feelings, confidence, self-esteem, or other emotions. For example, someone can pretend to be delusional or claim they were not in their right mind and don't remember when they got involved in abuse, dysfunctional behavior, or betrayal. They make the victim doubt themselves and their memories and play the victim to the third party so they don't have to face the consequences.

Some employees call in sick or make up an emergency at home to get out of work. They exaggerate the importance of whatever is on their schedule or claim to have a busy life in order to avoid duty.

Managers can blame their teammates for a failed project or criticize, blackmail, and frame an employee to get what they want. They employ gullible and desperate people who will believe whatever they say so they won't complain about their working conditions while the managers continue in their deceit without being called out.

5. For Social Gains

Many people lie about their standards and lifestyle to fit a particular clique or company. It is very common among teenagers. For example, they lie about their parents' status and indulge in acts they normally wouldn't do to keep up their social life. Some have low and fragile self-esteem. Hence, they mask it with fake confidence and pick on the weak, or someone they think is below their class to feel empowered. Others lie about their social influence to eliminate threats. They strategize and build a fake life of importance so that no one dares to challenge them to not be on the wrong side of powerful influencers or to gain their favor when they lie about something.

For example, they do wrong and claim that it's not their fault, the offended party deserved it, they didn't mean to do it, it wasn't that terrible, it's no big deal, or worse, they can pretend it didn't happen. The victim has to accept everything, not step on the wrong foot, and be unsure of how much social influence they have.

Some of these lies start as a conscious denial, but over time, they become so addictive that they continue to live it as their reality and believe that as long as they go on, they will be fine and have nothing to worry about.

6. To Protect Themselves

Sometimes, you agree that telling lies to protect yourself is good, whether the lies result from intentional wrongdoings or honest errors. These lies are mostly about personal things or serious matters.

Lies are important to protect yourself in risky circumstances, like a threat or where you suspect someone wants to harm you. Similarly, keeping information to yourself and hiding items can help you avoid harmful people.

For instance, a youngster might lie and tell an outsider their parent is asleep. They should come at another time out of fear that something terrible would happen if the stranger finds out they are home alone.

Children often lie to avoid punishment or getting into trouble, which is another typical lie. They learned the lie and can readily fabricate it when they have done something wrong or failed to do something they were told to do.

7. To Maintain Privacy

Almost everyone would like ultimate control over their lives, and one way most people keep this independence is by being deceptive. They lie whenever matters concerning their lifestyle come up and prefer to cover up their secrets.

These lies are told to protect their privacy, like their career and finances, because they are shameful or because of their friends and relations. It is mostly fear of jealousy, envy, or future failure.

Through deception, it is possible to control and decide who, if at all anyone, can discover your hidden lives.

Secrets include the purposeful concealment of personal data. To cover up these secrets, you conceal information from a specific person or in a particular circumstance, which can be viewed as a lie.

The most frequent secrets where lies are used to cover up include a physical or emotional affair, sex orientations, romantic aspirations, embarrassing events, sexual passions or fantasies, and dependence on drugs.

Some private matters are not considered bad to others, like ailments, family history, financial circumstances or debt, or future goals or fitness ambitions. However, some people would still prefer to lie about them.

How to Identify Untruthfulness

The ability to tell a lie from the truth is fascinating. In this case, you can keep a smile or a straight face because you know the person is telling a lie without their knowledge. Lies are evident in different forms, and they can be complete deception, dishonesty, exaggeration, half-truths, or precise omissions. Fishing out a dishonest person is not as easy, but there are signs to look out for.

Do you notice the person's gaze shifting all the time? Do they shout rather than communicate calmly? Are they always clearing their throats to rearrange their speech? This section reveals the cues of a verbal and non-verbal deceiver.

Verbal Indicators

When a person talks, how they sound and relay the story can easily give them away if they are liars. They usually speak in generalized terms and beat around the bush, giving you all the information you need to hear.

Below are some verbal indicators to detect deceit:

1. Speech Patterns

Most times, immature liars mix their words, chew on their tongues, take a long time before answering, stutter, and correct almost every word they say. They try to change the subject and rearrange questions so their answer sounds believable.

They jump into answering without fully hearing the question, with the notion that if they give you all the information, you won't question them anymore. They often end up spilling more information than intended.

2. Choice of Words

They mix up their words, especially if it is an impromptu lie. Where they might have prepared to lie, their exaggerated details can give them away. A dishonest person might repeat your question before answering it, ask you to rephrase or repeat your questions, and play dumb by saying they need more information before they can give you an answer. They usually use words suggesting they are the victims, talking more about themselves than answering the question.

They could say things like "the way I see it," "to tell you the truth," and ask you a question like "Would I do such a thing?" to convince you.

3. Vocal Tones

When someone lies, their voice becomes shaky, especially under great pressure and tension. Their vocal pitch changes, and they try to sound pitiful and helpless. It might sound like they've lost their voice or it is strained, so they pretend they said something, only you didn't hear them. They also sigh a lot. They sound less refutable and more powerful by talking in an enforced, rehearsed manner as if offended.

Non-verbal Cues

Some people can easily be caught in their lies, while others are so careful that only their body language can give them away and provide subtle hints of dishonesty. When reading non-verbal cues, it's necessary to treat them as an insight rather than proof of deceit because some people do them out of stress and not deceit. Consider the following non-verbal cues to detect deception:

1. Facial Expressions

This is one of the easiest ways to detect a lie. Things like exaggerated blinking, frequent random eye movements, such as looking from side to side or away from the interviewer, and unstable eye contact can be indicators of deceit. Some dishonest people put their fingers over their mouths to prepare lies in their heads or cover their mouths as if the lies would escape if they didn't.

Some give facial expressions which are completely off, having no relation to the conversation.

2. Gestures

Normally, people make hand motions to illustrate a point and facilitate communication. However, if a person changes their gesture due to pressure, it might be a sign of deception. Some gestures can hint at deceit, like unclasping the hand, picking at the hem of a dress, and playing with a piece of jewelry.

3. Body Language

An honest person will lean closer to the interviewer as the questioning gets more serious to understand them better and explain their facts.

A deceptive person leans away, changes their positioning sporadically, suggesting discomfort, and adopts a completely different sitting style when the questions get too tough. Sometimes they fall silent, act like they can't hear you, and are easily distracted, so you must constantly repeat your questions, or they feign tears.

The Science of Micro Expressions

Micro expressions occur for a split second, and no matter how hard a person tries to control it, this involuntary leakage of emotion exposes their real feelings. The universally understood micro expressions are fear, disgust, happiness, contempt, sadness, surprise, and anger. Sometimes, you must look intently at how the person expresses their emotions to read the hidden ones. For example, when a liar tries to cover whatever they are trying to hide with a smile, the eyes usually don't participate in the expression. This is an indicator that they are being disingenuous.

Another example is a person trying to make their situation look pitiful, but their lips curl up in a smile for a fraction of a second, which is a slip in their false display.

Also, they usually become sensitive to temperature. As the question gets hotter, they are thrown off balance, and their body temperature gets hotter. Although they try to act cool, it doesn't last long, and they sweat profusely, touching their necks constantly, getting thirsty, and often tugging at their collars.

However, these micro-expressions are not always reliable, as they can be masked, exaggerated, minimized, or neutralized.

Detecting Lies

When a criminal is being interrogated, the investigator ensures that the criminal is comfortable to enhance communication and that there are no barriers to gaining a full view of the subject. The investigator ensures that there is no obstructing furniture, not even a table, so they can read the accused's body language and non-verbal indicators.

Just one sign is not enough for a judgment, so the strategy is to gather all the clues and use tactful and smart questioning (such as directly accusing rather than asking and being a little threatening) to pin down the accused.

The following are some techniques used by professional lie detectors, like law enforcement officers and interrogators, to detect lies and deceit:

1. The Eye Technique

Certain parts of the brain are for specific information, and the direction in which the eye is moved is to recall whatever information is kept on that side. Hence, professional lie detectors focus on the subject's eyes, even when they try to avoid their gaze.

2. The Grammar Technique

Law enforcement officers construct their questions so they can't be rephrased and stick to them even when the subject tries to change them. The dishonest person avoids using personal pronouns, disowning their guilt, and placing the blame on themselves.

Detectors watch out for overused words like "our team" rather than "I" and the change of pronouns into an indefinite article, like "I opened the house" rather than "I opened my house."

3. The Accusing Technique

This technique reveals to the accused that they have been identified as the culprit. For example, rather than say, "Did you take the wallet?"

An interrogator says, "Why did you take the wallet?" It gives the liar room to fabricate why they took it, which automatically acknowledges they took it rather than denying it. If they play dumb, they might say, "What are you talking about?" You can ask them the exact question again, truly or falsely, and the moment they begin explaining, they could be involved in the offense.

4. The Smarter Technique

Often, the person likes to play dumb or outsmart the interviewer. They might ask the interviewer, "Why do you want to know that?" and "Don't you have something better to do?" Your replies should be "I just want answers" and "No," respectively. You don't have to play with them. If you have one, write down details of their story, and contrast it with the original story. Also, jot down their answers and repeat the questions to see if their answers change.

Exercises to Hone Lie-Detection Skills

The following are practical tips to use in real-life deceptive situations:

- Gather enough facts first
- Stick to your question
- Directly accuse as if you are overconfident
- Be in control of the conversation
- Practice micro-expressions and how to identify them
- Demand details
- Get skilled in awkward silences to inflict intimidation
- Practice reading body languages
- Take note of sarcasm and humor used to avoid the question and distract your attention. You did not come to play.

Lying comes in many forms, from enormous and ugly, to tiny, seemingly harmless, delicate white lies. This chapter has detailed practical examples and tips on being a good lie detector. Since an investigator seeks to determine credibility, they should also consider a subject's mental state. Dishonest people that are mentally ill, drunk, or under the effects of psychoactive substances do not provide accurate clues. In reality, interviewing people when they are under the influence is never a good idea.

Chapter 5: Understanding Proximity

Confusion is common with the concept of proxemics. Proxemics refers to the study of how humans use space and how we perceive and communicate through it. Understanding proxemics is important because it impacts how we perceive and interact with others and communicate effectively. This chapter delves into the concept of proxemics and its relevance in our daily lives and explores the four levels of proxemics, including intimate, personal, social, and public. Additionally, the chapter highlights the role culture plays in shaping our understanding and use of space. By the end of this chapter, you'll have a deeper understanding and appreciation for the power of proxemics.

The level of proximity differs depending on the type of relationship.
https://unsplash.com/photos/kxTmX59VqEE?utm_source=unsplash&utm_medium=referral&utm_content=creditShareLink

What Is Proxemics?

Proxemics is a branch of non-verbal communication focusing on the study of how people perceive, use, and structure space during interpersonal communication. It examines how people use physical distance, body language, and other non-verbal cues to convey meaning and establish relationships. This concept considers the space between individuals, the proximity in which people stand or sit, and how humans communicate through non-verbal cues, such as eye contact, body posture, and gesture.

Anthropologist Edward T. Hall introduced the study of proxemics in the late 1950s. He coined the term proxemics and defined it as studying the spatial aspects of non-verbal communication. He considered it an essential part of human behavior, shaping how we interact with others in different contexts. It includes how individuals use physical space to communicate social messages, establish power dynamics, and express emotions.

Hall's research showed that humans are highly sensitive to space, and physical distance can convey important information about people's relationships. For example, in Western cultures, close proximity often signals intimacy, whereas in some Eastern cultures, standing far apart shows respect or deference.

Hall identified four personal space zones; intimate, personal, social, and public. The intimate zone, from 0 to 18 inches, is reserved for close relationships such as parents, children, and romantic partners. The personal zone, from 18 inches to four feet, is used in communication with friends and acquaintances. The social zone ranges from four to twelve feet and is considered for formal social interactions. The public zone extends beyond twelve feet and is for public speaking and social events.

Proxemics also uses body language and other non-verbal cues, such as eye contact, tone of voice, facial expressions, and hand gestures. These signals convey a person's attitudes and intentions toward others and can influence the perceived relationship between two individuals. For example, standing too close to someone can signal aggression or intimacy, while standing too far away can signal disinterest or discomfort.

In addition to interpersonal communication, proxemics has applications in architecture, urban planning, and design. It is used to design public spaces promoting social interaction and in buildings and homes to create a sense of community.

Proxemics offers valuable insights into how people use space and non-verbal cues to communicate and establish relationships. Understanding the intricacies of proxemics can lead to more effective communication and better social interactions.

The Importance of Proxemics

Proxemics' importance is immense and cannot be ignored in conversation. Proxemics help us understand how an individual intends to communicate. It can help gauge the other person's feelings, thoughts, and intentions based on their body language and distance.

Proxemics can tell us a lot about a person's comfort level in a particular situation. If someone keeps a greater distance or stands farther away than usual, it could mean they are uncomfortable or threatened by the conversation. Conversely, if someone stands very close to you or touches you, it might mean they are comfortable and open with you.

Proxemics can influence power dynamics in a conversation. If you stand too close to someone who does not perceive you as an intimate partner, they might become anxious and uncomfortable and see you as a threat. On the other hand, standing too far could denote disinterest, lack of confidence, or disrespect. Therefore, understanding the appropriate distance during a conversation is crucial in establishing a positive and productive interaction.

At an interpersonal level, proxemics can help create positive feelings between two individuals and strengthen their relationship over time. When people feel comfortable in each other's presence, whether through physical proximity or non-verbal cues like eye contact or facial expressions, they are more open and willing to have meaningful conversations, leading to deeper understanding between them both.

Four Levels of Proxemics

1. Personal Space

Personal space is a fundamental aspect of proxemics, the study of how humans use space to communicate. This zone measures between 1.5 and 4 feet and is often called the intimate or personal space. It is reserved for friends, family, and close acquaintances a person feels comfortable around. Within this zone, people enjoy having close individuals around, interacting with them, and sharing sensitive information.

Usually, people are uncomfortable or feel violated when someone enters their personal space without permission. Therefore, this zone is highly regulated and is subject to cultural differences. The personal space required is often linked to cultural upbringing, personality, and gender. Individuals from cultures that value individualism prefer more personal space than collectivist cultures.

The level of proximity in personal space is highly dependent on the nature of the relationship between individuals. For instance, individuals sharing a close relationship are more comfortable being within a closer range, whereas those who do not share this relationship require more space. Social interactions in the personal space zone, like greetings, handshakes, hugs, and other subtle touches, are considered normal and friendly gestures.

The interpretation of personal space differs depending on the context. For instance, people might perceive distance differently depending on the circumstances. A speaker who understands their audience's cultural diversity will adjust their proximity to accommodate the audience's expectations. Various professions negotiate personal space differently. For instance, a health professional has to come closer to perform a physical examination while maintaining a professional demeanor.

2. Public Space

Public space is the furthest level of proxemics, extending 12 feet from an individual's body. This zone is typically used in professional settings where a person speaks to a large audience or addresses a group of people. The distance intentionally creates detachment, providing individuals with a comfortable space to move around and establish their presence.

Public figures, like celebrities and high-profile individuals, are known for maintaining a public space for safety reasons and asserting their power. This strategic move allows them to remain visible while maintaining a safe distance from their fans and the paparazzi.

Some examples of public space are political rallies, conferences, and seminars where the speaker delivers a speech. The audience is typically seated at a comfortable distance from the speaker, allowing them to hear the speaker's message and avoiding intrusion or discomfort.

Another example of public space includes crowded areas like airports or train stations. In these situations, individuals typically move past each other maintaining a respectful distance, even in close proximity.

While public space is the furthest level of proxemics, cultural norms and individual preferences alter an individual's space. However, the general rule remains that public space provides individuals with physical distance and detachment, establishing their presence without feeling overwhelmed or crowded.

3. Social Space

The social space extends from 4 to 12 feet from a person's body and is characterized by normal social interactions between distant acquaintances and colleagues. However, as someone approaches closer to a person's social space, interactions become necessary.

The importance of social space can often be observed in various everyday situations. For instance, people stand a few feet away from other passengers on a crowded bus or train to maintain their social space. Similarly, standing in a group with people you know at a social gathering, but not within each other's personal space. This space is crucial to maintaining privacy and personal agency while also fostering social interactions and connections.

Furthermore, cultural background significantly determines an individual's perception of social space. For example, those from Western cultures might feel more comfortable with a larger social space, preferring to maintain distance between themselves and others. In contrast, those from Eastern cultures usually feel more comfortable with a smaller social space, as close personal interactions are often more common.

4. Intimate Space

Intimate space is a crucial aspect of proxemics, the study of human communication and interaction through space. It refers to a person's surroundings and interactions with people within that space. This zone is considered intimate as it extends only up to 1.5 feet or less in distance.

People usually reserve this intimate space for their romantic or intimate partners, closest friends, and family. Other people entering or closing in on this zone can result in emotions like comfort, happiness, nervousness, discomfort, or fright. The proximity of someone within the intimate space can be a powerful tool for influencing emotions and feelings.

Due to its close proximity, intimate space is reserved for only those who most closely relate to you emotionally, physically, or mentally. It is where people feel the most comfortable and safe with the least social and personal barriers.

For example, a couple in a deep, romantic relationship might enjoy being in close physical proximity within their intimate space while sharing a conversation or enjoying a moment together. On the other hand, if an acquaintance or stranger invades someone's intimate space, it can be discomfiting and create awkwardness, as personal boundaries are being invaded.

Role of Culture in Proxemics

The role of culture in proxemics is significant, as different cultures have different norms about personal space and physical touch. Culture is the shared beliefs, values, behaviors, and attitudes defining a group of people. Culture is critical in proxemics, shaping how people understand and use space. Different cultures have different norms regarding the acceptable distance between people when conversing or using touch when interacting with others. Understanding these cultural norms is critical to effective communication, as failure to recognize them can lead to misunderstandings or offense.

Let's examine some examples of how cultural norms can vary across different regions and societies to better understand cultural influence in proxemics.

Personal space is highly valued in some cultures, and people keep a significant distance between themselves and others when interacting. For example, in Japan, people are known for their preference for a greater distance between themselves and others. In traditional Japanese culture, respecting personal space is highly emphasized, and interpersonal touching is typically kept to a minimum. Furthermore, individuals often bow rather than shake hands when greeting one another, to maintain a greater distance. This behavior reflects the cultural emphasis on respect and deference to others' personal space.

In contrast, other cultures value physical touch more when interacting with others. For example, in Latin American societies, people stand closer to one another when interacting, often placing a hand on the other person's shoulder or arm. In these cultures, touch conveys warmth and intimacy and builds rapport and trust. People greet one another with a hug or a kiss on the cheek, which would be considered unusual in many other cultures.

Another example of cultural variation in proxemics is how people use eye contact to communicate. In some cultures, direct eye contact shows honesty and respect. In North America, people are expected to maintain steady eye contact when speaking to someone. In contrast, in many Asian cultures, direct eye contact is rude or confrontational. In these cultures, as a sign of respect, people avert their gaze or look down when speaking to someone.

Cultural norms regarding physical touch vary significantly. In some cultures, touch is used freely and often; in others, it is inappropriate or intrusive. For example, in many Middle Eastern cultures, men and women interact separately, and physical touch between members of the opposite sex is discouraged. In contrast, Latin American societies are known for their warm and affectionate interactions, with men and women freely hugging and touching one another in public.

Recognizing that cultural norms in proxemics change over time or vary is essential. For example, touch and personal space differ between younger and older generations or urban and rural areas. Furthermore, as cultures become more intertwined and globalized, norms in proxemics shift to accommodate new practices and interactions.

Culture is crucial in defining how people use space to communicate with each other. Different cultures have different norms regarding the acceptable distance between people when conversing, using touch when interacting, and the importance of eye contact. Understanding these cultural norms is vital to effective communication. Failure to recognize them can lead to misunderstandings or offense. Therefore, when interacting with individuals from different cultures, knowing these cultural expectations and accordingly adapting behavior is essential, building stronger relationships and avoiding communication barriers.

Psychological and Emotional Factors Influencing Proxemics

1. Attraction

Attraction refers to being drawn towards someone or something. Attraction is crucial in determining the distance maintained between individuals in their social interactions. Therefore, attraction is a central influence on proxemics.

The degree of attraction between two individuals generates cues indicating the level of intimacy and comfort in their interaction. These cues regulate the proxemic distances between them. For instance, in a romantic relationship, the intensity of attraction determines the degree of proximity individuals share; a greater level of attraction results in closer distances and vice versa. Additionally, the distance between individuals varies depending on the attraction they share. For example, people sharing a familial bond might feel comfortable being in close proximity to each other, while strangers typically maintain a greater distance.

Moreover, attraction can influence proxemics differently based on the cultural and social norms prevalent within a community. In Western societies, attraction and close proximity are often associated with intimacy and sex. In Eastern cultures, proximity has more platonic connotations. Additionally, cultural norms can regulate proxemics which do not always align with the level of attraction between individuals. For example, some cultures might promote physical distance in a professional setting, even if individuals have a strong attraction toward each other.

The influence of attraction on proxemics is demonstrated by how people modify their physical behavior based on their level of attraction towards someone. Individuals who are attracted to each other display positive body language, like smiling, leaning in, and eye contact. Similarly, individuals who find someone unappealing often exhibit negative body language, like crossed arms, frowning, and avoiding eye contact. It impacts proxemics, as the individuals' behaviors communicate their level of attraction toward each other.

Another example of the influence of attraction on proxemics is in romantic relationships. When two people are attracted to each other, they engage in behaviors like hugging, holding hands, and other physical contact. It influences their proxemics, as they are more likely to be near each other. In contrast, individuals less attracted to each other choose to maintain a greater physical distance.

Moreover, the level of attraction influences the perception of personal space. Personal space is the area surrounding an individual they consider their personal territory. The interpretation of personal space can be highly subjective and is influenced by cultural and individual factors. However, attraction is essential in defining personal space. For instance, individuals attracted to someone might accept them into their personal space more readily than those they are less attracted to.

2. Aggression

Aggression is defined as behavior intended to harm another person. Aggressive behavior can take various forms, from verbal aggression like name-calling or yelling to physical aggression such as hitting or pushing. Various factors can trigger aggression, including frustration, anxiety, or a perceived threat to physical or psychological well-being.

Aggression significantly influences proxemics by affecting the need for personal space. Personal space is the area surrounding a person and is considered "our own." The size of personal space varies depending on many factors, such as culture, gender, and individual preferences. However, research has shown that when individuals feel threatened or under stress, they increase the size of their personal space. This change in personal space might be a way to protect the person from potential harm or danger.

For example, when an individual feels threatened, like during a physical altercation, they would increase their personal space to defend themselves. The individual might move backward, put up their hands, or create distance between themselves and the aggressor. This increase in personal space is a protective measure, helping the individual feel more secure.

Another way aggression influences proxemics is through non-verbal communication. Aggressive behavior is displayed through non-verbal cues like a clenched fist, crossed arms, or a hostile facial expression. These cues signal to others that the individual is angry, stressed, or potentially violent.

For example, in a workplace setting, an employee feeling stressed or threatened by a colleague might increase their personal space and display non-verbal cues like crossed arms or a tense facial expression to signal their discomfort. The other person could interpret these cues as hostility or aggression and further escalate the situation.

Lastly, aggression can influence proxemics by influencing the interactions between groups. Where there are inter-group conflicts, individuals increase their personal space and interact less with opposing group members. This increased distance between groups can further exacerbate the conflict and increase tension.

For example, opposing party supporters have different personal space requirements at political rallies. Members of one party might create more distance between themselves and the other party's supporters to protect themselves from potential harm or attack. This increased distance could cause a lack of interaction between the groups, fueling the conflict.

3. Dominance

One of the most significant factors influencing proxemics is dominance. Dominance is the degree of power or influence a person has over another. It can manifest in various ways, such as wealth, physical strength, social standing, or job title.

More dominant people use space and distance to assert their power and reinforce their social status. Typically, they take up more physical space, stand closer to others, and use more expansive gestures and postures. In contrast, less dominant individuals occupy less space, keep their distance, and use smaller, more submissive gestures.

For example, imagine a CEO walking through a busy office. They are likely to stride confidently and purposefully, taking up much space and expecting others to make way for them. They stand closer to their subordinates and use forceful, commanding gestures to assert their authority.

On the other hand, a new intern would be more hesitant and uncertain, taking up less space and standing further away from their colleagues. They use smaller, less expansive gestures and postures to avoid antagonizing others and to show deference to those in more powerful positions.

Dominance can influence how people use personal space. It varies depending on cultural norms and individual preferences, but generally, personal space is larger for more dominant people and smaller for those less dominant.

For example, a high-status individual would feel comfortable sitting close to others and touching them on occasion, reinforcing their power and showing their confidence and control. In contrast, a low-status individual feels uncomfortable with physical contact and prefers to keep a greater distance from others to avoid being overly familiar or presumptuous.

Dominance affects how people use eye contact. Eye contact is an important aspect of non-verbal communication and conveys much about a person's intentions, emotions, and attitudes.

More dominant individuals use direct eye contact to signify assertiveness and confidence. They maintain eye contact for longer and use it to intimidate or challenge others. Conversely, less dominant individuals avoid eye contact and are submissive or deferential.

For example, imagine a job interview where the interviewer is a high-ranking executive. They use direct and prolonged eye contact to establish their dominance and assert authority over the candidate. Conversely, the candidate avoids eye contact or uses it sparingly, showing respect and deference to the interviewer's position.

Chapter 6: Tone of Voice and How to Understand It

Have you ever been conversing with someone but have been unsure of what they're conveying? Don't worry. You're not alone. The confusion emerging from body language and tone of voice is something many people struggle with. However, understanding tone is crucial in truly comprehending a person's message. This chapter looks into the different voice tones, their significance, and interpreting them to comprehend a person better. By the end of this chapter, you will be able to decode the hidden meanings behind a person's tone and convey your message more effectively.

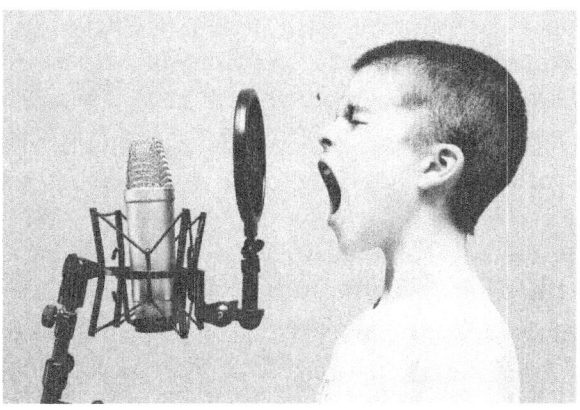

A person's tone can help you decode their body language.
https://unsplash.com/photos/ASKcuOZqhYU?utm_source=unsplash&utm_medium=referral&utm_content=creditShareLink

Role of Tone

In communication, body language is a crucial aspect that conveys much information. It comprises gestures, facial expressions, and tone of voice, revealing emotions and thoughts without spoken words. The tone of voice is significant in body language and crucial in conveying the message without relying on spoken words. The tone of voice refers to how someone speaks, including pitch, rhythm, and intonation. It is the key to understanding and interpreting underlying meanings and emotions behind the words.

The tone of voice is essential in conveying the message because it can significantly affect how the listener perceives the speaker. Research has shown that people pay more attention to tone of voice than actual spoken words because the tone reflects the speaker's emotional state, which can significantly alter the message's interpretation.

The tone of voice can convey a range of emotions, such as anger, happiness, sadness, and excitement, affecting how the listener perceives the message. For example, suppose you are angry and speak in a sharp, aggressive tone. In that case, your listener might feel attacked and become defensive even if your words are not necessarily aggressive. On the other hand, if the same words are spoken with a calm and assertive tone, the listener is more likely to be receptive and open to what you say.

Moreover, the tone of voice significantly impacts how someone is perceived. A monotone or expressionless tone can make the speaker appear disinterested or unenthusiastic, even if they are genuinely enthusiastic about the topic. Similarly, a high-pitched or nasally tone can make the speaker seem nervous or unsure of themselves, even if they are confident and knowledgeable on the topic.

The tone of voice affects the overall impression someone makes, especially in professional settings. For example, if you deliver a presentation to colleagues, speaking confidently and authoritatively will make you appear more competent and credible. Conversely, a timid or unsure tone makes you appear unsure of yourself and your message.

The tone of voice is not always easy to interpret. Understanding tone requires careful listening and attention to the words and how they are said. So, paying attention to the tone of voice when communicating with others is crucial to ensure that the message is accurately conveyed.

The tone of voice is a crucial aspect of body language, significant in conveying emotion and meaning in conversation. It affects how the listener perceives the message and the speaker and significantly impacts the overall impression someone makes. Pay close attention to tone when speaking and know how your tone of voice can affect the listener's interpretation of your message.

Different Tones Convey Different Body Language

Body language is a crucial communication component, helping convey thoughts, feelings, and emotions. One key element of body language is tone, referring to the words articulated and expressed through pitch, intonation, and other vocal qualities.

Different tones convey different meanings and emotions, each with unique impacts on the receiver. The tone of voice accounts for 38% of a message, making it a critical part of effective communication.

One of the most common tones in body language is the assertive tone, which conveys confidence and authority. When you speak assertively, you express your opinions and ideas clearly and confidently without appearing aggressive or defensive. This tone is often used in leadership and management roles, where communicating effectively and confident decision-making is vital. For example, you firmly state your opinion in a team meeting or when you give your employees instructions.

The opposite of an assertive tone is a submissive or apologetic tone, often used to avoid conflict or when afraid of hurting someone's feelings. When you speak with a submissive or apologetic tone, you appear hesitant or uncertain, conveying a lack of confidence or self-assurance. This tone can be detrimental to your growth and progress, as people undervalue your opinions and ideas. For example, you say, "I'm sorry" excessively, even when unnecessary.

Another tone in body language is the empathetic tone. This tone conveys that you understand and care about someone's feelings. When you speak empathetically, you demonstrate putting yourself in someone's shoes and offering support or encouragement. It is often used in counseling, coaching, or mentoring roles, where showing empathy and compassion is essential. For example, you say, "I understand how you feel," or "I'm sorry, that must be tough for you," when someone confides in you about their challenges or struggles.

The opposite of an empathetic tone is a cold or dispassionate tone, which conveys a lack of interest, concern, or care. When you speak with a cold or dispassionate tone, you appear distant, aloof, or uninterested, conveying that you don't care about someone's feelings or experiences. This tone can damage relationships and make people feel unimportant or disregarded. For example, you respond to someone's emotional story with an expressionless or monotone voice, conveying a lack of connection or empathy.

A conversational tone is another common tone in body language, conveying friendliness and approachability. When you speak with a conversational tone, you invite people to engage with you and express themselves freely. This tone is often used in social situations or networking, where making a good impression and establishing rapport are essential. For example, when you ask someone about their weekend or hobbies or make small talk at a party.

On the other hand, a monotonous or flat tone conveys boredom or disinterest and can be off-putting. When you speak with a monotonous or flat tone, you appear unenthusiastic or uninspired, conveying that you are disengaged or uninterested in what is said. This tone can harm interactions, as people feel disheartened or neglected. For example, you respond to a question with a simple "yes" or "no" without inflection or elaboration.

Body language is a critical component of communication to help convey thoughts, feelings, and emotions. The tone of voice is a significant aspect of body language, conveying various meanings and emotions. The different tones in body language include assertive, submissive, empathetic, cold, conversational, and monotonous. Understanding these tones and when to use them helps you communicate more effectively and authentically.

Elements Affecting Tone of Voice

1. Volume

Understanding body language is an important tool for effective communication. One aspect often overlooked is the volume of tone a person uses during a conversation. Learning to interpret this aspect of a person's communication style can give you important insight into their background context, personality, and emotions.

Three main tone volumes are used during communication: low, normal, and high. Each tone volume reveals different aspects of a person's body language, providing important insight into their communication style.

A low-volume tone is generally associated with shyness, insecurity, or introversion. Someone speaking at a low volume could be hiding their emotions and not drawing too much attention to themselves. In some cases, they might be afraid of being misunderstood or ignored. In addition to their low-volume tone, they appear nervous, fidgety, and avoid eye contact. When interpreting a person's body language with a low-volume tone, it's important to allow them time and space to speak without pressurizing them.

A normal tone volume is often associated with someone confident and comfortable in their skin. These individuals usually speak clearly and with purpose. They might exhibit certainty in their words and use eye contact, hand gestures, or other non-verbal cues to emphasize certain points. People using normal volume tones have open and welcoming body language. They usually make eye contact, and their facial expressions reflect their words and emotions.

Lastly, individuals using a high-volume tone during communication are often perceived as assertive or aggressive. They speak loudly and without inhibitions, making others feel intimidated or uncomfortable. People with high-volume tones have intimidating body language, like crossing their arms or standing too close to others. However, a high-volume tone does not always signal aggression. Sometimes, individuals with this tone are just enthusiastic or passionate about a subject and express themselves fully. Therefore, approach communication with a person using a high-volume tone with caution and respect.

Understanding the tone volume in a person's body language can provide valuable insight into their communication style, emotions, and background context. By paying attention to a person's tone, you can anticipate their feelings and reactions and adjust your body language and communication style accordingly. Whether a low, normal, or high volume of tone, interpret it in the broader context of the person's non-verbal cues and spoken words. This way, you achieve more effective communication and better interpersonal relationships.

2. Articulation and Vocalization

As you observe a person, you can gather important clues about them by listening to their tone of voice. How a person articulates or vocalizes can give you a unique insight into their body language and how they communicate. Often, you can determine if someone is approachable, friendly, or secretive by the sound of their voice.

When a person articulates their words clearly, it usually suggests they have mental clarity and are open to communication. They convey a message and want to be understood. They are engaged in the conversation and want to participate fully. Clear articulation is often the hallmark of effective communicators who convey their intended message with precision and clarity.

In contrast, imprecise articulation indicates deceit or mental confusion. Slurred or unclear speech can signal that a person is hiding something or cannot articulate their thoughts coherently. People who lack confidence in their message might mumble or stutter, confusing the listeners. In some cases, imprecise vocalization indicates a person is not invested in the conversation and has no desire to be fully engaged.

Very clear vocalization, while impressive, can signal negative emotion. For instance, the narcissism evident in this communication suggests the speaker is overly self-absorbed or more focused on making themselves heard rather than listening to or responding to others. These speakers are more focused on their point of view than the conversation. Additionally, tension can often cause a person's voice to become clear and precise, suggesting the person is anxious or nervous.

Stumbling over words can indicate inhibitions or aggressiveness. Nervous or uncomfortable people stutter or trip over their words, while those who feel strongly about an issue become aggressive and stumble over their words in the heat of the moment.

A person's vocalization tells a powerful story about their communication style and interactions with others. Clear vocalization suggests a person is open to conversation and engagement, while imprecise articulation hints at deceit or confusion. Very clear vocalization, while often impressive, can suggest narcissism or tension. Stumbling speech can indicate inhibitions or aggressiveness. By paying attention to a person's vocalization style, you can get a sense of their personality and communication tendencies, allowing you to better understand their body language and how they interact with others.

How a person vocalizes and articulates says a lot about their communication style and interaction with others. By listening closely to a person's tone, you can sense their mood, confidence, and openness to communication. Each person's vocalization is unique, so identifying patterns and tendencies can give insight into their personality and help interpret their body language. By paying attention to verbal and non-verbal cues, you gain a more comprehensive understanding of a person and build more effective communication strategies.

3. Pace

The pace of tone refers to the speed the person talks. It varies from person to person and even situation to situation. However, considering the pace of tone in relation to the context is essential. A slow pace of tone can indicate a lack of interest in the conversation or disconnection from the world. A person speaking slowly might be bored or disinterested in the discussion. Their body language exhibits disinterest in this scenario, like slouching or avoiding eye contact.

On the other hand, a fast pace of tone can indicate the person is anxious or tense. They might desire to hide information or feel uneasy about the topic. In this scenario, the body language exhibits nervousness, like fidgeting or avoiding eye contact. Be mindful of these cues since they can indicate the person is withholding information or feeling uncomfortable.

A regular pace of tone is difficult to interpret since it might not exhibit obvious emotion. However, it is essential to understand that a regular tone indicates the person is holding back or bottling up their emotions. They might be maintaining composure, which will be evident in their body language. They avoid fidgeting or slouching, maintaining upright posture and steady eye contact, indicating that the person is trying to control their emotions and might not be entirely engaged in the conversation.

An irregular pace of tone is the most challenging to interpret since it could indicate a range of emotions. It can indicate confusion, anxiety, or communication breakdown. A person with an irregular pace of tone exhibits conflicting non-verbal cues, making it challenging to interpret the body language accurately. In this scenario, paying close attention to their facial expressions and body posture, which provides additional context, is essential.

Understanding the pace of tone provides valuable insight into a person's emotional state. By analyzing the pace of tone, you can gather information about the person's interest, tension levels, and willingness to communicate. This information, combined with other non-verbal cues, like body posture and facial expressions, provides a wealth of information about the individual's emotional state. Be mindful of the pace of tone and its relationship with the conversation's context to interpret the person's body language accurately. You will improve your communication and understand the individuals better.

Step-by-Step Guidance

Accurately interpreting the tone of voice is an essential skill for effective communication. The tone of voice conveys the speaker's emotional state and intentions and significantly impacts the receiver's understanding of the message.

Here are practical tips for interpreting tone of voice accurately:

- **Pay Attention to Changes in Tone:** Tone varies during a conversation. Recognizing these changes provides insights into the speaker's emotions and intentions. For instance, sudden shifts from a neutral or friendly tone to an angry or defensive tone can indicate the conversation has triggered negative emotions in the speaker. On the other hand, a gradual progression from a hesitant or uncertain tone to a confident and assertive tone can signal the speaker has gained more confidence or conviction in their message.

- **Analyze the Pitch and Intonation:** Pitch and intonation are critical elements of tone, revealing the speaker's emotional state. A high-pitched tone and rising intonation indicate excitement or enthusiasm, while a low-pitched tone and falling intonation signal sadness or disappointment. Changes in pitch and intonation convey sarcasm or irony, revealing the speaker's true feelings about the topic or person discussed.

- **Observe Non-verbal Cues:** Non-verbal cues, like facial expressions, gestures, and body language, are valuable clues to interpret tone. For example, a speaker who fidgets nervously or avoids eye contact could be anxious or uncomfortable. Conversely, a speaker who stands tall, makes eye contact, and uses expansive gestures is usually confident and assertive.

Observing these non-verbal cues with tone gives a more comprehensive picture of the speaker's emotions and attitudes.

- **Consider the Context:** The conversation's context or background significantly impacts the tone. For example, a speaker uses a sarcastic or ironic tone in a light-hearted conversation or jokingly criticizes a close friend. In contrast, the same tone in a serious discussion or professional setting can come across as rude or disrespectful. Considering the context helps interpret the tone more accurately and avoid misunderstandings.

- **Listen for Emotionally Charged Words:** Emotionally charged words or phrases can indicate the speaker's emotional state. For example, a person using "hate," "love," "angry," or "happy" frequently reveals their emotional state. However, consider the context and tone of voice to determine whether the words are intended literally or sarcastically.

- **Identify Patterns in Speech:** Identifying patterns in speech, like repetition, hesitation, or filler words, gives clues about the speaker's emotional state or thought process. For example, a speaker who frequently uses "um," "uh," or long pauses might be searching for the right words to express themselves, while a speaker repeating certain phrases or ideas might be emphasizing a particular point.

- **Practice Makes Perfect:** Finally, practice interpreting the tone of voice. As with any new skill, accurately interpreting tone takes time and consistent effort. Talk to people and pay attention to their tone changes. Identify variations in tone and correlate them with the physical or emotional cues you observe. The more effort you put into practice, the more skilled you will become in accurately interpreting tone.

Chapter 7: Cultural Context and Non-verbal Cues

This chapter focuses on understanding non-verbal communication cues within different cultures and delves into how cultural norms and values significantly influence peoples' communication, gestures, and body language. Reading this chapter, you'll understand the cultural context and learn its importance when perceiving and interpreting non-verbal cues.

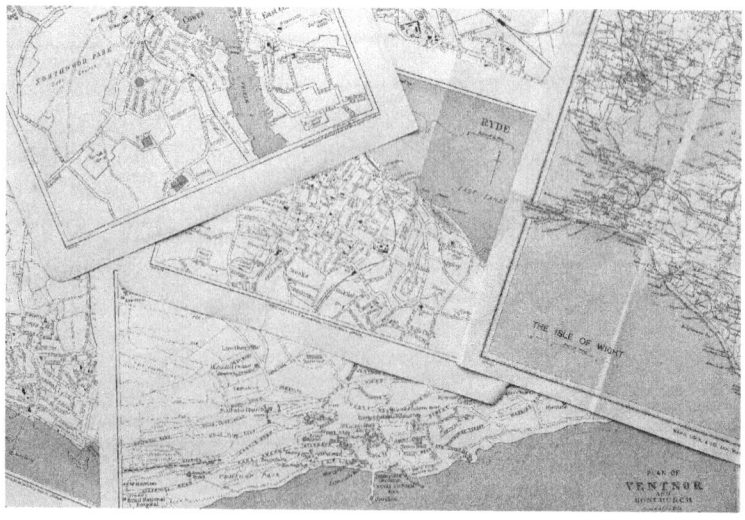

Non-verbal cues may have different meanings in different cultures.
https://unsplash.com/photos/AFB6S2kibuk?utm_source=unsplash&utm_medium=referral&utm_content=creditShareLink

You'll learn various factors to account for when communicating with someone from a different background and how each factor affects their communication habits. You learn about communication challenges, such as differences in the perception of gestures, body language, eye contact, space, time, and touch.

Cultural Context and Communication

Communication is essential for the creation and functioning of societies. It builds relationships with people, expresses thoughts and feelings, and shares ideas. Non-verbal communication can be very helpful when communicating with someone who doesn't speak your language.

Hand gestures help get your point across, narrowing the language barrier. Your facial expressions also give insight into how you feel and think. By examining your facial reactions, others can tell whether you're happy, confused, angry, sad, or concerned. Your tone of voice can reveal your intentions and feelings, even if the person doesn't understand what you're saying. By observing several non-verbal cues, people can tell whether someone is asking a question, complimenting, expressing their frustration, or being friendly regardless of their language.

How people communicate is heavily shaped by their society and culture, whether verbally or non-verbally. Therefore, it's imperative to be aware of cultural context when interpreting communication cues. Cultural context refers to the significance of culture and background in how people perceive the world and, accordingly, communicate with others.

You might encounter several obstacles and misunderstandings if you're not mindful of a person's society and upbringing's influence on their communication style. Besides language, a group's cultures, values, customs, and traditions affect nearly every aspect of their life, including gestures, facial expressions, body language, tone of voice, and other non-verbal cues. It substantially impacts how groups of people communicate among themselves and with others.

Have you ever wondered why you were getting weird looks from locals when traveling abroad? The chances are you did something considered offensive, even though it was totally normal everywhere else. In the same way that you look up the weather forecast and the most interesting sights to see when planning your trip, you must familiarize yourself with the locale's acceptable and unacceptable behaviors and verbal and non-verbal communication cues.

Each culture has unique differences, and these distinctions aren't meant to create greater gaps between people. Making an effort to understand a person's background, beliefs, customs, and cultures can bring you closer and foster mutual appreciation and admiration. It makes it much easier to connect with them, regardless of your differences. Cultural differences should also be considered in the workplace, as they affect how people do things, approach big decisions, and interact with their co-workers.

The following are a few things to consider when communicating with someone from a different background:

Do They Come from a High or Low Context Culture?

Whether a culture is a high- or low-context greatly impacts how they communicate. In high-context cultures, people rely on their relationships with others, rather than their words, to deliver certain messages because they mostly use indirect or implicit communication.

These cultures understand messages based on their shared knowledge, connection, and history. To foster deeper mutual understanding, they mostly pay attention to non-verbal communication cues, such as body language and facial expressions. Most Middle Eastern Countries, including South and North Korea, China, and Japan, are a few examples of high-context cultures.

On the other hand, low-context cultures use direct and explicit communication. They rely on carefully selected words to ensure their messages are communicated effectively. People from low-context backgrounds usually value individualism and don't leave room for ambiguity. They don't stress non-verbal communication cues, deeming them less important. Northern European countries, Germany, and the United States are among high-context cultures.

Consider Their Communication Style

Social norms, values, and culture shape a person's communication style in various ways, including their intonation, how formal or direct they are, and their non-verbal communication cues. In some cultures, indirect communication, the excessive use of metaphors and euphemisms, and using implied or double meanings are normalized. In other cultures, straightforwardness and frankness are highly valued.

Each culture has its expectations regarding non-verbal communication cues. For instance, some cultures consider crossing their legs a sign of disrespect. In many parts of the world, you'd be expected to maintain eye contact as an indication of attentiveness and respect, but in other places, maintaining eye contact for too long is perceived as aggression.

Each culture has unwritten rules regarding hierarchy and formality, depending on age or social standing. For example, skipping certain honorifics or formal titles when addressing someone older or people you don't know well is considered a sign of extreme disrespect in some countries. In other cultures, people commonly use informal language. The meaning of certain facial expressions, postures, and hand gestures can vary from one country to another, and you might accidentally offend someone.

Understand Their Cultural Beliefs

A person's cultural beliefs and values influence how they perceive and interpret others' behaviors. Exploring these beliefs helps you avoid miscommunications. For instance, some cultures encourage expressing your opinions. Others consider expressing emotions and personal opinions impolite, especially when they oppose someone else's. In most cultures, you're expected to greet others before you initiate a conversation. The form of greeting also varies depending on the context and situation.

Account for Customs and Habits

Each culture has unique communication habits and norms. While silence in the United States can be perceived as an awkward pause during conversations, it's tactfully used to indicate messages in other cultures. In Japan and some Arab countries, silence indicates respect and agreement. An Arabic saying translates to "silence is a sign of approval." Negotiation styles vary among different groups of people. In some cultures, people prioritize assertiveness, and others opt for compromise because they prioritize harmony over self-interest.

Using humor is common in various communications. It can help deliver certain messages or lighten the mood. However, this tactic's effectiveness differs from one nation to the other. Australians and Americans encourage using humor during communication. They believe it's a way to break the ice and relieve heavy, uncomfortable emotions. People prefer to be more reserved in other cultures, like China and Japan. They're very mindful of how and when they incorporate humor into their interactions.

When talking to someone, you must be wary of their cultural taboos. Each culture considers certain subjects offensive to discuss openly. In some parts of the world, talking about money or asking someone about their income is considered inappropriate. Topics like sexuality, religion, and politics are also taboo in some cultures. Also, always be aware of their cultural norms regarding personal space. Keeping a small distance during conversations is normal in Latin American and Middle Eastern countries. While in Northern American and European countries, people prefer to keep a greater distance.

Understand the Geographical Impact on Communication Style

A country's geographic location can impact its people's communication style. Each country has a unique blend of natural resources, terrain, and climate, interestingly affecting how its inhabitants communicate and interact. For instance, people raised on islands or coastal areas are often more connected to the sea. Their economy likely relied on seaside activities like maritime trade and fishing. They might also have lived in smaller communities where people valued cooperation, friendliness, and unity. Therefore, these individuals might communicate similar values and build similar relationships with their friends.

People living in rough climates and terrains might rely on communication styles reflecting their hardships. They might be overly defensive, straightforward, or hyper-independent because they were raised to practice self-sufficiency and survival techniques. People's experiences and environment shape the way they interact with the world.

Determine the Degree of Cultural Freedom

Countries have varying degrees of cultural freedom, meaning people from different backgrounds might fear being subject to censorship, repression, discrimination, or prejudice if they practice their cultural activities and traditions. Not everyone is free to celebrate and express themselves and their cultural identity.

Cultural freedom affects the extent to which people can communicate authentically and openly. When their ability is limited, they'll build less meaningful relationships. They might have to suppress certain thoughts and feelings and avoid talking about certain topics, making them come across as less reserved or non-genuine and creating misunderstandings.

When people can freely discuss their perspectives, they are more open to hearing about other people's opinions, views, and experiences. It encourages cultural exchange and allows people to learn from others' backgrounds and life events, connecting more deeply, inhibiting unhelpful views and stereotypes, and enhancing mutual appreciation. High cultural freedom leads to direct and open conversations, improving communications and allowing people to get their points across more effectively.

Consider the Societal Frankness Level

How frank and candid people are is a trait affected by their cultural and societal norms. Candor leads to more honest and stronger relationships because it allows people to lead more honest conversations. Being candid doesn't necessarily mean you must be impolite or call people out for their slightest shortcomings. However, too much politeness, to the point where you avoid giving people your honest opinion, can lead to a lack of trust. When communicating with someone, you must determine the frankness and candor they are willing to accept in a conversation. What you might think is simply being honest might be considered disrespectful to others.

Consider Your Cultural Lens

Understanding the key differences between other peoples' cultures and your own isn't enough. You must also analyze your cultural lens, the unique way you absorb and interpret information about other cultures. People give meaning to cultural aspects based on what they know, essentially influenced by their culture. A person's cultural lens is the expectations, beliefs, values, behaviors, and actions they've been raised to have or do. People who have never gone outside their cultural bubble often struggle to differentiate between their assumptions and reality.

Think of when you were outside your comfort zone. Meeting people with different values and beliefs makes you more aware of your own. You realize your morals, values, and beliefs shape your perceptions and opinions about these individuals. In other words, you are observing and evaluating them through your cultural lens.

Learning about another person's culture and background through your cultural lens leads to misconceptions. You must let go of everything your culture has taught you to truly grasp their cultural context. Approaching a culture through your background's perspective inevitably causes you to interpret their cultures and traditions in ways that don't reflect their actual meaning. It can lead to misunderstandings and the perpetuation of harmful stereotypes.

For instance, if your culture values productivity and punctuality, you might view slower-paced cultures as lazy and judge them accordingly. However, you might not realize their lack of punctuality is because they prioritize relationship-building and socialization or believe tardiness is a way to show that you're not putting your needs before others.

Challenges of Cultural Context

Unfortunately, few people can achieve flexibility with non-verbal cues, especially if they were raised to perceive certain actions and behaviors as disrespectful or offensive. Additionally, non-verbal cues usually happen unconsciously. While you can think before you speak and carefully ponder the effects of your verbal communications, you can't do the same with your facial expressions, body language, or intonation, which makes it hard to control or change them.

Here are some challenges resulting from the impact of cultural context on non-verbal cues:

Differences in Hand Gestures

Hand gestures are among the easiest and quickest ways to communicate without words. However, many people don't realize that hand gestures that they once thought universal, like a thumbs up, the equivalent of the middle finger in some cultures, don't necessarily have the same meanings everywhere in the world. Even nodding your head, a sign of agreement, means the opposite in some parts of the world. Some gestures are only known to certain cultures.

Generally, gestures can be divided into 7 categories:

1. **Gestures signaling that you've arrived or are about to leave:** Shaking hands, waving, hugging, or blowing a kiss are among the most popular gestures. Pounding a fist to the chest is among the lesser-known gestures.
2. **Gestures signaling approval:** Clapping or applauding, nodding the head up and down, and giving a thumbs up are commonly used to signal approval. Some people give high fives or simply raise their arms.

3. **Gestures signaling disapproval:** Folding the arms, moving your finger left and right, wrinkling the nose, and right and left head-nodding often signal disapproval. Yawning, choking, and holding your nose are more sarcastic ways to show disapproval and are usually deemed disrespectful.
4. **Examples of profane gestures that offend others include the middle finger, nose-thumbing, and flicking the chin.**
5. **Gestures as alternatives for words:** Extending your thumb and little finger over your ears to mimic a phone instead of saying, "Call me." Upturning your palm and moving your fingers toward you instead of saying, "Come here." Putting your index finger over your lips instead of saying, "Shut up."
6. **Gestures to attract someone's attention:** Winking, holding hands, fluttering the eyelids, wiggling the eyebrows, and staring are often used in an effort to attract someone's attention (particularly for romantic purposes). However, some of these gestures are considered offensive in some cultures.
7. **Gestures to emphasize or make a point:** Making fists, snapping the fingers, shrugging, stroking the chin, and drumming fingers commonly deliver certain messages.

Differences in Body Language

A person's body language can reveal much about their personality, engagement in an interaction, and feelings. Most of these movements come naturally and don't require much thought. However, other body movements are culturally exclusive and fulfill certain expectations. For instance, Japan and South Korea are cultures that follow a strict hierarchical system, and age, social status, and relationships dictate how you interact with people. You must bow to certain people in these cultures as a sign of respect. Special attention is paid to the angle of the bow, its duration, and how often it is done.

Some cultures, particularly high-context ones, are more expressive in non-verbal cues than others. You might notice that Italians or Middle Easterners use gestures and talk with their bodies more than the British or Germans. The Japanese are very contained and mindful of their body while speaking. They're often careful not to wave their hands around a lot or use whole-body gestures when interacting with someone. It could be because of their harmony-seeking nature, which makes them less confrontational and more cautious not to offend anyone.

How They Approach Time

People also view and approach the concept of time differently depending on their culture. Some cultures considered monochronic, like the United States, perceive time as segmented. They schedule their day and allocate certain portions to specific tasks. They live by the adage "time is money" and try to make the best use of this precious resource. They highly value efficiency, work-life balance, and punctuality. Monochronic individuals have a low tolerance for tardy or slow people and perceive them as unreliable.

Latin American, Arab, and African cultures are examples of polychronic cultures. These cultures perceive time as more fluid and flexible. They don't feel pressured to schedule their day down to the last minute and are generally more easygoing. They're multi-taskers and believe several activities and tasks can take place simultaneously. Polychronic individuals are more intuitive and like acting whenever they feel like "the time is right."

Polychronic people try to use time to accommodate their needs and the needs of others. For instance, they might find it disrespectful to end a conversation if the other person still has things to share, even if they have something else to do. Some cultures have mixed views on time, depending on the situation. For instance, in China, it's common to delay wedding receptions for a couple of hours to consider those running late. However, when it comes to work-related matters and other important meetings, punctuality is a must. The use and perception of time vary significantly, depending on the circumstances and situations in all cultures.

How They Perceive Space

The acceptable personal space differs in cultures. People usually feel comfortable with limited personal space during interactions in high-context cultures. People might feel uncomfortable in other cultures when someone maintains less space than culturally preferred. People who need more personal space than their society usually accepts are often perceived as shy or cold.

Dealing with Touch

How different cultures deal with the concept of touch during interactions relates to how they perceive personal space. In low-context cultures, individuals rarely hug or touch each other unless they're very close. Cultures considered non-contact include Germany, some Asian countries, North America, and England.

Other cultures, such as South European, Arab, and South American countries, are more expressive and affectionate and often use touch to express their emotions. Touching is often considered normal in professional relationships. Contact cultures feel comfortable with less personal space and find it respectful to maintain eye contact with others.

Accidental touch is dealt with differently in non-contact countries. Some Asian countries, especially those densely populated, are more accustomed to accidental touch and don't necessarily feel offended. People in Western cultures are more likely to feel irritated or offended when a stranger touches them, even if it is unintentional.

In some cultures, heterosexual men hold hands and greet each other with hugs and kisses as a sign of friendship. This behavior is considered highly intimate in Western cultures. In some conservative cultures, touch between individuals of the opposite sex is frowned upon. Patting a child's head is a way to show love and care in several cultures. Touching anyone's head is considered inappropriate in some Asian countries because the head is considered sacred. Shaking someone's hand using your left hand is also considered offensive in some cultures.

How Gazing and Maintaining Eye Contact Is Perceived

In Western cultures, people are expected to maintain eye contact when interacting with each other. Looking someone in the eye is considered an indicator of attentiveness. If you avoid eye contact while speaking, people might think you're being dishonest.

Individualistic cultures with low power distance value eye contact, especially in romantic relationships. Looking your partner in the eye signifies a sign that you perceive them as an equal. On the other hand, in collectivist cultures with high power distance, individuals who rank lower on the social scale avoid looking their "superiors" in the eye as a sign of respect. Avoiding eye contact signals humility.

Each culture responds differently to public staring or gazing. For example, it's considered rude to stare at someone in the United States, but the Chinese do it whenever they stumble across a beautiful or eccentric person.

You must consider a plethora of things when interpreting a person's non-verbal communication cues, especially if they come from a different background. Cultural context is significant in how people communicate and interact. Each culture ascribes unique meanings to certain hand gestures and body movements. How people perceive time, space, and eye contact is also shaped by their society and upbringing.

Chapter 8: Intuition: Trusting Your Gut

Have you ever been conflicted, trying to decipher someone's body language and what it could possibly mean? It's not uncommon to rely on intuition or "gut feelings" to help make sense of non-verbal cues. But what are these instincts, and how do they work? Understanding intuition can be a vital tool in improving communication and relationships. This chapter delves into the importance of intuition, how to interpret it, and combine it with rational thinking. So, let's dive in and unravel the mysteries of the human intuition.

Intuition is a process within human nature.

https://unsplash.com/photos/j5itydU55FI?utm_source=unsplash&utm_medium=referral&utm_content=creditShareLink

What Is Intuition?

Intuition is a complex cognitive process deeply embedded in human nature. It refers to an individual's ability to perceive, understand, and interpret information so that it seems effortless, automatic, and spontaneous. Intuition is often referred to as a hunch, a gut feeling, or a sixth sense and is usually perceived as a rapid and effective cognitive tool for decision-making.

The scientific study of intuition suggests it is a complex mix of different cognitive processes, including but not limited to perception, memory, attention, and problem-solving. Intuition is the unconscious mental process operating outside your awareness yet significantly influencing behavior and judgment.

Intuition can be developed and refined through practice and experience. Expert intuition results from years of deliberate practice and training in specific domains. For instance, experienced chess players can perceive patterns more quickly and accurately than novice players, allowing them to make better and faster decisions.

Intuition is influenced by factors like emotions and is considered an emotional response triggered by external stimuli. In some cases, intuition can lead to biases or errors in judgment, particularly when influenced by personal beliefs or past experiences. However, research suggests that intuition can be improved through techniques like mindfulness meditation, which promotes self-awareness and clarity of thought.

How Does Intuition Work?

Intuition is a fascinating phenomenon of the human mind enabling decision-making, problem-solving, and interpreting information without conscious reasoning or deliberate thought. It is a non-linear, non-rational, and non-verbal process occurring spontaneously and often unconsciously, relying on past experiences, expertise, emotions, and perceptions. Intuition is not a supernatural power but rather an innate ability present in everyone and can be improved with practice and training.

The essence of intuition is in the processing of implicit knowledge – the information a person is unaware of but is stored in the memory and influences behavior and judgment in subtle and complex ways. This implicit knowledge is acquired through life experiences, education, upbringing, culture, and environment and can be accessed and used by the subconscious mind to guide people in various contexts.

One of the most natural examples of intuition is the gut feeling or hunch often felt when faced with a decision or problem. It is a sudden and inexplicable sense that something is right or wrong, good or bad, without logical or rational justification. For instance, imagine you are interviewing a candidate for a job, and a voice in your head tells you this person is untrustworthy without tangible evidence or reason. You can ignore this feeling, hire the candidate, or follow your intuition and reject the application. Later, you might discover the person had a history of fraud or dishonesty, and your intuition was accurate.

Another example of intuition is expertise-driven decision-making, which relies on the vast knowledge and skills experts acquire in their respective fields. Experts often make intuitive judgments based on their holistic understanding of the situation, pattern recognition, and inductive reasoning. For instance, a doctor diagnoses a patient's illness based on symptoms that might not seem related to the disease but have a characteristic pattern only the expert can recognize. Similarly, chess players intuitively make a move based on their experience and intuition rather than logically calculating possible moves.

Intuition can operate through emotional cues, the subtle signals the emotional state sends to the conscious mind. Emotions are an essential source of information and feedback and convey valuable messages about you and the environment. For instance, when you meet someone for the first time, you get an intuitive sense of whether they are friendly or hostile based on their tone of voice, body language, and facial expressions. These emotional clues activate your intuition and quickly evaluate the situation before the logical brain takes over.

Another way intuition works is by triggering unconscious biases and prejudices, influencing your perception and judgments through a heuristic or mental shortcut. Your biases are the automatic and unconscious mental processes categorizing and evaluating people, objects, and situations based on your preconceptions and stereotypes. For instance, if you see a person wearing a business suit, you might assume they are successful, competent, and knowledgeable, even if you have no evidence to support your judgment. Your intuition relies on these biases and stereotypes to make a quick decision or judgment, even though it may not be accurate or fair.

Intuition is a complex and multifaceted process through implicit knowledge, expertise, emotions, biases, and heuristics. It is a powerful tool that can enhance creativity, problem-solving, and decision-making abilities, but it has limitations and risks. To develop intuition effectively, you must be aware of your biases and prejudices, challenge assumptions and beliefs, and balance intuition with conscious deliberation and critical thinking. Intuition is not a substitute for rationality or evidence-based reasoning but rather a complement to expand your perspectives and enrich your life.

The Importance of Intuition in Understanding a Person's Body Language

Body language is crucial in interpreting the underlying meaning behind conversations in human interaction. How people position, move and express themselves affects how others perceive them. Therefore, reading body language is an essential skill for anyone aiming to be an effective communicator or negotiator. However, intuition is another aspect often overlooked in understanding body language.

Intuition is an inherent ability everyone possesses. It's an instinctive cognition to make quick judgments about people or situations based on subtle signals. Intuition helps you interpret your surroundings more easily and quickly, even if you don't have all the facts or information. For reading body language, intuition is a powerful tool for a better understanding of what's happening behind spoken words.

One reason intuition is so important in deciphering body language is that the signals you pick up through body language are often subtle and sometimes subconscious. It can be challenging to interpret these signals without the help of intuition, as they might not be immediately noticeable to the conscious self. For example, you notice someone crossing their arms or avoiding eye contact. In social situations, intuition can help decipher subtle cues such as discomfort or withdrawal.

Furthermore, intuition helps you to sense when something seems off or inconsistent in someone's body language, even when they attempt to be deceitful. For example, someone claims they are perfectly happy and relaxed, but their body posture or subtle facial expressions suggest otherwise. Your intuition can help you detect these inconsistencies and potentially reveal ulterior motives or hidden agendas.

Another important role of intuition in reading body language is it helps personalize interpreting the signals. Some universal body language cues most people display, the context affects the meaning. For example, a person fidgeting in their seat could indicate restlessness or signify nervousness or excitement, depending on the circumstances. Intuition can help factor in the unique person or situation to interpret the signals more accurately.

Intuition in reading body language can be highlighted from a cultural perspective. Different cultures have varying interpretations of body language. For example, a gesture signifying gratitude in one country might be impolite in another. So, understanding and factoring in culture while reading body language cues in unfamiliar contexts is crucial. Your intuition can guide you to decipher the non-verbal cues' correct interpretation in cross-cultural communications.

Intuition is an instrumental tool in interpreting body language cues. It taps into the subtle, subconscious signals people give off, personalizes the interpretations, and detects inconsistencies in peoples' expressions. Although body language is not a sure-shot predictor of behavior or motivations, combined with intuition, it can significantly improve the accuracy of insight. Developing intuition in body language interpretations is a gradual process of consciously noting body language cues and verifying your interpretation. As Malcolm Gladwell aptly said, "Intuition is not some magical property that arises unbidden from deep within our minds. It is a product of long hours, intelligent design, meaningful work environments, and particular rules and principles." Therefore, strive to develop your intuition continuously, and it will transform into your sixth sense unveiling the mysteries of body language.

The Role of Subconscious Processing and Emotional Cues in Intuitive Decision-Making

Subconscious processing in intuitive decision-making is important for quickly processing large amounts of information that would otherwise require lengthy analysis or deliberation. The brain can take in far more data than you could ever consciously consider, and the unconscious sorting of this data enables quick and accurate decisions. For example, when you drive a car, your brain processes the speed limits, other drivers around you, construction signs, and road conditions simultaneously while all you do is focus on steering. This automatic processing happens without any active effort on your part but allows you to make decisions while driving safely.

Simultaneously, emotions are important in intuitive decision-making. Without realizing it, the emotional brain constantly encodes and decodes signals from your environment. As a result, you unconsciously pick up on warning signs or subtle cues to help you decide without consciously considering all the relevant factors. For example, suppose you enter a room that feels tense or uncomfortable. In that case, your body instinctively sends you signals indicating something is off without requiring conscious thought processes. Your intuition kicks in and helps guide your decision-making by sending you a clear signal to leave the situation, even if no obvious external signs of danger are present.

In addition to subconscious processing and emotional cues, intuition can be informed by personal experiences and the stories you tell yourself. Past experiences shape your decisions. Similarly, internal narratives can help you unconsciously interpret what is happening around you and inform your intuitive decision-making. For example, suppose you're contemplating whether to take a particular job opportunity. Your past experiences might lead you towards one decision or another, but so do the stories you tell yourself about the position or yourself.

Ultimately, understanding how subconscious processing and emotional cues affect intuitive decision-making can help you make more accurate decisions without relying too heavily on conscious thought. By understanding how the brain processes information and responds to environmental cues, you can better understand why certain decisions feel right and make more informed decisions to reach your goals. This knowledge can be incredibly useful when making important life choices or navigating complex situations without spending a lot of time analyzing every detail.

Ultimately, intuition involves subconscious processing and emotional cues which inform your intuitive decision-making. By understanding these processes better, you learn to trust your gut more and become a wiser decision-maker.

Combining Intuition with Rational Thinking

Intuition and rational thinking have much to offer in reading body language. While rational thinking can help you read context cues and answer questions quickly, intuition helps you pick up on subtle nuances in body language which might otherwise be missed. These together can effectively decode non-verbal communication and make accurate judgments about the meanings.

Intuition is a powerful tool to help you pick up on subtle cues that are not immediately obvious. It allows you to tap into your inner sense of knowing and make quick assessments based on your instincts. For example, you might get a gut feeling that someone is disingenuous or hiding something, even when their words and actions suggest otherwise.

However, relying solely on intuition can be problematic since it is subjective and prone to bias. Past experiences and personal beliefs can affect how you interpret body language, leading to inaccurate readings. Hence, rational thinking is significantly beneficial.

Intuition is relative as it helps you pick up on subtle cues that rational thinking might miss. For instance, a person's body language shows signs of anxiety, such as fidgeting, sweating, and avoiding eye contact, but their facial expression could appear relaxed. In this case, intuition is essential for accurately judging a person's feelings. It won't necessarily give you the exact answer, but it will guide you in making an appropriate decision.

Rational thinking is necessary when reading body language. Additionally, it can help make sense of the data collected by intuition and conclude its meaning. Rational thinking uses logical reasoning and objective observations to assess body language. Combining your intuition with rational thinking, you make more well-rounded assessments considering emotional cues and cold, hard facts. For example, suppose someone sits rigidly with their arms crossed and avoiding eye contact. In that case, rational thinking tells you they are uncomfortable or angry. It could be further confirmed by looking at other clues, like tone of voice, facial expressions, or word choice.

Combining intuitive and rational thinking when reading body language is advantageous in understanding what another person is conveying non-verbally. The key is to be consciously and subconsciously aware of the signs to accurately decode them, even in difficult conversations. Additionally, body language does not necessarily give you the entire picture. It should be used with other communication forms, such as verbal or written communication, to better understand the situation.

So, take time each day to observe the people around you and practice honing your ability to read body language.

To grasp intuition and rational thinking in action, consider the following scenario. You are interviewing a potential job candidate, and while they seem confident and capable, something about their body language makes you uneasy. Your intuition tells you something is off, but you're not sure what it is precisely.

Instead of dismissing your gut feeling, you take a moment to analyze the situation more objectively. You examine their body language in greater detail and note specific behaviors supporting your intuition. For example, you might notice they repeatedly cross their legs or fidget, suggesting they are nervous or uncomfortable.

Based on this more well-rounded assessment, you ask a follow-up question allowing the candidate to elaborate on a particular aspect of their experience. This additional information helps shed light on your gut feeling and confirms your intuition that the candidate is not the best fit for the role.

In this scenario, by combining your intuition with rational thinking, you read the candidate's body language more accurately and made a more informed decision. You tapped into your inner sense of knowing while using logical reasoning and objective observations to support your intuition.

Another example of this combination in action is in social interactions. You attend a party and meet someone new. While they seem friendly and engaging, something about their body language makes you question their sincerity. Your intuition tells you that there's something off, but you're not precisely sure what it is.

Instead of disregarding your intuition, you take a moment to observe the person's body language more closely. You look for specific behaviors supporting your intuition and note inconsistencies in their behavior. For example, you might notice that they maintain eye contact for longer than what is comfortable or stand too close.

You pick up on specific behaviors that violate social norms or personal boundaries by objectively analyzing the situation. This realization helps you decide how to interact with this person further. You could politely end the conversation or excuse yourself from the situation.

When reading body language, there are times when your intuition can be your best friend. However, there are also times when relying solely on intuition can lead to misinterpretations and misunderstandings. Therefore, combining your intuition with rational thinking to accurately assess body language is vital.

Combining intuition with rational thinking is crucial for accurately reading body language. Intuition can be a powerful tool, but relying on logical reasoning and objective observations is essential to avoid subjective interpretations. A more well-rounded approach to assessing body language better equips you to make informed decisions and navigate social situations more confidently.

Tips to Harness Your Intuition

- **Self-awareness:** Get to know yourself better. Take time to observe and reflect on your thoughts and feelings and how you react to the world around you. Pay attention to physical sensations in your body that could signify tension or anxiety during an important decision or conversation. Knowing potential emotional triggers is important to prevent them from overwhelming you and cloud judgment.
- **Mindfulness:** You can practice mindfulness through meditation, yoga, or even sitting quietly for a few minutes each day and focusing on your breath as it moves in and out of your lungs. This will help you calm down and access your intuition more easily. It allows you to become more aware of your body so that when faced with a situation, you instinctively know how to respond without thinking too much about it.
- **Learn from Others:** Observing the body language of others can give you valuable insight and help you understand their feelings better. Pay attention to facial expressions, gestures, and posture. These signals can indicate whether someone is truthful or deceptive. When interacting with people, don't jump to conclusions based on what they say or do. Instead, consider what their body language tells you.
- **Listen Intently:** Listening intently means paying close attention to the words, the tone of voice, and the context of conversations. You can catch hidden meanings behind peoples' words and gauge their true feelings.

- **Journaling:** Writing down your thoughts and feelings is a great way to connect with what's happening internally. It clarifies confusing decisions, allowing you to make better choices when trusting your gut.

- **Pay Attention to Dreams:** Dreams might seem random or disconnected from reality, but they contain valuable clues about intuition, body language, and emotions of which you are unaware. Keep a dream journal by your bedside to record insight or messages revealed through dreaming; this will help you understand yourself better and make informed decisions.

- **Trust Your Instincts:** When faced with a difficult decision or situation, trust your instincts and don't be afraid to act on them. Often people second guess themselves and ignore their gut feeling, leading to regrets. Instead, assess the situation using all the tools mentioned, listen to your intuition, and act accordingly.

- **Practice Self-care:** Caring for yourself is essential to access your intuition effectively and accurately understand others' body language. Get enough rest, eat healthy meals, exercise regularly, and find ways to relax, like spending time in nature or engaging in creative activities. It will help balance your body and mind, which is key for intuitive decision-making.

By incorporating these tips into your daily life, you will be better equipped to access your intuition, understand others' body language, and make confident decisions. Remember, trusting your gut is important and necessary to make wise choices and move forward in life. So, don't be afraid to take risks; it could lead you to success.

Chapter 9: Applying Your Knowledge

Body language is an important aspect of communication, mostly underappreciated and even neglected. Non-verbal communication conveys attitudes, intentions, and emotions. This book has shown you the different components of body language and how a proper understanding of their usage leads to a better understanding of human behavior.

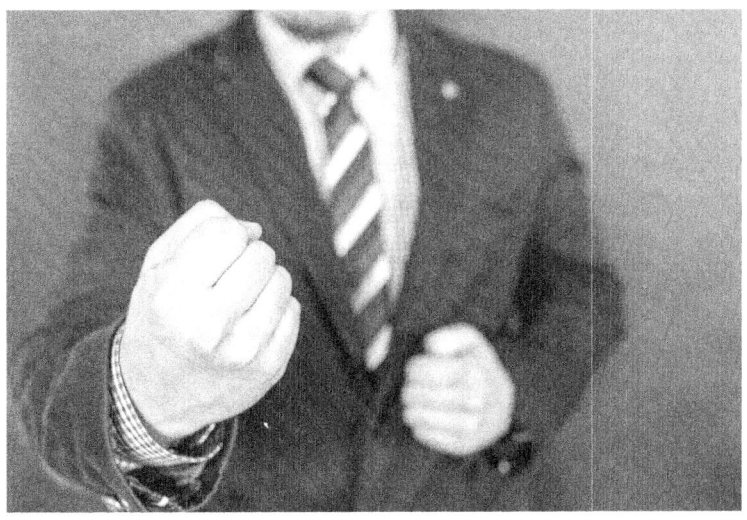

Body language is a vital aspect of communication.
https://www.pexels.com/photo/men-s-black-blazer-652348/

This final chapter focuses on the practical application of body language skills. You will be guided in applying the body language skills you learned in your relationships, workplace, and social situations. It provides tips and strategies to improve your communication, build stronger relationships, and gain insight into human behavior by applying your knowledge of body language.

Understanding Body Language in the Workplace

Every successful workplace is built on effective communication. It encourages cooperation and builds healthy relationships to increase productivity. Nevertheless, verbal exchanges are only one form of communication. When conveying information to ensure effective communication, body language is vital.

You can better grasp non-verbal cues from your coworkers, superiors, and subordinates by learning to read and understand body language in the workplace. Reading and understanding visual clues improves your ability to connect and engage at work to understand others' feelings and thoughts better.

Why Is Body Language Important in the Workplace?

Understanding body language in the workplace is essential for the following reasons:

Conveys Emotions and Attitudes

You can know a person's emotions, intentions, and attitudes when you understand how to read their body language. For instance, a smile might imply friendliness and openness, whereas crossed arms can suggest a defensive demeanor.

Enhances Communication

Non-verbal cues support verbal communication by elaborating on meaning and offering context. For instance, a nod can indicate that you agree, whereas a furrowed brow can denote confusion or disapproval.

Builds Relationships

You can build rapport and trust with your coworkers, clients, and customers by using body language. Making a good impression and establishing connections can be facilitated by maintaining eye contact, using open gestures, and showing interest.

Influences Perceptions

You can influence how others see you by using non-verbal cues. Slouching or avoiding eye contact can imply that you are insecure or lack confidence. Similarly, an authoritative demeanor, firm handshake, and assertive gestures can communicate to others that you are competent and in control.

How to Read and Interpret Body Language in the Workplace

After familiarizing yourself with the fundamentals of body language, the next step is to practice interpreting and reacting to non-verbal cues in formal settings. Follow these guidelines to learn to read and interpret body language in the workplace:

Observe

Observation is the first step in learning to read a person's body language at work. You should focus on the person's gestures, postures, and facial expressions.

Here are some useful tips to look out for:

- **Gestures:** A person's hand and arm movements can reveal anxiety, excitement, or enthusiasm. Pay attention to tapping, twitching, or arm crossing at the office.
- **Posture:** A person could show confidence or unease through their posture. Watch your colleagues. Are they sitting with a stooped back or standing tall with their shoulders back?
- **Facial Expressions:** You can tell a lot about how someone feels by their facial expressions. Be observant of people with raised eyebrows, scowls, smiles, or squinted eyes.

For instance, you observed a colleague refusing to make eye contact during a meeting. This body language shows they are either nervous or uncomfortable about a situation.

Contextualize

Contextualization is the second step in understanding body language. Consider the circumstances of the event and the person's actions during the event. While dealing with contextualization, you must consider the following:

- **Personal Habits:** Body language can be influenced by a person's normal conduct. Please take note of their normal demeanor and how it differs from their current actions.
- **Environment:** A person's body language can be influenced by their immediate surroundings. Check to affirm if they are in a pleasant or unpleasant environment.
- **Cultural Norms:** Body language can communicate in several ways across cultures. Keep these differences in mind and adjust your understanding as needed.

For example, you see your colleague behaving out of character in a meeting. Knowing they are the confident and engaging type, you will quickly notice something is off with them because it is not their usual modus operandi.

Cluster

Clustering is the third phase in interpreting body language. Instead of focusing on specific signs, search for behavioral patterns. Here are a few things to think about:

- **Repetition:** If the person repeats a behavior like crossing their arms or caressing their face, it could suggest a more serious emotional condition.
- **Consistency:** Is the person's verbal and non-verbal communication in sync? If not, notice inconsistencies.
- **Timing:** Keep track of the person's particular actions. Does it answer a specific question or topic?

For example, while discussing a specific project at your workplace, you notice your colleague behaving in an increasingly agitated fashion, like repeatedly crossing their arms and avoiding eye contact. This action can indicate that they are uncomfortable or opposed to what is discussed.

Avoid Assumptions

Avoiding assumptions is the fourth step in understanding body language. To avoid making assumptions, you must keep an open mind and refrain from snap judgments since non-verbal signs can be misunderstood.

- **Check for Context:** Ensure the issue's context is understood before assuming anything. Ask questions if you require further information.
- **Look for Additional Cues:** Consider the speaker's words and tone of voice. Non-verbal clues should not be relied on alone.
- **Consider Multiple Interpretations:** Consider other meanings a non-verbal cue might convey.

For example, if your coworker avoids making eye contact during a meeting, you might assume they are bored or uninterested. However, after weighing various explanations and looking for additional cues, you discover they're merely feeling under the weather.

Self-Awareness

Self-awareness is the final step in reading body language. Take note of your non-verbal communication and how it influences the situation. Here are some pointers:

- **Adjust Your Non-Verbal Cues:** Ensure your verbal expressions and the situation are reflected in your non-verbal cues.
- **Be Conscious of Your Body Language:** Understand how your body language can affect the conversation.
- **Practice Active Listening:** Pay attention to verbal and non-verbal signs to understand the situation.

For example, you observe the other party acting forcefully during a negotiation. You become aware that your body language might be contributing to the tense situation, so change your tone and posture to ease the tension.

Recognizing Non-Verbal Clues in Social Situations

Using non-verbal cues in social communication is crucial. Non-verbal cues give information about a person's thoughts, feelings, and intentions, helping you relate to them better, especially in social settings. When meeting new people, you rely heavily on non-verbal cues for creating impressions and building relationships.

The Significance of Body Language in Networking

Networking is key, whether you're looking for a job, expanding your social network, or marketing your business. Connecting with others is essential for networking, and body language is as important as verbal communication.

Body language can convey assertiveness, openness, and confidence, which are important for successful networking. Using the right body language can create a positive first impression, connect with new people, and project confidence and reliability.

Reading Body Language to Improve Your Networking Skills

For effective social communication, you must be able to read body language. To help you improve your networking abilities, consider the following body language reading techniques:

Take Note of Eye Contact

Eye contact is a potent non-verbal cue conveying sincerity, trust, and curiosity. Don't let your gaze wander while conversing with someone. Instead, maintain eye contact. Avoiding eye contact could indicate discomfort or apathy while making excessive eye contact can come across as hostile.

Take Note of Your Posture

Posture can convey openness, assertiveness, and confidence. Keep your shoulders back, stand straight, and avoid slouching or hunching. Good posture can help you project a confident and friendly personality.

Keep an Eye Out for Mirroring

Mirroring is the act of someone imitating your actions, gestures, or facial expressions. Mirroring signifies bonding since it shows the other person is paying attention to you and is fascinated by what you say.

Pay Attention to the Tone of Your Voice

Tone can convey emotions such as excitement, confidence, and honesty. Adjust the tone of your voice to the person you're conversing with by paying close attention to them. If you communicate clearly and confidently, it might be easier for you to appear more trustworthy and confident.

Take Note of Hand Gestures

Hand gestures can denote zeal, sincerity, and a thirst for knowledge. Do not fidget or cross your arms, as this could signify defensiveness or discomfort. Instead, use open-handed gestures and keep your arms at your sides.

Using Body Language to Establish a Connection with New Acquaintances

For networking to be successful, building rapport is essential. You can connect with someone you do not know and establish confidence and trust using good body language.

Here are some tips on using body language to build rapport:

Smile

One of the simplest ways to connect with someone is to smile. A sincere and welcoming smile could help establish a positive first impression and put the other person at ease. Smiling shows you are friendly, kind, and interested in the other person. Your smile must be sincere when using it to connect. A fake smile can raise suspicion because it is obvious, as your lips follow your eyes when you smile. It shows you are absorbed in the topic when you smile and maintain eye contact simultaneously.

For instance, you are applying for a job and want to impress the hiring manager. Approach the room with a warm smile, open body language, and an expression of your joy for the job offer. Focus on keeping eye contact, paying attention, and using the tone of your voice to convey your passion for the position.

Show Your Enthusiasm

Enthusiasm is contagious and can help a person develop fondness quickly. When you demonstrate excitement, you communicate interest in what the other person says and value their point of view.

To effectively express enthusiasm in your tone of voice and facial expressions, do it with lively speech. Make eye contact, smile, and nod when the other person speaks.

Use Touch to Demonstrate Warmth and Sincerity

An effective method for non-verbal communication is touch. It shows you are honest, warm to be around, and trustworthy. It is equally a method that must be used with utmost care and politeness to avoid sending the wrong message. Please ensure that the other person is comfortable being touched physically and you are not invading their personal space. Shake hands or touch them lightly on the arm or shoulder to establish a connection. If they appear uncomfortable, avoid contact and respect their personal space.

Make Use of Open Body Language

You need not say much before your body language gives you away. For instance, when your legs or arms are crossed, it is a sign you feel indifferent or defensive.

Keep your posture open, your legs and arms uncrossed, and use receptive body language. Face them and lean in slightly to show you are paying attention to what the other person says. It helps develop a sense of comfort and trust with the object of your conversation.

Use the Mirroring Technique

The mirroring technique means subtly imitating another individual's posture, gestures, and attitudes. It is one of the quickest ways to build relationships and rapport. To use mirroring, observe and imitate the other person's body language. For instance, you could lean forward if they lean forward. Use your hands to emulate their gestures if they use theirs as a cue. Use mirroring sparingly and in moderation to avoid appearing fake or manipulative.

Suppose you want to leave a good first impression on a potential business partner at a networking event - use open body language, a genuine smile, and words of appreciation when introducing yourself. Use minimal physical contact, like a light handshake, and emulate their body language to build rapport.

Understanding Non-Verbal Communication in Romantic Relationships

Non-verbal cues are frequently more effective than verbal communication in romantic relationships.

Here are a few instances where non-verbal cues are used in relationships:

Be Observant of Body Language

Your partner's posture, walking patterns, and mannerisms reveal much about their emotions. For instance, crossing their arms or legs could be a sign of discomfort or defensiveness. Furthermore, it suggests interest or attraction if they lean toward you or mimic your movements.

Pay Close Attention to Facial Expressions

A person's facial expressions convey a lot about how they feel. Your partner is likely happy and engaged in the conversation if they smile and make eye contact. However, if they avoid your gaze or scowl, it could indicate they are disturbed or uneasy.

Listen to Their Tone

How someone speaks reveals a lot about their feelings. For instance, a soft and sensitive tone can imply love, but a harsh and strong tone might represent annoyance or fury. Observing these non-verbal cues gives you valuable insight into your partner's emotions and improves your ability to interact with them.

How Body Language Can Help in Conflict Resolution

People's emotions take over and shoot through the roof when upset, and they frequently say or do things they regret. There will always be arguments in relationships. Conflicts will worsen if handled inappropriately, whether in small disagreements or full-blown fights. Disputes can be resolved amicably and even help the relationship grow if handled properly.

The following tips will help you overcome disputes using body language:

Remain Calm

It's normal to experience a sudden surge in emotions when disagreements occur. Impulsive responses can worsen the problem and sour relationships. Your judgment will become clouded by rage, irritation, and anxiety. At this point, you must maintain your composure and tackle the matter rationally. Controlling your breathing is one technique to help you remain calm. Take deep breaths and softly exhale to regulate your heartbeat and relax your muscles. You'll feel more in control and less impulsive due to this exercise.

Using open body language is another method to maintain your composure. Keep your arms relaxed and ensure your partner can see your eyes. It will let them know you are willing to listen to them and work things out.

Acknowledge Your Partner's Feelings

When resolving a dispute, showing empathy and respect for your partner's feelings is best. It could calm the tension and show your willingness to negotiate a settlement.

Here are a couple of tips for acknowledging your partner's emotions:

- Use "I" statements to express your understanding of your partner's perspective.
- Use active listening strategies like echoing your partners' words or paraphrasing them.
- Saying, "I understand why you feel that way," or "That must have been difficult for you," will help validate your partner's feelings.

Your partner will feel understood and validated if you consider their emotions. It also helps the conversation advance toward a conclusion.

Consider the following example to show how body language can aid in conflict resolution:

Six months into their relationship, Jane and Tom started to fight more frequently. Tom's arms were crossed, and he avoided Jane's eyes during a tense debate. She became aware he was on the defensive and unwilling to hear her point of view. She inhaled deeply, uncrossed her arms, and looked Tom in the eyes. While considering Tom's viewpoint, she expressed her feelings in "I" clauses. She made it an effective dialogue, and they settled their dispute not long after the open body language and respect for Tom's emotions techniques were applied.

Use Open Body Language

Without saying a word, your body language conveys a plethora of information. Open body language when resolving a dispute can promote trust and express your willingness to consider your partner's viewpoint.

The following are examples of open body language:

- Show you are listening to your partner by nodding your head
- Maintain eye contact with your partner

- Your facial expressions should be relaxed
- Do not cross your arms or legs
- Slightly lean towards your partner. This shows that you are invested in working things out.

Open body language establishes a safe and welcoming environment for your partner to express their thoughts and feelings. It can assist in removing obstacles to communication.

Recognizing Dishonesty

Dishonesty is bound to rear its ugly head in a relationship, even with trust in your partner. Through body language, you can see deception for what it truly is and can recognize and tackle challenges that might appear with the following useful tips:

- **Not Maintaining Eye Contact**

Dishonest people shy away from direct eye contact. It signifies they are uneasy or not completely truthful. When you look into their eyes, they feel you are looking into their soul and would do anything to avoid your gaze.

- **Body Language Is Not Consistent**

Inconsistent body language is frequently the outcome of dishonesty. For instance, a person lying might hold a smile, but their body language shows stress or discomfort. Knowing these warning signs, you will better determine when your partner might lie, helping you deal with your relationship problems.

Nervous Movements or Fidgets

When your partner lies, they usually fidget, touch their face or hair, avoid being still, or exhibit other nervous behaviors.

Developing Your Body Language Reading Skills

The ability to read body language is not a natural talent. The learning process requires patience, effort, and desire. Here are some suggestions to help you become more adept at reading body language:

- Keep an eye on how people hold their bodies and move their hands, mouths, and eyes. These convey various feelings and ideas.

- Observe clusters and patterns of body language.
- Notice how people move their bodies during social events, meetings, or watching movies or television.
- Learn to read body language in everyday situations. Keep track of the body language of those you interact with and attempt to correlate it with their speech and behaviors.
- Research how body language varies between cultures. Certain gestures or postures have different connotations in various cultures.

The Importance of Context and Clusters

Understanding context and clusters is necessary for reading body language. Body language can be complicated and have multiple connotations depending on the situation.

The following suggestions can help you analyze body language in context:

Understand the Relationship and Setting

Understanding a body language signal requires understanding the context in which it was used. It entails considering the situation, the parties involved, and other relevant details. For instance, a smile could be welcoming in one case, like meeting a new acquaintance, but mocking or false in another situation, like during a serious conversation.

The relationship between two individuals can strongly influence the significance of body language cues. A close friend's touch on your arm can be perceived as consoling, whereas a stranger's touch on your arm might be perceived as intrusive or improper. By considering the relationship and context, you can prevent misunderstanding body language and drawing the wrong conclusions.

Be Abreast of Details

Timing and order are important aspects to consider when understanding body language. Paying attention to these nuances is crucial to preventing misconceptions because little changes in the timing or order of gestures can substantially alter their meaning. For instance, a nod and a shake of the head can signify conflicted emotions, whereas a shake of the head and a nod might imply agreement after initially resisting.

Considering how body language complements verbal communication is best. Comparing two signals is crucial to establishing which is more accurate when someone says one thing while expressing another through body language. For instance, if someone says they're happy, but their body language suggests they're not, you should probe further to understand their true feelings.

The Influence of Combined Cues

While specific gestures can hint at someone's emotional state, combining several cues can help you understand someone's thoughts more precisely. Insight into someone's opinions or intentions can be gained through groups of non-verbal clues or clusters of movements occurring together. During a conversation, someone leans away from you, crosses their arms, and avoids eye contact. This collection of behaviors could indicate they are uneasy or defending themselves. However, a person smiling, nodding, and maintaining constant eye contact is engaged and interested in the conversation.

To further understand the role of context and clusters in body language interpretation, let's examine a few real-world scenarios:

- **Public Speaking**

When speaking to an audience, a speaker stands straight, makes eye contact, and moves their arms expansively. The audience might be more inclined to believe the speaker with these clusters of gestures, implying the speaker is confident and knowledgeable.

- **Job Interview**

During a job interview, the interviewer leans in, nods, and maintains eye contact with the candidate. The candidate's chances of obtaining the job might increase with these clusters of gestures, showing that the interviewer is attentive and interested in the applicant.

Learning to read and analyze body language is excellent for developing your conversational skills, forging deeper relationships, and better understanding people's behavior. Reading body language in various contexts, including work settings, social settings, and intimate relationships, is highly useful. It can significantly affect how people interact with one another in certain circumstances.

Developing your body language reading skills will help you build meaningful relationships, gain people's trust, and make lasting impressions.

Conclusion

Now that you have read this book, you know everything about reading people like a book. You've gained sufficient knowledge to understand and interpret body language and non-verbal cues effectively. When you know how to pick up on these signs accurately, you naturally gain more insight into the intentions, thoughts, and feelings of others. Learning these signs will help you become a better communicator and determine when someone is lying or has ill intentions.

Non-verbal cues are key to building trust and rapport between individuals. People subconsciously look for clues in an individual's facial expressions, body language, and tone of voice to determine whether they can be trusted. Do you ever get an off-putting feeling about someone for no apparent reason? You might have picked up on a non-verbal cue that they have ill intentions. At the very least, understanding non-verbal cues allows people to determine when it's their turn to speak or signals they should speak in a softer tone or put on a friendly smile to help someone feel at ease.

This book has covered the importance of observation, interpretation, and intuition in reading people's body language. You've learned the skills and strategies to master differentiating between various body language cues, such as posture, facial expressions, and gestures, and determine what each means. You've come across indispensable tips and tricks you can always revisit to observe these cues and identify the messages and hidden emotions a person's voice carries.

By reading this book, you've discovered how a person's cultural background and personal values can heavily influence their communication skills, behaviors, and body language. You've explored the fascinating yet alarming world of deception and understood how many use this art to steer conversations in their favor. Fortunately, learning about deception allows you to easily determine when someone is untruthful or doesn't have your best interest at heart.

This book has explained the role of your intuition in reading body language. You should trust your instincts and pay attention to your gut feelings when understanding others. Intuition is a crucial aspect of communication because it helps you read between the lines and uncover information not directly revealed. Intuition allows you to determine how others could react to your messages and how your words and actions are perceived. Over time, trusting your intuition will help you build stronger relationships and create stronger boundaries.

You are now ready to apply the skills obtained in several contexts, such as the workplace, social situations, and personal relationships. Human communications are very complex. Often, there are underlying elements people don't pick up on, which is why misunderstandings and miscommunications are always likely. Having a book to help you read body language is especially handy.

Remember, each person communicates uniquely. Some body language cues might indicate different meanings depending on the context and the person's personality. Therefore, you should interpret these signs sensibly and note individual differences when observing people's body language.

Mastering the art of non-verbal communication requires a lot of practice, dedication, effort, and patience. However, this powerful and rewarding tool is worth the trouble. Incorporating these strategies into your daily life and interactions allows you to predict the behaviors of others and understand them on a deeper level.

Here's another book by Andy Gardner that you might like

Free Bonus from Andy Gardner

Hi!

My name is Andy Gardner, and first off, I want to THANK YOU for reading my book.

Now you have a chance to join my exclusive email list related to human psychology and self-development so you can get the ebook below for free as well as the potential to get more ebooks for free! Simply click the link below to join.

P.S. Remember that it's 100% free to join the list.

Access your free bonuses here:
https://livetolearn.lpages.co/andy-gardner-how-to-read-people-like-a-book-paperback/

References

(N.d.). Inc.com. https://www.inc.com/lolly-daskal/learn-the-secret-into-decoding-people-s-emotions.html

(N.d.). Indeed.com. https://www.indeed.com/career-advice/career-development/improve-observation-skills#:~:text=Observation%20skills%20are%20qualities%20and,people%20and%20things%20around%20you.

. https://exploringyourmind.com/what-does-your-tone-of-voice-convey/

4 types of listening: Exploring how to be a better listener. (2021, June 2). Maryville Online. https://online.maryville.edu/blog/types-of-listening/

About Paul Ekman. (2013, May 15). Paul Ekman Group. https://www.paulekman.com/about/paul-ekman/

Ackerman, A. (2008, March 6). Emotion thesaurus entry: Jealousy. WRITERS HELPING WRITERS®; Writers Helping Writers. https://writershelpingwriters.net/2008/03/emotion-thesaurus-entry-jealousy/

Birch, J. (2021, August 29). Physical signs someone is in love with you: How to recognize body language. Well+Good. https://www.wellandgood.com/signs-someone-is-in-love-with-you/

Body language for intuition: Certified body language trainer. (2018, March 24). Nonverbal Science with Monica Levin; Nonverbal Science, LLC. https://www.nonverbalscience.com/speaker/intuition

Body language: Definition, examples, & signs. (n.d.). The Berkeley Well-Being Institute. https://www.berkeleywellbeing.com/body-language.html

Braillon, A., & Taiebi, F. (2020). Practicing "Reflective listening" is a mandatory prerequisite for empathy. Patient Education and Counseling, 103(9), 1866–1867. https://doi.org/10.1016/j.pec.2020.03.024

Busswitz, K. (2021, May 20). Which of the 5 posture types are you? BraceAbility. https://www.braceability.com/blogs/articles/types-of-posture-and-spinal-curves

Cherry, K. (2006, September 6). Types of Nonverbal Communication. Verywell Mind. https://www.verywellmind.com/types-of-nonverbal-communication-2795397

Cherry, K. (2015, January 5). Why empathy is important. Verywell Mind. https://www.verywellmind.com/what-is-empathy-2795562

Cherry, K. (2019, February 17). What Is Repression? Verywell Mind. https://www.verywellmind.com/repression-as-a-defense-mechanism-4586642

Cooper, C. (1677324168000). Macro and Micro Expressions: Understand the importance of them. Linkedin.com. https://www.linkedin.com/pulse/macro-micro-expressions-understand-importance-them-colin-cooper/

Cuncic, A. (2010, May 10). 7 active listening techniques to practice in your daily conversations. Verywell Mind. https://www.verywellmind.com/what-is-active-listening-3024343

Cuncic, A. (2013, April 28). How to read facial expressions. Verywell Mind. https://www.verywellmind.com/understanding-emotions-through-facial-expressions-3024851

EMEET. (2023, March 8). Importance of facial expressions in communication. EMEET. https://emeet.com/blogs/content/importance-of-facial-expressions-in-communication

Faces poem by Sara Teasdale. (n.d.). Poem Hunter. https://www.poemhunter.com/poem/faces-37/

Fox, E. (2022, September 12). Gut feelings: How does intuition work, anyway? Literary Hub. https://lithub.com/gut-feelings-how-does-intuition-work-anyway/

Gesture Types. (n.d.). Changingminds.org. http://changingminds.org/explanations/behaviors/body_language/gesture_type.htm

h24 CREATIVE STUDIO s. r. o. (2018, September 4). Cultural differences in nonverbal communication. Lexika. https://www.lexika-translations.com/blog/cultural-differences-in-nonverbal-communication/

Hammond, C., MS, & LMHC. (2018, March 10). 30 reasons why people lie. Psych Central. https://psychcentral.com/pro/exhausted-woman/2018/03/30-reasons-why-people-lie

Hwang, R. (2022, January 18). 8 powerful ways to tap into your intuition (that work!). Science of People. https://www.scienceofpeople.com/intuition/

Imam, R. (2020, February 25). The power of body language in the workplace. Forbes. https://www.forbes.com/sites/forbesbusinesscouncil/2020/02/25/the-power-of-body-language-in-the-workplace/

Interpreting Body Language. (2011). In Qualitative Market Research (pp. 199–201). SAGE Publications, Inc.

Kardec, R. (2020). Body language: Read and analyze people. Learn how to influence anyone through behavioral psychology secrets. Discover powerful verbal and non-verbal communication skills. Charlie Creative Lab.

Kelly, B. (2023, March 11). How does culture affect communication: Exploring the impact, importance & examples. Peep Strategy. https://peepstrategy.com/how-culture-affects-communication/

Kishore, K. (2020, September 7). Finding the right tone of voice in communication. Harappa. https://harappa.education/harappa-diaries/tone-of-voice-types-and-examples-in-communication/

Liebenthal, E., Silbersweig, D. A., & Stern, E. (2016). The language, tone and prosody of emotions: Neural substrates and dynamics of spoken-word emotion perception. Frontiers in Neuroscience, 10, 506. https://doi.org/10.3389/fnins.2016.00506

Lumen Learning. (n.d.). Cultural context. Lumenlearning.com. https://courses.lumenlearning.com/suny-esc-communicationforprofessionals/chapter/cultural-context/

Martinez, A. M. (2019). Context may reveal how you feel. Proceedings of the National Academy of Sciences of the United States of America, 116(15), 7169–7171. https://doi.org/10.1073/pnas.1902661116

Maya, V. (2022, January 23). Tone of voice in communication: How to use it effectively at work. CustomersFirst Academy. https://customersfirstacademy.com/tone-of-voice-in-communication/

McKinney, P. (1647870992000). Should you trust your gut? Linkedin.com. https://www.linkedin.com/pulse/should-you-trust-your-gut-phil-mckinney?trk=public_post_content_share-article

Menzies, F. (2015, June 15). You're cramping my style: Cultural differences in nonverbal communication. Include-empower.com; Culture Plus Consulting. https://cultureplusconsulting.com/2015/06/15/cultural-differences-in-non-verbal-communication/

MindTools. (n.d.). Mindtools.com. https://www.mindtools.com/acjxune/8-ways-to-improve-your-powers-of-observation

Monte, J. (1416921086000). Observation, empathy & insight: Tools for elicitation. Linkedin.com. https://www.linkedin.com/pulse/20141125131126-202979673-observation-empathy-insight-tools-for-elicitation/

Monu Borkala, L. K. (2022, July 14). Importance of observation skills and how to develop it. CollegeMarker Blog. https://collegemarker.com/blogs/importance-of-observation-skills/

Muletown Digital. (n.d.). Two types of gestures: Illustrators and emblems – Ethos3 – A presentation training and design agency. https://ethos3.com/two-types-of-gestures-illustrators-and-emblems/

No title. (n.d.). Study.com. https://study.com/academy/lesson/understanding-the-tone-and-voice-of-your-message.html

Nonverbal communication and body language - Helpguide.org. (n.d.). https://www.helpguide.org/articles/relationships-communication/nonverbal-communication.htm

Nonverbal communication and body language - Helpguide.org. (n.d.). https://www.helpguide.org/articles/relationships-communication/nonverbal-communication.htm

Okorobie, D. (n.d.). Importance of body language at work. Betteryou.Ai. https://www.betteryou.ai/importance-of-body-language-at-work/

Owen, S. (2014, February 17). Trust your instincts to read body language: 10 tips. Relationships Coach UK; Relationships Coach. https://www.relationshipscoach.co.uk/blog/trust-your-instincts-to-read-body-language-10-tips/

Patel, D. (2018, October 10). 10 telltale phrases that indicate somebody isn't telling the truth. Entrepreneur. https://www.entrepreneur.com/living/10-telltale-phrases-that-indicate-somebody-isnt-telling/321282

Paul Ekman ph.D. (n.d.). Psychology Today. https://www.psychologytoday.com/us/contributors/paul-ekman-phd

Pease, A. &. B. [@peaseinternational]. (2020, May 10). Intuition vs Body Language - how to tell what others are really thinking. Youtube. https://www.youtube.com/watch?v=h29U8Bw2gK4

Posture. (n.d.). Physiopedia. https://www.physio-pedia.com/Posture

Proxemics and its Types – Explained with Examples. (2022, July 6). Communication Theory. https://www.communicationtheory.org/proxemics-and-its-types-explained-with-examples/

Schueneman, T. (2023, March 10). Cultural differences in nonverbal communication. Point Park University Online; Point Park University. https://online.pointpark.edu/business/cultural-differences-in-nonverbal-communication/

Situation awareness: Making sense of the world. (2020, May 16). Human Factors 101. https://humanfactors101.com/topics/situation-awareness/

Situational awareness and survival. (n.d.). Psychology Today. https://www.psychologytoday.com/us/blog/hope-resilience/202010/situational-awareness-and-survival

Spirit Land

* * *

The Peyote Diaries of Charles Langley

Against Witchcraft and Evil Ones

Charles Langley

Copyright Charles Langley, 2017
All rights reserved.

ISBN: 1544896751
ISBN-13: 9781544896755
Library of Congress Control Number: 2017904657
CreateSpace Independent Publishing Platform
North Charleston, South Carolina

The Peyote Diaries
of
Charles Langley

Edited

*For lust of knowing what should not be known
We take the Golden Road to Samarkand.*
—James Elroy Flecker

Contents

Preface xi

I 1
II 19
III 43
IV 63
V 79
VI 94
VII 109
VIII 127
IX 147
X 172

Preface

This is the first in a planned series of *Spirit Land* books that are an attempt to preserve the past while, at least for the moment, it is still part of the present. Recorded here is the world of a North American Navajo Indian medicine man named Blue Horse, the origins of whose shamanistic art and beliefs stretch back to the Ice Age. It will not be long before the last practitioners of these ancient ways are gone; and gone with them will be a tradition that has been handed down for thousands of years. Within these pages readers will find many extraordinary and, frankly, unworldly events and occurrences, involving witchcraft, peyote visions, divination, cursing and healing, and no one can be blamed for finding some of them hard to believe. Yet this is not a story book, nor is it a collection of half-remembered tales from long ago. This book is a living record of our time and everything written here—no matter how extraordinary it may seem—I witnessed and took part in.

In my first book, *Meeting the Medicine Men*, I occasionally took a number of episodes of a similar nature and wove them into a single event, largely as a device to protect the identities of those involved. In this book, I took a different approach and opted to turn the field notes of my diary into a readable narrative. Every event recorded here is entire in itself, although names and places have once again been scrambled to protect privacy. Blue Horse is a pseudonym, but unlike in my first book where "Blue Horse" stood for an amalgam of medicine men; here he steps forward in his own right, as one outstandingly powerful Navajo medicine man whose apprentice I became. From the beginning, it was decided that I should document his work in detail, so that at least one reliable record of the world of a Navajo medicine man might survive as a witness to the future. It is my dearest hope that, in this, I have succeeded.

While this book is intended for the general reader, so that as many people as possible may hear of the feats of which Navajo medicine men are capable; it comes at a time when historians are rediscovering the enormous influence that magic, divination and witchcraft exerted in Europe and the United States until surprisingly recent times. Galileo cast horoscopes, Sir Isaac Newton was an alchemist, and for many centuries science and magic were indistinguishable. Well into the 20th century, many villages and settlements in Europe and the United States contained wise men and women—witches to an earlier time—who knew charms, spells and potions intended to cure the sick, both human and animal.

That tradition has almost all gone now and cannot be reconstructed. But my exploration of a still powerful, still living and still largely untouched and untainted tradition of witchcraft, divination and healing among the Navajo people of the American Southwest, has been in time to record at least some of its wonders. If nothing else, my work as a medicine man's apprentice demonstrates that strange powers and events, inexplicable by any logic that I know, are not all marvels of the past—not yet, not quite—and for the moment remain a living part of a large and vibrant 21st Century Navajo society.

Charles Langley
Albuquerque, New Mexico, 2017.

I

After a trip to England that had lasted far longer than intended, I was back on the Navajo Indian reservation in the American Southwest. A territory so vast it stretches east to west across Arizona and New Mexico, north into Utah, south as far as Zuni and the Puerco River, and east as far as the Colorado border. Within its boundaries are such extraordinary natural phenomena as the Grand Canyon, Monument Valley and the great Navajo redoubt of the Canyon de Chelly. In total an area bigger than several European countries; bigger than the Republic of Ireland, bigger than the US state of West Virginia, and just a little smaller than Maine or South Carolina.

But while the Republic of Ireland, West Virginia and South Carolina count their populations in millions, the Navajo reservation has about 150,000 people living on it. There are endless tracts of the most beautiful country you could ever imagine, entirely unspoiled by the presence of human beings. To me, this is one of its most attractive features and it was here, in this land of outstanding beauty and great emptiness, that I once more took up my duties as apprentice to the powerful Navajo medicine man Blue Horse.

I was more than happy to be back among the Navajo, and arrived to find a peyote medicine meeting being organized for the purpose of strengthening and refreshing Blue Horse and his wife Baa. It was being prepared by the Yazzie family, who live on the outskirts of Gallup, New Mexico, a town that straddles the main I-40 east-west highway. New Mexico styles itself—not without good reason—as the Land of Enchantment and Highway 1-40 was formerly, and far better known, as Route 66: the Mother Road, the Road of Dreams. What better place to be, than on the Road of Dreams in the Land of Enchantment. New Mexicans, with their wry sense of humor, refer to their state as the Land of Entrapment; but this is praise not denigration, and in this praise I must join. For I am but one of thousands, tens of thousands more likely, who after one healthy dose of New Mexico was never able to leave.[1] Entrapment? Perhaps, but who would not wish to be trapped in a land where the enchantment is real.

Now I was about to experience another sort of magic, the magic of the peyote medicine, and it was with this meeting that I re-entered the extraordinary Navajo world of peyote visions, witchcraft, divination and healing. And so, I again picked up my pen as Blue Horse had asked me, to record the many extraordinary occurrences I witnessed, starting with this medicine meeting and my experiences during that long night.

* * *

The hogan[2] at the Yazzies' home was the biggest and most elaborately decorated I had seen. It was made of big logs, with a kind of concrete mix between them, which took on a strange kind of half-green color as the night wore on and my peyote content went up. The roof was of modern plywood with a waterproof cladding tacked over it; it had a big hole in the middle through which a shiny metal chimney had been suspended on chains above a fire that burned brightly in the middle of the hogan. Traditionally, smoke from the fire would go up through the smoke hole in the thick earthen roof, but the substitution of flammable modern materials for traditional ones, makes the metal chimney vital if a stray spark is not to start a conflagration.

Hanging from the walls were woolen rugs and blankets of the type still woven on hand looms by Navajo women. Behind the seat of honor, where

---

1 I once shocked an East Coast immigration officer by telling him I didn't want to live in the USA, I wanted to live in New Mexico.
2 A hogan is a traditional six or eight-sided single-story building made of timber and originally roofed with a dome of earth four feet thick. Up until the 1950s and 1960s, the majority of Navajos lived in hogans. Today, they are mostly for ceremonial use, and modern building materials are increasingly used in their construction.

the medicine man sat on cushions on the floor, hung a large rug with a diamond pattern that had been deliberately left unfocused and fuzzy. Navajos call this a "dazzle rug" or "dazzler" because, as the peyote gets to work, the pattern starts to buck and jink around and continually changes shape and color. As the night wore on, this dazzler took on a life of its own: first turning into a 3-D version of itself, before transforming into a liquid of bright and brilliant colors, that poured slowly down the wall until it reached the floor. Nailed to the walls were expensive Pendleton blankets, whose colors glowed like neon as the medicine took hold. A big rug with a jagged black, red, and white pattern had been tacked to the wall behind the sponsor's seat.[3] When I first entered and took my place cross-legged on the earthen floor, I thought this rug looked terrible. But it had become hugely attractive by the morning, once its red and black patterns and colors had merged to take on the brilliant hues of a setting sun. Red as blood, black as night, and very beautiful.

The meeting was run by the medicine man Leonard Tsosie, whom I had met before; Ronny, husband of Baa's daughter Cecelia, was the fire chief,[4] and it was a fabulous meeting that I greatly enjoyed.

The medicine was exceptionally powerful that night—so powerful that Leonard sent it around only twice. Three times is more usual, sometimes four, but I think he decided that twice was enough. It certainly was for me. There was the usual dried type, then fresh peyote buttons from near the Mexican border, and then there was peyote tea. Having three different types of medicine is unusual, and I don't think I've seen three kinds at one meeting before.[5] It was likely because we had three types of medicine that Leonard sent them around only twice, because if one sampled all three on both rounds—and I did—that was a lot of peyote to ingest.

---

[3] All peyote medicine meetings have a sponsor—the person who has organized the meeting either to ask for prayers for the sponsor's own sake, or for help for someone else. The sponsor sits immediately to the left of the officials who run the meeting.

[4] A medicine meeting has four officials: the medicine man, the cedar chief, the drum chief, and the fire chief. This book will not go into details of how medicine meetings are organized as these can be found elsewhere.

[5] I later discovered that this was not that unusual, but two forms of medicine (and sometimes only one) is more the norm.

While this was probably a wise decision on Leonard's part, given how strong the medicine was, for me it was unfortunate. By the time we had the break, after Leonard had gone outside to pray to the four directions at about three in the morning, I felt a vision coming on. Although I hovered on the edge, I knew that without more medicine I would not be able to break through to the other side. Or so I thought.

After a while spent hovering, I began to have a few insights. The first was that having to some degree wasted a large portion of my life, I could not afford to waste more. That what I was doing among the Navajo was the most important task I would ever have; and that I should dedicate myself to it as much, and as fully, as I was able.

Then all sorts of things came pouring out of my memory as I sat in the hogan. Much of it, particularly that from my childhood and my life in England, I had thought (or more likely wished) I had forgotten. None of it was pleasant, and it seemed the medicine was reminding me that any thought of going back to England for good was a poor one and that abandoning, or even easing back, on this work of recording the spiritual world of the Navajos was not a thought I should entertain.

While I was thinking about this, a number of odd things began to occur. I didn't seem to be having a vision: it was more as if I were sitting in the hogan thinking with my eyes closed. But perhaps I only *thought* I was sitting in the hogan thinking to myself, while in fact the medicine had taken me elsewhere to show me something I needed to know. It seemed, after a while, that I had built a bridge over a wide river. It was poorly constructed, ramshackle, and in danger of imminent collapse, which was not surprising given that I am poor with my hands and know it. Despite its rickety structure, people were crossing my bridge in both directions. Not many, but a few.

While looking at this ramshackle creation of mine, and thinking that it would fall at any minute, I found myself standing on the riverbank talking with Wovoka, the Paiute messiah, whose preaching started the ghost dance movement of 1890. It was the ghost dance that led to unrest among the remnants of the plains tribes, which in turn led to the US Army's murder of more than two hundred largely unarmed Sioux at Wounded Knee, South Dakota, the great majority of whom were women and children.[6]

The ghost dance was a round dance, unlike any previous type of American Indian dance, in which the participants circulated in long lines around a fixed point. People believed that by dancing until they collapsed with exhaustion, they could dance the prophecies of Wovoka into being, and among those prophesies was one that the dance would restore the Indian world as it had been before the white man's arrival. The idea was that the old world would come sliding back over the top of this one, and that riding on top of it would be great herds of buffalo, and all those Indians who had died in wars with the whites. The ghost dance was intended to be peaceful, but the Indian agents and the US Army reacted violently, despite the fact that Wovoka had preached peace between Indians and white people.

Now, as I stood beside him, Wovoka told me not to worry about the temporary nature of my bridge. "You can see that a few people are passing in both directions," he said. "If your bridge collapses, it won't matter, because you will have shown people that it's possible to build a bridge here. Now they have the idea, they can come back and build their own modern super-highway bridge if they wish. If you tried hard enough, you might be able to build a modern steel bridge of your own with a big road going across it, instead of this wooden contraption that looks as if it will collapse at any minute. But that doesn't matter: the important thing is that you've shown that a bridge can be built here, and people can cross in both directions if they wish to."

Wovoka and I were standing on what might be termed the "Indian side" of the bridge, which was on the inside of a big bend in the river. I couldn't see what was on the other side, except that it was a tangle of forest. Of the Indian side, I saw nothing at all—despite standing there myself—because all my attention was focused on the bridge and its likely collapse.

---

6 The Navajo refused to have anything to do with the ghost dance movement, believing it to be nonsense.

In the morning, after the medicine meeting was over, I realized that while it didn't seem like it at the time, I was obviously having a vision, and a long and powerful one at that. That is how the medicine works on you sometimes. While it's working, you can be thinking one thing while the medicine takes you for a long and distant ride to show you things you never would have thought of alone. So, despite what I thought, I was not thinking—if you can follow this—I was having a peyote vision, and what it told me was that I should build a bridge between the Indians and white people. Wovoka was right that it mattered not whether I built it well or badly. The point was that it should be built so that others could follow and perhaps build something more lasting. The other important point was that the bridge allowed two-way traffic, and people could travel in both directions.

Later, on the way home, Blue Horse said that Leonard had told him to cancel all appointments for four days to give the ceremony and prayers time to do their work. This is a traditional period of rest after a ceremony, because it takes four days for the prayers to reach the spirit world and take effect.

"You have to respect the medicine, and then it will respect you," Blue Horse said when I told him about my vision. "If it wants you to build a bridge, you should build it."

"How?" I asked, hoping to benefit from words of unworldly wisdom and enlightenment. But all I got was, "I dunno. It's up to you."

With this sage advice ringing in my ears, we drove the rest of the way home in silence.

* * *

Despite the fact that Blue Horse had been told to rest for four days, we were at work again only three days later. A couple drove from Phoenix, Arizona, to see him and arrived at four in the morning. They were supposed to have arrived at ten the previous night, but had left Phoenix late.

I didn't hear the car pull up, but I awoke with a start from my little blow-up mattress on the floor at 4:00 a.m. precisely.[7] I could see the lights of a car through the window, but how long it had been there I didn't know. Blue Horse made coffee and then sent me to invite our visitors into the house, but I found them fast asleep in their car, which was not surprising after a six-hour drive.

When they eventually did come in, they explained they were the grandparents of a very sick baby named Annabelle who was being treated in a hospital in Norfolk, Virginia. Annabelle, who was four months old, had serious heart problems, her kidneys were seizing up and doctors suspected she'd had a stroke. The grandparents wanted Blue Horse to use his powers to divine what was wrong, and to see if he could do anything to cure her. To help him with this, the grandmother had brought a photograph of Annabelle with her, as well as a little suit of baby clothes she had worn, as items that have direct contact with the patient are believed to be an aid to divination.

As quickly as I could, I lit a fire outside to produce hot charcoal for the divination ceremony. These hot charcoals are placed in a sand-filled container about the size of the top of a large oil drum, which is set down in the middle of the house; and it is in these glowing coals that the Navajo medicine man divines the source of the troubles afflicting his patients. I see well in the fire—by which I mean I see well for an Indian, let alone for a white man—and can usually spot the symbols and signs that provide clues. The problem at this stage in my apprenticeship, was that I had not learned enough to accurately interpret their meaning.

On this occasion, however, I could see nothing—at least, nothing I could be sure about. Blue Horse kept saying that the problem was "up here," indicating a spot on the baby's photograph, which the grandmother held on her lap, on the child's left side above the clavicle, around the lower part of the neck. After a while he took out his sucking tube and went to work on the baby's picture. This tube, which is an essential part of the

---

[7] The blow-up mattress was a recent innovation and usually I slept on the bare boards. It didn't last long, however, and the mattress disappeared as mysteriously as it appeared.

medicine man's equipment, is a hollow wooden tube about six to eight inches long, through which he sucks "bad stuff" from the bodies of his patients. This bad stuff takes the form of various physical objects such as snakeskin, deer horn, bits of plants, fragments of bone, or even tiny arrowheads made of stone. These things have supposedly been shot into the bodies of patients by witchmen—*ańt'įįhnii* in Navajo—who wish to harm people, or even bring about their deaths.

I will go into this form of treatment in more detail later, but for the moment suffice to say that by sucking this bad stuff from the patient's body, Blue Horse is able to remove the cause of the illness. I've seen him do this on live patients many times, but this was the first time I'd witnessed a long-distance treatment using a photograph.

While the grandmother held the picture, Blue Horse sucked at the baby's neck until, after a great deal of effort, he managed to extract a long thread of something that looked like the hair that gets caught in the bath plug if you neglect to clear it out frequently; except this was dry. I find this aspect of Blue Horse's work most difficult, because I know you cannot suck things out of pictures or people. But it's a common practice of Navajo medicine men, and patients put great faith in this ability to draw evil from their bodies.

After he'd sucked out the bad stuff, Blue Horse and the grandmother took some pollen and went out to perform morning prayers. This ceremony should be conducted at dawn before the sun rises, and is intended to send back the evil, so it will rebound on the person who sent it, and also provide protection against evil in the future. It should be carried out before the sun rises, and because the sun was about to rise, Blue Horse was in a hurry to get it done. I was left alone with the grandfather and we had the chance to talk for a short while, during which time he naturally asked me what I was doing there. I explained briefly how I'd met Blue Horse while driving across the United States from coast to coast. I told him how I'd become his assistant—*akéé naagháii*—and added that I felt it was a good thing that Navajo people still had their ancient traditions to support them.[8]

---

[8] There is no Navajo equivalent of the English word "apprentice". Assistant is the nearest, and I have tended to use the two terms interchangeably, to preserve the implication of a learning

"All white people can do is pace back and forth on the carpet," I said. "At least Navajos are able to do something, and at least you know you're doing the best you can for the baby."

He pulled a wry face and said: "It would be OK if everybody (indicating the direction his wife had gone with Blue Horse) agreed to do something. But they don't always, and that's why it took so long to get here. I said, 'I've got Blue Horse's number; why don't we go,' but then nothing happens. And when it does it takes two hours for us to get out of Phoenix." Looking at the clock, he added: "I'm supposed to be at work in Phoenix at eleven this morning."

He did not say what work he did, but he had no chance of getting back to Phoenix by 11:00 am. I had the impression that the delay was caused by division in the family over whether the traditional methods were worth following. Shortly after this, Blue Horse and the grandmother returned, and then she and her husband left to drive back to Phoenix.

A few hours later, Blue Horse took a phone call from baby Annabelle's family, who said the baby had not had a stroke as the doctors feared, but had been suffering from a blood clot in her neck, which had been removed.

"See, I said the problem was in the neck," Blue Horse said, smiling knowingly, and tapping his wooden pipe.

✳ ✳ ✳

Later that same day we drove to one of the loneliest spots I had yet visited on the reservation, when we went to visit a Mr. and Mrs. Carlton. To get there we took Route 77 up toward Keams Canyon,[9] and after about twenty miles left the road and turned onto one of the hundreds of dirt tracks that crisscross the reservation, and then drove west for several more miles.

The Navajo reservation, or most of it, is off the beaten track, but large parts are so far off the beaten track that there is no track. Vast stretches

---

position in English, without abandoning the Navajo meaning of a helper.
9 Named after Thomas Varker Keam, 1842–1902, a Cornishman born in Kenwyn who married a Navajo woman. He set up a trading post there after the American Civil War and made a fortune.

contain no trace of human habitation, or activity, or any sign that human beings have ever been there. This was the countryside we were now passing through. Completely empty, it was the loneliest and loveliest I had thus far seen, and as pure and pristine as on the day of Creation, while the track we followed was no more than a single set of wheel marks in the sand. The pasture was sparse, but everywhere we could see swathes of desert flowers of the brightest blues, reds, and yellows bobbing their heads back and forth in the warm breeze. Tall buttes rose to the north and west and a broad wash, half a mile across, showed where torrents of water flowed with the rains. Beneath us the tires crunched over the loose desert sand, while the high vaulted sky, stretching from horizon to horizon, contained within its endless blue not a single cloud.

When we arrived the Carltons told me that apart from a couple of trailers out of sight miles farther down the track, they were the only people living here on what seemed to be the edge of the world. It was beautiful beyond all measure.

During all that follows, I was suffering from the drawback of *not* knowing that Mr. and Mrs. Carlton were the *other* grandparents of baby Annabelle. Blue Horse did not tell me, and there was no way I could have guessed from the events that were about to unfold. This was a common problem with Blue Horse. It's not that he's trying to hide anything from me; it's simply that sometimes he's a poor communicator. He has a tendency (which I've noted among other Navajo friends) to think that because he knows what is going on, I must know, too; which is very often not the case. Part of the problem is that Navajo is his first and preferred language, and he finds it difficult to express himself in English. Generally, it's better that I ask questions to which he can respond, but the problem with this approach is the difficulty of asking questions when you have no idea of what's going on. I was often left to extract details of a day's events from a tired and irritable Blue Horse, during long drives home that could last five or six hours or more, when his main desire was to sleep.

The Carltons raise and sell horses; and they apparently do so very successfully, judging from the smart trailer in which they now gave us coffee.

While we sipped our coffee, I tried to speak Navajo to a little girl of about six—another granddaughter, I suppose—only to find that she did not speak any.

"He's asking for your name in Navajo," Mrs. Carlton translated, but the little girl could not speak one word of her own language.[10]

After coffee we went to the hogan, which stood a short distance from the trailer, and began to prepare for the cedar ceremony. "Cedar" is the name given to the divination ceremony in which the medicine man looks into the red-hot charcoals placed in front of him, and sees the images, signs, and symbols that tell him what ails his patient: among the Navajo, what ails the patient is very often witchcraft.

Sitting cross-legged on the floor of the hogan Blue Horse reached into his *jish*, the medicine bag in which Navajos keep their sacred instruments, and began to set out the things he needed in front of him. There was his eagle feather, and his many-colored drop fan that blossomed like a chrysanthemum flower when handled correctly. He had his hollow sucking tube and his sacred and ornately carved drumstick, that was made from the black wood of an unknown tree. He had his eagle bone whistle, made from the leg bone of the only creature of the earth able to rise so high that it can gaze upon the face of the Great Spirit; and a little silver cup which he proceeded to fill with clear, fresh, water. Finally, he took out a piece of rock crystal, about the length of a man's thumb and only a little thicker, which he placed carefully in front of him. It is this crystal, correctly aligned with the charcoal, that enables the medicine man to observe past, present, and future.

Blue Horse carefully placed his instruments on a small rectangle of Navajo weaving that he'd laid out in front of him on the earth floor. When he was ready, he motioned to Mr. Carlton—a lean, spare, man who looked like someone whose business was horses—to fetch in the charcoal to begin the divination. This is usually my job, because it is important that: one, the pieces of charcoal be the proper size, which is about the size

---

10 A depressingly common situation, caused by Navajo parents failing to pass on the language in the mistaken belief their children will do better if they speak only English.

of a large pebble; two, there should be plenty of them and three, while they should be glowing red hot, they should not be smoking or aflame. It is an important function of the apprentice to make sure the charcoal presented to the medicine man conforms to the above rules, for if it does not, he will be unable to read anything in it.

Mr. Carlton was well versed in the ceremonies and knew exactly what was required, so I left him to it; and he soon presented us with two large shovelfuls of red-hot charcoal that were about perfect. For a few moments Blue Horse sat quietly looking at the heap of charcoal in front of him. Then, handing me a special fire stick for the purpose, he signaled me to shape the coals into a five-pointed star. A five-pointed star is the same shape as a man, with arms and legs and a head and a body, and the feet must always point east, and the head point west. These are the directions of the rising and setting of the sun and they represent the human journey from birth to death. This man-star is the preferred shape for divination, and when I had shaped it to his satisfaction, Blue Horse took a pinch of dried cedar fronds from a bag of white doeskin, and scattered them on the hot coals. A plume of aromatic blue smoke immediately curled upward, bathing the entire hogan in the sweet fragrance of burning cedar. Then, he bent forward slightly, and for a long time sat in silence looking deep into the charcoal. Eventually, he directed my attention to a face that had appeared in the fire. I'd already seen it, but now Blue Horse was about to reveal its significance.

When faces appear in the fire they can sometimes be extraordinarily detailed and clear. Some are so finely depicted that the person we are performing the ceremony for recognizes the face as the person they suspect of trying to do them harm, or "witching" them, as the Navajo say. This is not the same person as the witchman—who does the cursing—but is usually the person who has paid the witchman to do his evil work. In this case the face was not human. Instead, it was a rounded little white face with two little black eyes and a mouth, that seemed to be poking out of a hole in the side of a jumble of black rocks. To me it looked like a puffy-faced white maggot with two eyes and a mouth, which is why I paid little attention to it, until Blue Horse identified this face as a snake; a sign of great evil among the Navajo. As I watched the face inflate and deflate in the heat, it gave the impression of popping out of its hidey-hole to look around, before darting back inside to hide.

"It's like a snake looking out from a pile of rocks," Blue Horse said. "That's the one we have to find."

What he meant was that the fire was showing us that a curse assailing the Carlton household had been hidden somewhere in a pile of rocks nearby; when we found it, the curse would look like the snake, or fat maggot, we could see in the fire. Among the Navajo a curse is not a form of words, but a physical object. Often, we find a bundle containing several parts that make up a single curse, and this bundle is usually hidden in, or near, the home of those the curse is directed against. These bundles are generally about four to eight inches long, wrapped tightly in animal hide, often deer hide, and bound with string or rawhide. Frequently, they have lain hidden for years, and Navajo families who suffer a run of setbacks and unforeseen tragedies, such as the illness of baby Annabelle, will often conclude they have been cursed; and that is when they send for a medicine man like Blue Horse.

The witchmen who make and plant these curses are usually medicine men who once worked for the good, but sold out to the dark side in return for the power and wealth it brings them. These men, and they are always men, are paid high prices to put curses on people, and it is only the most powerful medicine men—and Blue Horse was an extremely powerful one—who are strong enough to confront the evil of the witchmen, and have the ability to find and destroy the curses, and the evil they contain. Knowing this, the witchmen take great care to hide their curses among the vastness of the empty countryside, which offers endless hiding places among its rocks, gullies, canyons, and hills.

If Blue Horse and I had been Sherlock Holmes and Dr. Watson, or even Batman and Robin, the sight of a fat maggot in a fire wouldn't have been much of a clue. But Blue Horse possessed powers beyond the merely deductive, and once the fire had shown him what to look for, he blew his medicine man's whistle to call the spirits to his aid. He says that when they answer his call, he hears an inner voice that points him in the right direction. Using this method, he often discovers curses in seemingly impossible places: thirty feet up a tree on one occasion, and in the lantern of a tall floodlight that was illuminating a paddock on another. But calling on the spirits is not the only way he finds curses. He also practices hand trembling, a Navajo technique by which the hand trembles, apparently involuntarily, sometimes moving so quickly it resembles a fluttering bird. Good hand tremblers, like good dowsers, can locate lost valuables or lost people or, in the case of a powerful medicine man like Blue Horse, the hiding place of curses.

Taking Mr. Carlton with us, we left the hogan and set off into the desert in Blue Horse's truck. Bumping along, following a single set of wheel tracks that to the untrained eye seemed to stretch to infinity, after only a couple of miles Blue Horse came to a sudden halt beside a pile of black volcanic rocks that rose about forty feet from the desert floor. The rocks were the remains of a volcanic plug, one of many in the area, and was strongly reminiscent of the black cliff and rocks I'd seen in the fire. Volcanic plugs are the remains of small volcanoes, the outer parts of which weathered away hundreds of thousands or even millions of years ago, leaving only the hard basalt of the interior plug still visible.

We all got out of the truck and Blue Horse began to walk this way and that blowing his whistle, while his other hand trembled back and forth. Earlier in the day he had given me a pair of soft *kélchi*, Navajo moccasins, which I'd put on not knowing we were going into the wilds. Now the sharp desert stones and thorns began to rip my kélchi apart and stab into my feet, but there was nothing I could do except put up with it. Blue Horse indicated we would find the curse on top of this rock pile; but because he is rather portly and nowhere near as fit as me, he told me to climb up the rocks and see what I could find. I took a spade with me in case the curse had been buried up there, but the top didn't have much soil, and the few places where I could dig yielded nothing. Soon, I switched my attention to a patch of dry, scrubby, desert grass about a foot tall. The patch was no more than three feet long and a foot wide, and was growing where a little moisture could accumulate in a narrow channel only a few inches deep in the rock; but, again, after probing with the spade I found nothing.

Frustrated by my lack of progress, Blue Horse now began to climb up the stack. But it was hard going for him, and he stopped on a ledge just below the summit where the grass patch I had searched was about waist high to him. There he began to pull at the dry grass, while urging me and Mr. Carlton, who had climbed up to join me, to move on and search elsewhere. I did as he said, looking back a few times to see Blue Horse poking at the grass patch. Then, after a minute or two, he called to me.

"It's here!" he shouted, indicating the scrubby grass patch and pulling at what looked like a tangle of old twine.

I was not impressed, to be honest; not at first. I'd looked at that patch of grass only a minute earlier and seen nothing. Then Blue Horse had distracted my attention by sending me to search elsewhere with Mr. Carlton—so I had my back to him—and I'd seen him fiddling around in the grass moments before he claimed to have found the bundle. I want to make it plain that just because I'm his assistant doesn't mean I stop using my brain, and I'm naturally suspicious of hocus-pocus. While I'm fascinated by Navajo culture, medicine, and traditional ways, that doesn't mean I suspend reason or disbelief. It most certainly doesn't mean I blindly accept that unseen or occult forces are in play, just because I can't immediately find a more conventional explanation. Blue Horse's work among his people is invaluable to them, and the witchcraft and curses are real, whether you believe they have any power or not. But no serious-minded man working in this area can remain blind to the possibility of trickery. Then, as events unfolded, they quickly turned into an impressive demonstration of Blue Horse's powers as a medicine man.

I walked rapidly over to where he was still pulling at the bundle to free it from the grass. The first thing I noticed was that the bundle was wrapped in tangles of twine that had grass growing through them, which was why he was having difficulty extracting it. If the bundle had been placed recently, then grass could hardly have grown up between the bunched coils of twine. Seared by the desert sun, many of the grass stalks were brittle and crumbled into fragments when I handled them; meaning that it would have been impossible to manhandle such fragile vegetation to fit between the twine. The only way the grass could have got where it was, was if it had grown up through the twine over an extended period; and when I examined the bundle it had every appearance of being there for a long time. The twine was weathered and yellowed by the sun, until it was the same color as the grass growing through it, which explained how I'd missed it. This was not an accident, nor was it an accident that the curse had been placed in just the right position that it overlooked the Carlton family home, visible a couple of miles away. Whoever put it there knew what they were doing and hid it with great skill. Navajos would know it was hidden where it was, to see what the family was up to, what was going on in and around the home, and who came and went—information it would pass to its creator, who would know how best to use that information against the family.

When Blue Horse finally untangled the curse bundle from the grass we neutralized its evil in the traditional way by placing it in a bag of fine wood ash. Curses found outside a dwelling are never taken inside, because that would risk introducing the evil into the home. Instead, they are dealt with in the open air, and when we opened this one we did it standing outside the hogan door—and then I really did have a surprise. When Blue Horse took the bundle apart, out came a white stone that was exactly the same shape as the head I'd observed in the fire; and what's more, it had two eyes and a mouth drawn on it. What astonished me was not that the stone and the face drawn on it looked a bit like the face in the fire, nor that it looked a lot like the face in the fire; what was truly shocking was that this was *exactly* the same face we had seen in the fire.

I had another surprise when we turned the stone over. On the other side, in relief, were the head and coils of a rattlesnake, an evil omen indeed among the Navajo. I thought at first that the rattlesnake had been made of some glue-like substance and then stuck on to the stone, but when I looked more closely, I saw that it was an integral part of the stone itself. Whether created by nature or carved by the hand of man, I couldn't say for sure; but either way it must have cost a fortune to get a witchman to make a curse with a fetish so complicated and difficult to obtain as this one.

As we continued to examine the curse we saw a second stone inside the bundle, which also closely resembled the face in the fire, although not so closely as the first. This stone was colored green and it had the face incised on one side, while on the other side were three tiny black lines. These lines, made of some kind of tar, were stuck so tightly to the stone they could not be pried off, even when Blue Horse exerted considerable pressure with the tip of his drumstick.

"It's the three sisters," Blue Horse explained, pointing to the three lines.

While we'd been talking over coffee earlier, Mrs. Carlton had told us about her three grown-up daughters, one of whom could not have children, one whose marriage was in deep trouble and a third who, in ancient Navajo style, had married a man she had never met. Mrs. Carlton said of her third daughter: "She told me, 'No one seems to want me, so I'll do it the old-fashioned way'." Oddly—or perhaps not so oddly—this marriage was doing fine. But whoever placed that curse must have known about the three sisters, while Blue Horse and I had no idea of their existence until we arrived at the Carlton home only an hour or so earlier.

As the examination proceeded it didn't take long to confirm that this curse was primarily aimed at the women of the household. Between the tangles of twine, we discovered a piece of frill from a pair of women's panties with some black pubic hair wrapped inside. Both of which were sure signs that the curse was aimed at women.

"They'll have stolen the panties," Blue Horse told me quietly while Mr. Carlton was out of earshot.

"But how did they get the pubic hair?" I asked.

"Someone close to them did this," Blue Horse said.

Regrettably, among the Navajo it is frequently those nearest a family—often their closest relations—who from jealousy, envy, spite, or a hundred impure motives, curse those who ought to be most dear to them. But I didn't understand at the time that all this was connected to baby Annabelle who was, of course, the latest female addition to a family whose female members were under attack from witchcraft. Once again, I did not know because no one bothered to tell me.

II

Some days later Blue Horse and I were due to return to the Carltons' home, where Blue Horse was to hold a peyote medicine meeting for little Annabelle. But first we held a sweat lodge ceremony for ourselves, partly as a purification, but mostly because Blue Horse enjoys a sweat more than anything. When it was over, and as we were clearing up, I reached down to pick up one of the heavy volcanic rocks Blue Horse had thrown out of the sweat lodge. Just as I did, he threw another one, and the two heavy stones banged together trapping the tip of the third finger of my left hand. The smashed finger end bled profusely through the broken nail and the pain was enough to make me yelp: after that, things became progressively worse.

With my bandaged finger still bleeding and throbbing, I drove into Gallup and ate at a restaurant where I got hash browns, two eggs, two sausages—and a bad bout of food poisoning. Opinions were divided as to whether it was the eggs or the sausage that did the damage but, whichever it was, by four that afternoon I felt as if an iron bar was being rammed through my innards.

By now I'd become aware of the Carlton's connection to Annabelle, but in the state I was in, I had my doubts about going to the medicine meeting. Blue Horse insisted, although by the time we got there I was in no condition to go into the meeting, which was being held in a tepee on a lonely part of the Carltons' ranch. Instead, I staggered into an old trailer parked nearby that was being used as an HQ for the meeting, but it had no running water and no sanitation. Eventually, I was directed to an old-fashioned earth closet outhouse that faced south, away from the trailer, but which turned out to have no door, and there I stayed for a few hours. When I inquired later why the outhouse had no door, I was told that as no one lived south of there for twenty miles, a door had not been thought necessary.

Later, the family let me rest on a bed inside the trailer for a while, but then the fire chief came in and said Blue Horse wanted me to come into the tepee when the morning water came in. Bringing in the water is one of the most solemn parts of the ceremony, so I could hardly refuse, and once inside the tepee I was able to stick it out to the end, despite the throbbing of my injured finger and the rebellion in my bowels.

Not long after this, Blue Horse heard from the Carlton family that baby Annabelle was recovering nicely, and on the point of being released from hospital to go home.

* * *

One dark and moonless night, Blue Horse and I found ourselves riding the "Devil's Highway", also known as the "Highway of Death"; both local names for Route 666, which goes north through Navajo territory from Gallup toward the town of Shiprock. At this time Route 666 was officially one of the most dangerous roads in the United States, if not the most dangerous. This was partly because little had been done to improve it over the years, but mainly because of the abnormally high number of drivers who were either drunk, or had taken drugs, or both. Many people think that 666 is the devil's number—the "number of the Beast" from the Book of Revelation in the Bible—and so the high casualty rate was commonly attributed to demonic influences. In fact, 666 in Revelation refers most probably to the Roman emperor Nero; although he was not much of an improvement on Old Nick, and was also a little crazy.

Eventually, it was decided to change the name of the road, but some Navajos objected. They pointed out that the Devil's Highway was a tourist attraction. That people came from all over the United States for the thrill of driving it, and to take pictures of themselves standing next to Route

666 signs. Unfortunately, some visitors did not stop at taking photographs and took the signs as well; digging them up to carry home as souvenirs. In the end, the name was changed not so much for superstitious or religious reasons, but because so many people stole Route 666 signs, it became financially prohibitive for the authorities to keep replacing them. Parts of the road have been improved of recent times and it now has a new name—the rather boring Route 491—but the death rate remains high: you have been warned.

Our journey tonight along this road of ill omen was taking us to the home of a family whose elderly grandmother, Dora Tso, had suffered a heart attack while weaving at her loom. Many people on the reservation still earn a living by weaving in the traditional way at a hand loom, and Mrs. Tso was an accomplished and well-known weaver.

Now she was seriously ill in a hospital in Albuquerque, and earlier in the day her family had come to Blue Horse's house seeking help. Blue Horse cedared for them and diagnosed various problems, of which the principal one was that Mrs. Tso had been witched. Looking into the fire he pointed out two boxlike square lumps, although I thought they could have been stubby pillars, one at each end of the arms of the five-pointed star. Next, he drew my attention to a *kachina* lurking in the coals near the crystal, but I found it difficult to see and recognized it only by its elaborate headdress.

Kachinas are not Navajo entities but part of the lore of the Pueblo Indians, who are the most secretive and most resistant to outsiders of all Indian peoples of the Southwest. Precisely what part kachinas play in the life of the pueblos is familiar only to their inhabitants, but it is known that there are three types of kachina. Some are true spirits that exist invisibly in the world around us and can be both helpful and harmful. Others are harmless dolls sold to tourists, and some kachinas are human dancers who take part in Pueblo Indian ceremonies and dress to resemble spirits. I had no doubt that the kachina in the fire was a spirit kachina, but this was not good news. Pueblo witchcraft is regarded as being so strong that other Indians—even powerful Navajo medicine men like Blue Horse—universally fear it.

"If that kachina flies to one of those boxes, she's as good as dead," Blue Horse said of Mrs. Tso, looking extremely serious as he pointed again to the big boxlike lumps at each end of the star's arms.

"Are those boxes?" I asked. "Could they be pillars do you think?"

"It's the curse," he said. "She's been cursed and that's why she got sick. But this has been goin' on for a long time now. She's a weaver, and I think they put something around her throat, like a thread from her weaving, so she couldn't breathe."

By this he meant witchcraft had been used to capture the spirit of the thread, invisibly bind it around Mrs. Tso's throat and tighten it; thus leading to breathlessness and her heart attack. Because woolen thread was so closely associated with her life and work, this personal closeness increased the power of the curse. So, when the cedar was over, Blue Horse announced that he knew the source of the trouble, and would have to go to the family's home to lift the curse that very night.

"People are jealous," he told me once Mrs. Tso's family had gone. "That's the problem with our people. They're just jealous of everyone, especially their relatives."

And so, we found ourselves driving through the dark along the Devil's Highway. After we'd gone a long way north, we turned west off the road onto a track, and followed it until it forked. Here we took the left fork. Then the track forked again, and then again, and again. Whenever the road forked, Blue Horse said to take the left fork and, eventually, we arrived at the family's little farm. It was pitch black, and even with the aid of the lights of my recently acquired fourth-hand Nissan Xterra, I could see little.

There was no moon and with only the stars for light we descended from my little truck. Blue Horse called to me softly through the darkness: "Always lock your vehicle around here. There's plenty of witches out here—and some of them are good, too." By "good" he did not mean beneficent, but skilled in the ways of bad medicine, and the many ways to curse a vehicle so that it might crash and burn.

As we approached the house we could see the fire for the charcoal was already burning outside, and when we entered we found the family gathered in one room waiting for us. The house had no electricity, and the only light came from a single oil lamp balanced on a battered dresser on one side of the room. I noticed a loom by the door as we came in, but there was no work on it, and it appeared to have been partially dismantled.

In the semi-darkness of the room the pale light of the lamp cast shadows that danced about the walls and ceiling. There were great pools of darkness where the flickering light did not reach, and for the most part I could see only the eyes of those present, and only then because their eyes reflected what little light there was. Gathered to meet us were the daughter of the sick woman, her daughter, Mrs. Tso's granddaughter, the granddaughter's husband, another man who spoke Navajo, but who I think from his accent was a Hopi Indian, a third man who was Mrs. Tso's son, and a grandson aged about fourteen. The details are sketchy because introductions were brief and, unlike the days when I was a newspaper reporter, I cannot go around the room asking people their names, relationships, and so on. Mrs. Tso's son told us he'd been present when his mother collapsed at her loom, and described how she'd suddenly slumped to the floor while weaving, and then tried to crawl weakly across the floor.

When we were done talking, I moved the oil lamp from the dresser and placed it on the floor; the better for Blue Horse to see when the charcoal was brought in. The son took a blue plastic milk crate, turned it on edge, and put a towel over it. Then he placed on it a photograph of his mother that had been taken at her loom. Next to this he placed the bundle of sticks that Navajo women are given after puberty, and which represent their mastery of the household and skills such as weaving and grinding corn. A large black metal dish a couple of feet across was filled with sand and placed in front of Blue Horse, who sat cross-legged on the floor, with me sitting cross-legged immediately to his right in the traditional place of the apprentice. The rest of the family took their places on the floor in a circle around the fire place, and then one of the men brought in the biggest shovelful of charcoal I've ever seen; so big it completely filled the dish.

Looking into the charcoal, I could see something that might have been a tree that had been struck by lightning—never a good sign and something guaranteed to cause sickness—but as I looked, the tree slowly began to change shape until it looked like the two slightly unequal-sized pillars I'd seen in the first divination. But now the pillars were not separated by the arms of the star, but bound together in an odd shaped oblong bundle. Blue Horse pointed out this phenomenon to me, adding that he was sure this was the curse we were looking for.

"Is it a box, or a pillar, or what?" I asked.

"Box, pillar; it's out there somewhere," he said. "Now I've seen it in the fire, I'll have to find it." And he pointed in the direction in which we did, eventually, find the curse.

With only the flickering oil lamp and the dull, red, glow from the charcoal for illumination, the room was, to put it mildly, already somewhat ghostly; unbeknown to me, events were about to take an exceptionally spooky turn. Blue Horse explained to the family what he'd discovered in the fire, and in which direction the trouble lay. After this, one of the men brought in a large bag of cold wood ash, which we would need to sanitize the curse when we found it, and I took charge of this in my capacity as apprentice. Then, after more talk, Blue Horse and I prepared to go out into the night accompanied by Mrs. Tso's son and the granddaughter's husband.

Before we went, at Blue Horse's instruction, we all dipped our hands in the ash, and coated our protection implements in ash for added safety. For protection against evil I was holding the fire stick that we use to shape the charcoals into the star, one of the men carried another fire stick that Blue Horse had given him, while the other was given a spear point made of black obsidian. Because of their close connection to the cleansing power of the fire, the fire sticks provide protection from witchcraft and evil, and the stone spear point has similar powers. These protection instruments are always carried in the left hand; however, it is not usual to add ash as a second layer of protection. Only when I saw Blue Horse rubbing ash on his drumstick and whistle, both of which are sacred and powerful implements in their own right, did I realize that tonight we might be facing witchcraft that was more than usually threatening.

When we stepped outside it was just after midnight. There was no moon, but the stars were indescribably bright. It is an awe-inspiring experience to walk under the stars on a moonless night in New Mexico. They blaze through the clean desert air with a clear, white-frosted brilliance, that makes them appear so close you need only stand on tiptoe to pluck handfuls from the sky; and so densely packed that hardly a finger's breadth of black space is visible in the entire expanse of the sky. Despite this, the stars shed little light, and so the men carried flashlights, and as we crossed the paddock the twin beams picked out a pen full of sheep, whose eyes glowed back at us through the dark with a ghostly phosphorescence.

Led by Blue Horse we clambered over a wooden fence into a field and walked on for a while before coming to a second barbed-wire fence. I held down the lower strand of wire with my foot, while one of the men pulled up the one above, to make the biggest possible gap for Blue Horse to climb through. He is not good at this sort of physical activity, but we got him through without mishap and pressed on, following him deeper, and deeper, into the dark. Soon we had left the farm far behind and were walking through the natural desert, in which rattlesnakes and black widow spiders abound, and where mountain lions are not unknown.

We had been walking for a while, and I still had no idea where we were going, when one of the flashlights picked out the unmistakable shape of a grave lying straight ahead. I suppose I should write that my hair stood on end, shivers ran down my spine, and that I gasped in horror. The two men with us certainly did, and when I took the flashlight from the granddaughter's husband, I could see they were both shaking and sweat was pouring down their faces. I can't blame them, but by this time I'd had so many strange experiences in Blue Horse's company that my reaction—on finding myself standing beside a lonely grave shortly after midnight, apparently in the middle of nowhere, on a pitch-black night with two decidedly panicky Navajos, one of whom had his shaking hand on a heavy-caliber pistol he'd surreptitiously shoved in his jacket pocket—was that it could have been worse.

"This is it," Blue Horse said under his breath as we came to a halt at the graveside. "This is where we'll find the curse."

The grave in front of us was a low mound of red earth. It bore no name, nor was there any stone to mark it and, in fact, Navajo graves seldom have such things; but it was surrounded by a double barbed-wire fence, which meant the family feared witchcraft. They had built the fence in an attempt to keep witchmen from interfering with their relative's burial place, because witches and "skin walkers"—another much-feared Navajo entity of evil—will dig up graves and take body parts to use in spells and curses.[11] We were way off the family's farm land by now, and I learned later that we had entered the land of one of their relatives. This was the grave of a great uncle of theirs, although how he died I don't know. What I also don't know, and never discovered, was how Blue Horse led us to this spot so unerringly through the dark. The men with us were completely taken aback when we arrived at the grave, and Blue Horse told me he had never met or visited these people before.

Navajo burials often take place on family land, so that the family can keep an eye on the grave site and keep witches and skin walkers away. But if that was the intention, in this case it had failed, as we were about to discover. The wire fencing consisted of an inner and an outer fence, and the men quickly dismantled the outer fence by lifting it off its posts, and holding it high enough for Blue Horse and me to duck underneath. But the inner fence was more solidly built, and the men had to pry off the wire holding shut a narrow gate that provided the only entrance. Once the gate was open Blue Horse had to go in alone, because there wasn't room between the wire and the grave for both of us. So, I moved to one side with the flashlight and played it on the grave, to give him as much light as possible as he went to work.

Blue Horse went down on his hands and knees and began digging with his bare hands in the grave mound. At what I took to be the head of the grave someone had placed a bunch of pale pink plastic roses, and after a

---

11   Skin walkers are human shape-shifters able to transform themselves into animals or birds in order to move around swiftly to do evil.

while Blue Horse stopped digging and began to pull the plastic roses away to feel underneath. Then I heard him say in English, "I've got it." And, still on his hands and knees, he began to back out through the wire, clutching something between his hands. I couldn't see much until he had shuffled out through the inner wire, backside first. Then he rocked back on his heels and rubbed his hands together to break up the earth clinging to the object he was holding: and there was the curse. In outline it looked much the same as the shape we'd seen in the fire, like one pillar and a slightly shorter one, wrapped together.

We didn't look closely just then, because we needed to get out of there fast. In circumstances like these you never know who might be watching from out of the dark. Mindful of the danger of discovery by the evil ones, either now or later, Blue Horse insisted no one should know we'd been to the grave, and he asked me to cover our tracks. I put the roses back as near to the way we found them as I could then, in true Indian style, set about erasing our tracks by brushing them out with a bough of green juniper torn from a nearby tree. I saw how to do it in a film, and by the time the men had wired the gate shut and put the fence back together, and I'd walked backwards for twenty yards sweeping away our footprints, I'd covered our tracks pretty well.

When we reached the house again, we stopped outside to examine the curse under the flashlights. It looked like the twin pillar shapes seen in the fire, and when Blue Horse unwrapped it, the two pillars proved to be two pieces of wood, bound together with a woman's black elastic hair band that still had some hair sticking to it. At one end, both pieces of wood had been carved slightly to resemble a head, and the hair band was wrapped around the neck. This was significant, given that Blue Horse had predicted that witchcraft had been used to strangle Mrs. Tso.

Mrs. Tso's daughter and granddaughter emerged from the house and came over to join us. We showed them the curse and they identified both the hair and the hair band as belonging to Mrs. Tso. Then, when we took the hair band off, the two pieces of wood came apart and we could see a long lightning symbol carved on the inside of one of them. The significance of the lightning symbol was that it was intended to direct the deadly power of a lightning stroke at Mrs. Tso and kill her. The second piece of wood had several odd-looking marks on it, that may have been aimed at other members of the family. It was difficult to tell for sure in the artificial light, but the marks looked as if they had been burned into the wood with a piece of hot metal.

An unusual feature of this curse was that it looked new, while most of the curses we find seem to have been in place for years. It was a testimony to its efficacy that it had worked so quickly, and faced with a curse of such unusual power, Blue Horse decided to burn it immediately, so as to destroy its power in the cleansing flames. I carried the curse away from the family's compound to a safe distance, where I lit a fire as fast as I could. Mrs. Tso's son came to help me, but he was so nervous after his experiences, that he built the fire far bigger than was necessary and it became a veritable bonfire. This reassured the family that the evil was being destroyed, but the man was in such a state of panic, that he accidently threw into the flames the obsidian spear head Blue Horse had given him for protection. While the curse burned, fresh water was brought and we washed the ash from our hands and our implements. Then, when all was finished, I drove Blue Horse away into the night.

One the way home he reminded me of the partially dismounted loom we'd seen as we entered the home. He told me: "She's been trying to finish that piece of weaving for four years, and usually it takes about a year. But she couldn't finish it because of the curse. When she collapsed, she still hadn't finished it, so the family finished it for her and took everything down. It's bad to leave something like that unfinished, particularly if the person making it dies so it can never be finished. The family had to hurry and finish it before she died."

"But that curse looked new," I said.

"Yes," he agreed. "I think they had one and it only slowed her down, that's why the weaving took so long. Then, when that man died, they took the old curse away and put a new one in the grave, and that's what did the damage to her."

There was silence for a while before Blue Horse suddenly asked me: "Did you see that band was wrapped round the throat of the wooden pieces back there? That was to stop her breathing, and that's what happened."

When we went to Presbyterian Hospital in Albuquerque the next day to perform a healing ceremony at Mrs. Tso's bedside, I found she had been given a tracheotomy, an incision into the windpipe to bypass blockages that prevent the patient from breathing naturally. It was the only way the doctors could save her life.

It is a more than three hundred mile round trip from Blue Horse's place to Albuquerque, and when we drove to the hospital it took ages longer than it should have, because the road was blocked by a burning truck near Laguna Pueblo. When we eventually reached the Presbyterian, no one from the family was there to greet us and this somewhat offended Blue Horse's *amour propre*; particularly because we'd driven for so long in very hot conditions. We settled down to wait, or rather Blue Horse did, while I went in search of pop and gummy bears to offset the rigors of the journey. By the time I got back there was still no sign of the family and Blue Horse was in revolt.

"I've been waiting two hours and it's time to go!" He declared crossly. It had been less than thirty minutes and I tried to counsel a little patience, but he stumped off to the nurses' station to leave a message that he'd been and gone. As he was doing this a man approached, and then another, both of whom were from the family.

They took us to see Mrs. Tso, who was lying unconscious in the critical care unit on the seventh floor, breathing through a plastic pipe that had been inserted into her windpipe. I pointed this out to Blue Horse, who'd never heard the word "tracheotomy" before. But when I explained what it meant, he nodded knowingly. "Can't breathe, just like I said," he replied.

He was not in the least bit awed by the banks of hi-tech hospital equipment that surrounded the bedside with its drips, monitors, screens, tubes, wires and alarms, and he decided to perform some traditional healing on Mrs. Tso. To make sure we would not be disturbed, he sent me to inform the nurses' station of what we were doing.

Even though they were helpful and understanding—hospital staff in the Southwest are well accustomed to ancient native ceremonies being performed on their hi-tech wards—the Navajos did not want the white doctors and nurses seeing what was going on. The blinds in Mrs. Tso's room were lowered to keep out prying eyes and everything seemed hurried and furtive as the screens were drawn shut around her bed. When we lowered the sides of the bed so that Blue Horse could get at Mrs. Tso, there was a decidedly surreptitious air about it. Blue Horse blew his whistle and sucked bad stuff that looked pretty horrible from her neck and chest. I wrapped this in paper towels ready to throw it in the Rio Grande, because some bad stuff is better destroyed by free running water—but one of the men threw it down the lavatory before I had the chance. As soon as we'd finished, I drew back the curtains and opened the blinds, and then Blue Horse and I left straight away and drove back to the reservation.

And how much did we get paid for all this, including the cedar ceremonies, the midnight perambulation to the grave, and the total of nearly six hours of driving to Mrs. Tso's sickbed and back? We received the princely sum of fifty dollars, of which most went on fuel. The family may have promised more, but we never got it. I say "we", I mean, of course, Blue Horse: as bag carrier, apprentice, and general factotum, I don't get paid at all. Medicine men work for donations and don't charge fixed fees, but in return the people they serve are beholden to provide a suitable reward for the effort involved. Sometimes they do and sometimes they don't; and in this case Blue Horse definitely gave a lot more than he received.

* * *

Not long after this we were getting ready for a peyote meeting at Blue Horse's place, and Blue Horse, me and Ronny, who is married to Baa's daughter Cecelia, were putting up the tepee. I was videoing this when, just as I was providing a running commentary with the words, "in the hands of experts, putting up a tepee looks easy …", we were interrupted by a loud and ominous tearing sound, and a rip a couple of yards long opened in the canvas.

Panic! The meeting was due that night and Baa was frantic. She refused to accept the preferred male solution, which was to tape up the rip with duct tape, and instead insisted on sewing the tepee back together again. So down came the tepee, out came the sewing machine, and we lugged nearly one thousand square feet of heavy canvas into the living room. There, to my astonishment, in only a few minutes Baa had sewn a big patch onto the tepee and it was as good as new. I wonder how many women in London or New York could have done that? Ronny tried to make light of it all, suggesting that Indians would see the tear as a good thing that would allow the patient's illness to depart more rapidly. I thought he was pulling my leg and said so, but Ronny insisted that Indians always try to find something positive in every disadvantage. Since the arrival of the white man, I suppose Indians have had a lot of practice at that; but I still think he was pulling my leg.

One of the great things about tepees is how adaptable they are. This one was twenty-five feet high, and could easily seat thirty people in a circle around the inside, with ample space for a good fire in the middle; yet it packed into a plastic box small enough to shove under the bed.[12]

The patient that night was CJ, one of Baa's sons, [13] a large man who was clearly in pain. I thought he was suffering from arthritis, but it turned out he'd been struck by lightning! More precisely, he was in his house when the house was struck by lightning, which to the Navajos is pretty much the same thing. They fear lightning, which they see as a terrifying phenomenon that spiritually pollutes anyone who gets near it, and is sure to lead to serious, even life threatening, illness. They will studiously avoid going anywhere near a tree that has been struck by lightning; making a fire from lightning struck wood, or cooking on a fire made from lightning struck wood, is taboo. Anyone who does such a thing, even by accident, needs to seek purification immediately, or disaster will inevitably follow.

---

12   This does not, of course, include the tepee poles, which are often more than thirty feet long and usually stored outside on a special rack.
13   Blue Horse and Baa have several children from different marriages.

Since being struck, CJ had progressively lost the use of his arms and his hands, and as he was a carpenter by trade this meant he had also lost his living. The Navajo interpretation of CJ's suffering, and his obvious pain, was that the lightning had entered his system and was poisoning him. CJ said the storm had been some way off in the mountains, so he thought it odd that his house had been struck from such a distance. The implication of his reasoning being that the lightning strike had been guided by witchcraft; and in the last chapter we discovered inside the curse aimed at Mrs. Tso, lightning symbols intended to direct the deadly power of a lightning bolt towards her. CJ believed something similar had happened to him and, whatever the truth of the matter, it was universally acknowledged that it would take exceptionally strong medicine to counter the powerful effects of lightning. This is why he'd come to seek his step-father's aid and healing, and Blue Horse had promised to doctor him inside the tepee during the medicine ceremony; something that would give the healing extra power.

It was a good ceremony, and Blue Horse sucked some vicious looking stuff from CJ during the healing part, which seemed to do him good. Unfortunately, I was tired that night from other activities and had difficulty staying awake, which is why my description of events is somewhat perfunctory. I remember that at one time all the blues in the tepee, particularly those in the women's dresses and ceremonial blankets, turned such a deep and vibrant hue, that the color itself seemed to be alive. Cecelia was wrapped in a green Pendleton blanket that after a while began to shimmer as if made of silk; then it turned into a peacock's tail, and I found myself staring into eyes of Hera's watchman.

The unusually strong medicine from the meeting at the Yazzies' hogan had been presented to Blue Horse and Baa at the end of that ceremony, which is usual, and they had kept it to use tonight. This, combined with some dried medicine sent up from near the Mexican border, ensured that there was plenty of good, strong, medicine to go round. But if you want the medicine to show you something, or you have a problem to ask about, it's best to have that clear in your mind before the meeting begins, and I didn't. I was tired out and I'd gone solely with the intention of helping CJ, with my main focus being to try to stay awake until the morning. So, I didn't have anything to ask, or so I thought; but the medicine knew better.

I was struggling to fend off another wave of sleep inducing fatigue, when someone helpfully pulled back the tepee door and let in a stream of fresh air. It was a relief from the heat of the tepee, where the fire chief was keeping up a lively blaze, to feel that cool breeze blowing over my face and body. It was only when I turned to give a wave of thanks, that I found the cool breeze was blowing from a range of snow topped mountains towering above me, and I was walking down a path towards a green valley which, wherever else it was, wasn't in New Mexico. It felt like South America, but I could not be sure.

I was holding a staff to help me walk and there was a pack on my back, as I marched along on a hot day with my throat parched with dust. I wasn't concerned about my journey, thirst or fatigue, because I knew the path was leading me to the pleasant valley floor, where I could rest among its green bowers and luxuriant pastures, and slake my thirst from it streams of crystal waters. I marched on in happy anticipation, but the path did not lead me to the valley; or, rather, the path went there, but I did not.

Instead, I kept finding myself turned around and marching back the way I'd come towards the grim and forbidding peaks topped with snow, that towered so high they disappeared into iron-grey clouds that overhung that forbidding range. I couldn't work it out. No matter how hard I tried to descend into the valley, whenever I looked up to check the way, I was going in the wrong direction; up instead of down. Soon, I had a plan: I decided to walk backwards. That way I could look at the mountains and walk down to the valley at the same time. "That'll fool 'em," I thought. But it was to no avail, and instead of finding myself relaxing in the soft and verdant pastures, drinking the clear waters, and bathing my weary body in the crystal streams; I was back among the grim, snow and scree covered slopes of the mountains. A snowstorm began to blow, and without a coat or blanket, shivering and numb to the bone, I took shelter behind a large granite boulder.

While I was trying to figure it all out, the snow turned to rain and a little stream of water began to flow around the base of the boulder, where I watched in fascination as the little stream carried bits of earth and tiny pebbles and debris down the slope. Somewhere close at hand, I heard a voice uttering Frundsberg's words to Martin Luther, "Little monk, little monk, you take a hard road," over and over again. Not like a human voice, but like a short, rapid, staccato burst from a short-wave radio on an endless loop. I'm no monk (if I had been, I wouldn't have been so tired that night), and I'm certainly no intellectual like Martin Luther; so, I thought the voice must be referring to someone else, and I stood up and looked about to see if anyone was on the path; but I was alone.

Then, the vision faded, and I found myself back in the tepee, sitting cross-legged on the same piece of earth floor I'd been sitting on for the last nine hours, and which now seemed every bit as hard as any slab of granite could ever be.

I wondered later if the medicine was telling me that the only road worth taking would take me to a hard place, a place of granite. That I was not to live at ease, avoiding the hard places, if my work was to endure. I'm not going to attempt further analysis; I'm pretty sure I know what it meant.

The meeting did CJ good and in the morning when it was all over, he said he felt a lot better and his pain had eased. But Baa confided that she believed the only way to help him recover fully was to hold a Lightning Way ceremony for him. This ceremony would free him from all the evil effects of the lightning strike, but Baa had a problem: despite a search of several months, she had not been able to find a medicine man who knew how to do Lightning Way.

"It's getting so hard now to find anyone who can do these things," she complained. "They used to do it all the time, but now the medicine men don't know how to do it anymore, and those who do know are getting so old they don't want to do it anymore. Even when I find someone who says he knows how to do it, they say they're so busy it's going to be months." All I could do was sympathize.

Later, Baa shared something that reminded me again of how little some Navajos understand the white man's world, even to this day. She had a relative who was in jail on serious charges, she said, who when asked by the court if he wanted to plead guilty or not guilty, was unable to answer because he didn't understand the difference between the two.

"He's not an educated man, and he doesn't understand what's going on," Baa explained. "He had to call Blue Horse to ask what the difference was. They say he's got to have a trial to see if they send him to jail, but he's been in jail all this time anyway."

* * *

A couple of mornings later we went to cedar at the home of Jimmy Naakai. His is a traditional Navajo name that, as with a lot of Navajo words and names, is not easy to translate. In this case, based on the sound alone, Naakai could mean either "the Mexican" or "the wanderer." Whichever it was, Jimmy turned out to be a thoroughly likable man.

He and his two adult daughters were present for the ceremony and because the elder of the two sisters spoke little Navajo, most of the ceremony had to be in English; which was good for me as it was much easier to understand. She had a bad case of eczema on her face (actually, I thought it looked more like lupus), which she had suffered from for years. She also had a problem with her right leg, which often seized up so badly that at times she couldn't straighten it, while the younger sister had a bad back.

As we all sat cross legged in a circle around the charcoals in the fireplace, Blue Horse asked a lot of questions, particularly about the women going swimming as children and, oddly, about cacti. He eventually said he believed the women may have been witched while swimming; a local man's name—which I won't give here—came up several times. Blue Horse also felt that some interaction between the older sister and a cactus was to blame for the eczema, but I couldn't fully understand this part as by now he was speaking with Jimmy in Navajo. As this talk was going on the smoke went around as usual, but the Nahkais didn't realize I was part of the cedar and didn't pass the smoke to me. When Blue Horse gave it to me, and I blessed myself in the correct way, they were surprised a white man knew the ceremony.

The divination ceremony cannot begin until all the participants have been ritually purified and blessed with tobacco. To achieve this, the medicine man rolls what is known as a "smoke." This is a hand-rolled cigarette filled with extremely strong tobacco mixed with herbs to give the smoke a sweet smell and flavor. Theoretically, the tobacco should be wild native tobacco, but this is not easy to come by, so strong pipe tobacco is often substituted.

After the charcoal is brought in, but before I form it into the five-pointed star, I make it into a circle. This should be as perfect a circle as possible—and is another one of those things easier said than done. After this, my next duty is to pass Blue Horse the tobacco, which he keeps in a soft deer-hide bag with a beautiful beadwork design painstakingly sewn onto it. I also hand him packs of stiff brown cigarette papers of a kind I've never seen anywhere outside the Navajo reservation. The medicine man then rolls by hand a big fat cigarette, and it is this that is known as the "smoke" or, "a smoke". When he is ready, he signals to his apprentice, who then lights a special "fire lighter" stick from the east side of the charcoals, the side of the rising sun, and passes the stick to the medicine man so he can light the smoke. All this is done in a formal, ceremonial way but, again, it is not always as easy as it sounds.

For a start, some supposed "fire lighters" will do anything except catch alight. This is to the intense embarrassment of the apprentice, who can spend several anxious minutes blowing on the hot charcoals in an attempt to light the stick; until he is so out of breath he feels about ready to faint. The lighter, which may be as much as two inches in diameter and eighteen inches long, must not be allowed to heat up to the point where it bursts into flames. Instead, the apprentice has to ensure that the lighter smolders until every last bit of the end is glowing red hot—but not actually on fire—before he passes it to the medicine man. If all this is not done correctly, and the full face of the lighter is not glowing uniformly red hot, the medicine man may hand it back and tell the apprentice to try again. (More embarrassment and humiliation!)

Provided the fire lighter has been correctly lit, it is then passed to the medicine man who lights the smoke and hands the lighter back to the apprentice, who carefully places it on the east side of the fireplace, with the glowing end pointing directly toward the medicine man. It has to be placed in just such a way that it will not catch fire in the hot charcoals, but will go out gradually and naturally. In this day and age, an added hazard is carpet—an item entirely unknown to a previous generation of medicine men's apprentices—and I have to place the fire lighter exactly right, so it can't roll off and burn a hole in the family's new and expensive carpet.

After the smoke has been lit, the medicine man smokes and then, after a while, hands the smoke to the patient (the person the cedar is being performed for), who sits on the medicine man's immediate left, and the patient is encouraged to smoke the tobacco, bless themselves in the smoke, and talk about what ails them. When the patient has finished, the smoke goes to the next person on the left, and so on. This ensures that the smoke travels around the circle sunwise, following the same direction that the sun goes around the earth. In this way the smoke travels in a holy direction to reach each person at the ceremony, so they too can smoke and bless themselves.

Among American Indians tobacco is holy, and its smoke confers blessings as well as carrying good thoughts and prayers up to the Creator. All participants, including me, must bless themselves in the tobacco smoke as it comes around, if they are to take part in the ceremony, and this is done in a standard way. When participants receive the smoke, the first thing they must do is to draw tobacco smoke into the mouth—this tobacco is not usually inhaled because it is so strong—and then blow a long stream of smoke downward as an offering to Mother Earth. Next, they blow smoke upward to Father Sky, and after that they blow smoke from side to side to the four directions. When all this has been done, some people blow smoke straight out in front of them, which is a smoke for yourself, but not everyone does this.

After this they must bless themselves with the smoke from the tobacco by blowing it into their cupped hands—left hand first for a man, and right hand first for a woman—and, starting at the feet, dab it all over one side of the body until the head is reached.[14] This is then repeated with the other hand, and the other side is anointed. Some people open their shirts, or blouses, and blow smoke inside over their bodies, but I don't do this. Only after all this has taken place, and the proper ritual with the smoke has been completed, is a person regarded as being ritually cleansed and blessed so they can take part in the divination. In the case of children too young to smoke, adults will blow smoke over them, which is considered sufficient.

The smoke goes around until I get it back, and then I have to hold it until Blue Horse is ready to take it back again. By this time the smoke is often so burned down that it is impossible to hold the stub without burning my fingers: yet hold it I must, and keep it alight by taking little puffs until the medicine man signals for it. This can be pretty tough because Blue Horse can be quite voluble on occasion, and I have to sit quietly holding the smoke and ignoring the pain. After getting the smoke back, the medicine man takes another puff or two, before handing the smoke back once more to the apprentice, who then buries whatever is left of it in the center of the red-hot charcoal. Because I am barred from using any implement in this procedure, readers may imagine that handling red-hot charcoal with the bare fingers of one hand, while holding a red-hot cigarette that has burned down to the very end in the other, is likely to lead to badly blistered digits: they have my assurance that it does.

Now that everything was ready, Blue Horse decided to make the star himself, and right away I saw a bad-looking face in the charcoal and it was pointing straight at the two women. Blue Horse saw it, too, showed it to them, and said he thought the face was a mask; but the sisters said they hadn't had anything to do with masks. I thought it looked more like a bear's face than anything else, but it could have been a bear mask.

---

14 This is much easier when sitting cross legged on the floor.

Then we discovered that the older sister—the one with eczema—had her *kinaalda* ceremony,[15] in which a girl comes of age, at the same time as the *yeibichei* ceremony was being carried out at her family's hogan. The yeibichei is the Navajo new year ceremony, held at various times from the end of October to the end of November. Yei means god, or gods, or holy ones in Navajo, and the ceremony essentially marks the end of the growing season, the harvest, and the onset of winter. Thus, the Navajo new year occurs at the time of the change of season as the winter sets in, and not to mark the middle of winter as is customary in Western societies, where the Christmas and New Year festivals are held shortly after the midwinter solstice on, or about, December 22. Important in the context of the problems of the Nahkai daughters, was that the yeibichei ceremony does include masks, some of which can appear bearlike to the untrained eye.

The yeibichei ceremony goes on for nine nights, during which the medicine man and his assistants sing and drum inside the hogan, praying that the winter should not be too harsh, and that the people will come through without hunger or starvation. On the ninth and final night, the yei themselves appear, heavily masked, and dance outside the hogan. The Navajos who perform this ceremony dressed as the yei make noises and sounds during their appearance, but as my friend the prominent Navajo medicine man Emerson Jackson told me: "You will hear no word of human speech."

One of the peculiarities of the yeibichei is that it is not held on a particular date, but rolls across the reservation roughly following the harvest; starting with the Shiprock Fair in the north-east of the reservation at the beginning of October, and not reaching some places until early in November. In its present form, marking not only the beginning of winter but the end of the harvest, the yeibichei ceremony cannot be older than the time the Navajos adopted farming; something they learned from Pueblo Indians sometime after the Spanish appeared in the Southwest.

---

15 Later I had the opportunity to attend kinaalda ceremonies. Descriptions are in later volumes of my diaries.

The Navajo arrived in what are now the northern parts of modern New Mexico, after migrating slowly south from arctic Canada for perhaps three hundred years or more. It is best to think of this migration as a slow drift towards the south, probably punctured by many long pauses, rather than as an Exodus style march. No one knows exactly when the tribe arrived in the Southwest, but it is conjectured they would have continued south towards Mexico and Central America, had they not met the Spanish coming north after their conquest of Aztec Mexico in 1521. This northern movement of the Spanish was probably the major reason the tribe's further southward migration was halted, and the Navajo settled down to farming, and herding sheep they acquired from the Spanish. Their arctic origins are obvious today in their Athabascan language, which they brought from what is now north-west Canada and central Alaska, and where similar Athabascan languages are still spoken.

While we were discussing all this, Jimmy Naakai produced some tiny fragments of turquoise and white shell, both of which have important properties in Navajo medicine, and told the girls to pick a piece each. They picked the white shell and began placing the tiny fragments on pieces of white paper towel, which they wrapped up and placed carefully beside the fireplace. Then Blue Horse, the two sisters and Jimmy, all went outside taking the little paper wraps of white shell with them. I was left to look after the fireplace and the sacred instruments, and in this I was ably assisted by the older sister's nine-year-old daughter Alex, who was a very pretty girl and had the most magnificent jet-black hair hanging so far down her back she could sit on it. She told me that when she'd been little she could speak Navajo well, but since going to school in Rio Rancho (a suburb of Albuquerque where she lived with her mother), she'd found it difficult to keep up, and could no longer speak much at all: a fate shared by too many young Navajo speakers, I'm afraid.

When they came back the sisters no longer had the white shell, and I wondered what had happened to it; but because I make a habit of not asking questions while ceremonies are taking place, I remained silent. When everyone had retaken their places on the floor, Blue Horse plucked a red-hot coal from the charcoal and put it in his mouth.[16] Then, holding the glowing coal between his teeth, he began to blow hot breath over the older sister, before taking his pipe and sucking out some black bits (which he later identified as deer horn) from her neck, and then more horn from the place where her right leg hurt.

"These two bits try to join up and pull themselves together inside you," he explained, showing her the two pieces of horn. "That's why you can't straighten your leg and why you hunch forward with the pain."

He then sucked a piece of deer horn from the younger sister's back before going to work on Jimmy, and sucking a large amount of black fluid from his knee, that poured out and flowed down the old gentleman's leg. His daughter quickly wiped it away with a paper towel, and then Blue Horse turned his attention to Jimmy's neck, and out of this he sucked a jagged piece of silver. I'd never before seen metal extracted during these sessions—stones, gunk, deer horn, bits of bear claw, snake skin and all sorts of weird-looking stuff—but never metal. When I was able to get a good look at it, I saw it was a sliver of silver about the length of my thumbnail, and very thin, that seemed to have been cut from a much larger piece.

"It's been cut from a silver bracelet dug up from a grave," Blue Horse explained, reminding us that witchmen loot graves to recover items they can use as curses, and also have the ability to shoot objects into people without the person knowing.[17] These objects can remain lodged in the body for years doing harm, until a medicine man discovers them and removes them.

"These people can do anything," Blue Horse warned us, and not for the first time. After this, I was dispatched to the waste drums at the side of the family home with some matches and lighter fuel, to burn and destroy the bad stuff he had sucked out.

---

16   This was something he did frequently, never once burning himself. The hot breath helps to cure, but Blue Horse was also demonstrating the shaman's traditional mastery over fire.

17   In my first book *Meeting the Medicine Men*, I recorded an incident in which we found a bracelet inside a curse. This bracelet was later confirmed by the widow as being the one she'd buried with her husband years previously.

Later, while we were driving home in the truck, I asked Blue Horse what had happened to the white shell the sisters carried outside.

"We presented it back to the cactus," he said.

"Does that mean the cactus takes the bad stuff back into itself?" I asked.

"That's it," Blue Horse said. "She's going to get better now."

III

At last Baa has found a medicine man to carry out the Lightning Way for CJ. Lightning Way is one of the most powerful Navajo healing ceremonies, and it goes on for two days. I was asleep on the floor when Baa burst in at about 5:00 am crying, "Charles, I have to apologize to you. We have an emergency, and we need to do a Lightning Way ceremony for CJ."

After searching for months she'd found a medicine man from near Keams Canyon in Arizona, who knew how to do the ceremony properly, and straight away the whole family, including me, was mobilized to get things organized. We had to move fast, Baa told us, because the medicine man had the narrowest of windows in his schedule, and could carry out the ceremony only if it was done immediately.

The patient, Baa's son CJ, whom we met in the tepee in the last chapter, had progressively lost the use of his arms after being struck by lightning; his condition had become so bad he could no longer raise his arms above the level of his shoulders, or use his hands very well. A carpenter by trade, he was unable to work and had fallen on hard times. The purpose of the ceremony was to free him from the evil the Navajo believe enters a person struck by lightning, and to restore the use of CJ's arms and hands so he could once more live a normal life and earn a living.

Navajo medicine is extremely complicated and some ceremonies last anywhere between two and five days—or even nine days in the exceptional case of the yeibichei, the ceremony that marks the new year—and all have to be performed flawlessly. The medicine man has to sing every song at its right place, and has to be word perfect in every song; because if he makes a mistake he has to begin all over again. There are a lot of songs to be sung, as well as a great deal of complicated ritual to be carried out in a ceremony performed over two days, let alone five. Because of this complexity, individual medicine men usually specialize in only one or two of the big ceremonies, such as Enemy Way, Squaw Dance, Beauty Way or Lightning Way; although some are reputed to know them all.

The only comparison I can think of, is of someone learning the whole of Wagner's Ring Cycle, the world's longest opera, including all the singing parts and all the orchestra parts, and then performing it all by themselves with no mistakes allowed. Wagnerian fans may think that a tall order—and they'd be right—but in total the Ring lasts only fifteen hours, while lengthy Navajo ceremonies can involve the medicine man in songs, prayers and rituals for eight or more hours a day for five days, a minimum of forty hours, nearly three times longer. Even a two-day ceremony like the Lightning Way, can involve ten or fifteen hours of work for the medicine man.

These highly specialized medicine men are perhaps analogous in the complexity of their work to modern brain or heart surgeons, while in the hierarchy of Navajo medicine, Blue Horse performs the role of family doctor with me as his intern. He deals with the everyday problems people bring him but, like family doctors everywhere, when faced with a serious and difficult case he refers it to those who specialize in such things. Blue Horse and I were not able to carry out the Lightning Way for CJ, for the simple reason that it was a job for a specialist.

Men capable of the extraordinary feats of virtuosity and memory needed to carry out these lengthy Navajo ceremonies, were probably never great in number, and they get fewer every year. Baa told me she had approached eight medicine men before she found Hastin Kee Manuelito, whom she managed to contact during the night as I lay sleeping on the floor. Some of the others she'd contacted knew the ceremony, but were too old to perform it, while others were too busy. Mr. Manuelito was busy too, but he had a two-day gap before the start of a squaw dance at which he was officiating.

While I constantly refer to medicine *men*, I should point out that there are medicine *women* among the Navajo. Women perform a different kind of medicine which is done both by and for women, and because of the strict demarcation between the sexes in areas of traditional Navajo life, men are not allowed to intrude in women's medicine. As a man, I am not allowed to know anything about women's medicine, and it would be impossible for me to become the apprentice of a medicine woman. So, I can write only about what I found among medicine men. Women's medicine, and medicine women, are an area closed to me, and I fully accept the traditional rules of the Navajo world.

We all dressed quickly and drove over to McDonald's on the north side of Gallup to wait for Mr. Manuelito. He turned out to be a very old man, who CJ said spoke no English, though I discovered later he spoke a bit. Well into his seventies, or more likely his eighties, he was a man of great dignity, who wore a large red paisley-patterned bandana around his head with a corner sticking up at the front. This is the traditional headband of a Navajo medicine men, but one that is rarely seen these days. His wife, who was extremely petite, appeared to be even older than he was. She had no teeth, although she obviously had a sharp personality, and she wore the traditional Navajo women's dress of a long-pleated skirt and velveteen blouse, that many older Navajo women still habitually wear.

When Mr. Manuelito was ready, Baa drove him and his wife, along with me and CJ, to CJ's house, which is on a Navajo Housing Association development. As this ceremony was the province of another medicine man, Blue Horse did not attend. As we drove, I observed that CJ was in considerable pain. He could hardly use his arms, one hand was so swollen it was unusable, and he was having trouble sitting still because his shoulders hurt so much.

We arrived to find that inside the house a space between the kitchen and the main room had already been cleared and scrubbed clean by CJ's wife Penny and their children. It was in this space that the ceremony was to be performed, and where the big sand painting that is integral to the ceremony would be created. Earlier, Baa had taken me to a sand pit where I filled two large buckets with fine, clean, yellow sand to form the base on which the painting was to be created. Many people will have heard the term "sand painting" in a Navajo context, but what is generally referred to as a "sand painting" is not as it sounds. It is not a painting made with sand: it is a painting made *on* sand, using white and yellow pollen and finely ground colored minerals. This is a vital distinction, because the whole point of painting *on* sand, is to emphasize the ephemeral nature of the images created during this ceremony, as I shall relate.

It took time for the family to assemble from all over Navajo territory, and so it was not until toward evening that the ceremony began. It began slowly and almost imperceptibly at first, and like so many Navajo ceremonies this one started with a good chat. We all sat in a circle cross legged on the floor while Mr. Manuelito established his authority with talk and humor. CJ sat in a corner on the medicine man's left, the traditional place for a patient and then, after a while, Mr. Manuelito asked for a rug to be brought in. A traditional Navajo-patterned hand-woven wool rug was fetched and spread carefully on the floor in front of him. Baa had brought with her a white buckskin and this was now spread on top of the rug. Then, as the old medicine man continued to talk he produced a small pocket knife and, casually at first, began to clean the surfaces of some hollow sticks he'd brought with him; scraping away any blemishes, dirt, or imperfections they might have had. When he was satisfied, he cut the hollow rods into ten equal lengths and began to paint them. As he did so, although he never ceased his casual-seeming demeanor and talk, it dawned on me that the ceremony was underway.[18]

Next, Mr. Manuelito painted the sticks in the traditional colors of the four directions: white for the east, turquoise for the south, yellow for the west, and black for the north. When he had painted each stick in its correct color, he and his wife began to paint intricate patterns on them, some of which looked like lightning strikes. Then they divided some sticks into small sections by painting lines on them, and then painting patterns in each section.

---

[18] Although I give a detailed description of parts of Lightning Way it is far from complete. No one will be able to reproduce this, or any other, sacred Navajo ceremony from the pages of this book.

While the sticks were drying, the medicine man carefully placed ten sheets of white linen on top of the white buckskin. The linen looked like the stained fragments of linen coverings from Egyptian mummies I've seen in museums,[19] and then a number of small feathers were laid on each piece of linen. Baa leaned over and whispered to me that these feathers were from many different kinds of birds. The idea being that "the feathers will carry away the evil in different directions, like the flight of many birds," she told me.

With the paint on the hollow sticks now dried, Mrs. Manuelito carefully plugged one end of each stick with a little ball of sage leaves she had rolled between her fingers. After this, one each of the ten sticks was laid next to the feathers on each one of the ten pieces of linen. The sequence now, from the floor upward, was: floor, rug, buckskin, linen, and then the painted sticks with the feathers. Now Mr. Manuelito began to chant in Navajo, while simultaneously tying the sticks together in pairs, using a thin cord to which more feathers had been carefully attached. Once he had completed this task, he picked up the sticks and placed each pair on various points on CJ's body, at the places where he was experiencing most pain. Carefully, holding the sticks in place with one hand, he suddenly pulled hard on the strings with his free hand. This lifted the strings of feathers sharply upward, so they hung shuddering and dancing in the air. As he pulled each string, Mr. Manuelito imitated a bird call to further encourage the evil to leave CJ's body and follow the flight of the birds. It this way it would be scattered to the four winds; just as a startled flock of birds will dart for the sky and scatter in all directions.

Once this had been done, the sticks and feathers were collected and placed on the linen squares once more, and then carefully folded and given to CJ. Next, still clutching the linen bundles, CJ was taken outside to a car and driven away by a companion to a remote spot. There he was to pray over the bundles, "Pray away" is the Navajo term, meaning that the evil is being prayed away by being prayed against in a spot remote from its source. Poor CJ was in such pain he had difficulty rising to his feet and I had to

---

19 I never discovered the significance (if any) of these coverings.

help him. Then, once CJ had gone, Mr. Manuelito continued to chant for a while, after which there was a pause in the proceedings until CJ returned.

During this lull, I was dispatched to collect a tub of earth from a corn field, which in this part of the world is not the field of wheat, barley, or rye many readers, particularly those from outside the United States, will be familiar with. In New Mexico and the Southwest "corn" means Indian corn—that is to say, maize—which the Navajo generally grow in well-spaced rows in small family lots. In New Mexico corn can be planted pretty well any time from March to July, but not being of farming stock myself, unless I can see big green stalks shooting skyward, I can't tell a corn field from any other kind of field. Thankfully, I was accompanied by Tim one of CJ's brothers who, like most Navajos, knew a corn field when he saw one, fallow or not.

It was important to get earth from a corn field, and not any other field, because corn occupies a central place in the lives and mythology of the Navajo. As well as being an important component in their diet, it is a ubiquitous image found on rugs and weavings, on the Navajo flag, and on the great seal of the Navajo nation. The corn "gives us our strength" as they say, and soil from a corn field is regarded as being endowed with power.

Tim and I drove a few miles before he spotted the right kind of field, and then we had to scramble through a wire fence, fill the tub with good earth, and drive back to the house as fast as we could. I figured the owner wouldn't miss a small tubful of his field, but Tim took a few small coins and scattered them about. "You have to give something for something," he said. "It's right to leave a gift if you've taken something for yourself."

A couple of hours later CJ returned and was reseated in his place on the medicine man's left. Then the rug and the buckskin were cleared away and the earth from the corn field was poured onto the floor, where it was shaped into a small circular mound. Boughs of green spruce were placed on top of the mound, each pointing towards one of the four directions, but deliberately set off-center, and sweet-smelling sage was interlaced between the boughs.

Baa fetched a traditional Navajo basket woven from split sumac, which she'd left soaking in the sink in an attempt to swell it and make it waterproof. This hadn't worked, so she placed clear plastic wrap on the inside,[20] and placed it at the center of the mound amid the spruce and sage. Next the basket was filled with cold water, to which Mrs. Manuelito added several different herbs until the surface was covered with floating greenery. Slowly and carefully, she began to scatter white, yellow, and red pollen across the surface of the bowl. When she'd finished, I saw she'd drawn the highly symbolic shape of a corn plant on top of the floating herbs. The level of skill needed to accomplish this—by scattering dry pollen on the leaves of green herbs floating on water—I found simply astonishing; if I hadn't seen it with my own eyes, I would scarcely have believed it possible. After the corn drawing had been made on the water, CJ had to leave the room because patients are not allowed to see the sand painting until it is completed; for if they do, they cannot benefit fully from its power.

With CJ banished to a bedroom, a couple of thicknesses of showercurtain were laid on the floor, and I carried in the buckets of sand and poured about a bucket and a half onto the plastic. Willing hands spread it evenly into a circle about five feet across and a few inches thick; while the medicine man and his wife painstakingly smoothed the top with the traditional wooden battens used in weaving. Only when the sand had been prepared to his complete satisfaction, did Mr. Manuelito begin to make the painting.

Taking pinches of yellow pollen between forefinger and thumb, he began with great care to scatter it upon the sand. Slowly, the pollen formed the outline of a long, thin, figure that was not immediately recognizable as either human or nonhuman. Then, once the outline was fixed, everyone joined in and began to add more pollen. I held back, because it can be a touchy thing for a white man to take part in a ceremony as sacred as this one. Even today, some older traditional Navajos consider the mere presence of a white man enough to ruin a ceremony; and while everyone here was family, I'd not met some of these relations before, and they didn't know me either.[21] A second reason for holding back was that I believed the Navajos

---

20 Baskets were traditionally waterproofed by a coat of pine pitch or resin smeared on the inside.
21 By this time I'd been adopted into Blue Horse's family.

had at least some idea of what they were doing, while I had none. I didn't want to do anything incorrect, or stupid, and perhaps in some way ruin the painting from ignorance. As it turned out I was wrong on every score; none of the family had made a sand painting before, they couldn't understand why I didn't want to help, and on the second day insisted I take part.

Today it's easy to find numerous photographs of Navajo sand paintings on the Internet, and it's easy to buy colorful, commercially made, sand paintings sealed with glue so they can be hung on the wall. What most people don't know is that none of these photographs are of real sand paintings, and none of the sand paintings for sale in shops or trading posts are real either. They are pretty, I agree, and I've bought several in the past, and I'd be the last person to stop you from buying one and keeping a Navajo artist in business. But vital aspects found in real sand paintings—the ones that give the painting power—have been deliberately left out of these commercial versions.

A genuine sand painting, like the one we were creating, is a sacred object that opens a direct connection between the human world and the world of the gods; the yei, or Holy People. This connection enables the Holy People to use the sand painting as a portal through which they can enter the profane world of human beings. Once here, they will restore *hozho*, which means something approximate to our English words *balance* or *harmony*; specifically, between a person and the surrounding world of the spirits. In another sense hozho is an inward concept that describes the way in which people strive to live their lives. The idea is much more powerful than English words can convey, and it is perhaps best to think of hozho as central to the Navajo universe and way of life; while at the same time residing within each person as an ideal.

The Navajo world is a balance between harmony and disharmony and if the balance of hozo is upset, even accidentally, bad things are sure to follow. The lightning strike that hit CJ's house caused disharmony but—equally likely—was the result of existing disharmony between him and the spirit world. As a result, he lost the use of his arms and thereby his living as a carpenter. Now the sand painting would open a door to allow a direct connection between CJ and the gods, who could enter to restore harmony and take away his suffering and illness.

When wrestling with these difficult concepts, it does not help that the English term "sand painting" obscures the whole idea of what is being done. The term has no meaning in the Navajo language and, in fact, the painting is not a painting at all; it is *iikááh*. The Navajo iikááh—another complicated word—can be translated as something like "the place where the gods' shrine is laid down," or "a place where the gods come and go". What iikááh indicts, is precisely what the English terms hides: that what is being created is not a painting, but a sacred place where humans and gods can interconnect. Just as a holy shrine is a place through which people can contact a saint in heaven, the iikááh allows direct contact between the world of the Holy People and ours.

I hope I have made it clear—and it is complicated, I agree—that the sand painting itself does not restore hozho. Instead, it allows the gods to enter and do so, and the most important part of the ceremony would come when CJ was placed on top of the iikááh to establish direct contact between him to the Holy People. By placing him on the sand painting, a physical junction would be achieved that would enable the Holy People to take away CJ's pain, suffering, and illness. When they had done their work, the yei would depart to their own world through the same iikááh, leaving behind the newly restored hozho. It is for all these reasons that photographs you see, or sand paintings you buy, are not real. If they were, they would not only be sacrilegious, but so overwhelmingly powerful as to be dangerous to humans, and Navajo tradition tells us why.

The first iikááh was created by the Holy People, but it was permanent and not made on sand. When the gods created the Navajo people—the all-too-human Diné [22]—and the people eventually entered the present world,[23] the gods recognized that the Diné would require their assistance, so they gave the people the right to summon them through the iikááh. But the gods knew that humans could not be trusted with the power the im-

---

22 Diné, or "people," is the name the Navajo call themselves.
23 To the Navajo our world is the fourth world, the Diné having already passed through three previous worlds before emerging through a hollow reed into Dinétah, the original heartland of Navajo territory near what is now their north-east boundary.

ages bestowed, and therefore decreed that the Diné could create the sacred images only on sand. In this way they could never be made permanent but, just to be sure, the gods further decreed that each image must be destroyed on the same day it is made.

For all these reasons the pictures now being created in front of me were, to the Navajo, not images of Lightning Beings but the real thing: Holy People, with one standing guard over each direction, east, south, west, and north. Before my eyes they slowly grew into spectacular creations that glowed with vibrant blues, reds and yellows. The colors were made from pollen, and finely ground sand and minerals, that were taken a pinch at a time to be carefully sprinkled onto the sand to create the many lines that made up each picture. As the paintings built up grain by grain, line by line, in layer after layer of color, they slowly came into focus; as if emerging through the portal of the iikááh, just as Navajo legend says they will. It took the better part of two hours to finish the painting, and when it was at last complete, these strange Beings did indeed seem to have emerged from another world.

I won't try to describe the Lightning Beings in detail—indeed, it would be beyond my power to do so—for these were complex and detailed representations. As with the yeibichei gods, who utter sounds but no word of human speech, the shape of the Lightning Beings was only partially human. They had discernable heads and arms and legs like humans, but their bodies were stretched and impossibly long. Their faces could not be seen, but their identity was made clear by the shafts of lightning that shot around them; and I noticed that each Lightning Being, at each cardinal point, was different in detail from each of the others.

When all was ready a glass tumbler and an abalone shell, both filled with the herb liquid from the basket, were placed at the western edge of the sand, along with a small feather fan. At last CJ, wearing only a pair of shorts, was led from the bedroom in which he had been cloistered, and was given white pollen with which to make an offering. This he did by scattered the pollen across the sand painting, making sure to sprinkle plenty on each of the Lightning Beings, while Mr. Manuelito did the same. The medicine man also anointed the Lightning Beings, using his feather fan dipped in the herb water. With my help—because by now he could not move unaided—CJ was led to the center of the sand, where I helped him to sit down facing the east.

This produced severe trampling of the painting and CJ, who is not a small man, did still more damage when he sat down in the middle of it. But this damage was beside the point, which was to create a physical bond between the gods and CJ, so the Holy People could reach him and remove all that ailed him. It was a moment in which our deeply flawed world was for a while united with the perfect realm of the gods. If in doing so, the painstakingly constructed pictures of the Lightning Beings were to our human eyes damaged or destroyed, this mattered little. The important thing was that physical contact between god and human had been achieved.

Mr. Manuelito began to chant accompanied by his rattle, which was made from soft leather, [24] and had a small red and blue stripe on the side to symbolized the Navajo red earth and blue sky. While he chanted, the basket filled with herbs and water was fetched, and I helped CJ to drink draught after draught from a small glass. I had to help him, because he could hardly manage for himself, with his useless hand, and his arms that he could scarcely raise to his lips. Even so, I wondered how he could get it all down; particularly as each glassful was filled with a thick mass of herbs. Yet, whenever the basket was close to being emptied, fresh water was poured in and CJ had to drink more.

Just as I thought he might burst, he was told to stop, and the rest of us were invited to take a drink. When I did, the liquid proved to be unbelievably bitter—so bitter that I had trouble keeping it down. It's worth noting that I drank one draught of a much-diluted liquid, while CJ had to drink quantities before so much as a drop of extra water had been added. How he managed this, I have no idea, as I know I couldn't have done it. But the theory behind the herbs was that their bitterness would help to drive the evil from him; and bitter they were indeed.

---

24 Navajo rattles are usually made from dried gourds filled with small pebbles, and make a characteristic high-pitched chinking sound.

While this was going on, the medicine man continued his chants, in which he sang of each of the Lightning Beings in turn, enumerating their good and bad points. Then he left his position on the floor, stood up, and still chanting took the abalone shell and the glass and made CJ drink yet more of the herb drink. After he had drained the last bitter drop, I helped CJ to stand up, and guided him to a chair where he sat covered from head to foot in sand and pollen. However, he was warned by Mr. Manuelito that he must on no account shower or wash that night, for fear of washing away the power of the magic that was now upon him, and after this warning CJ was led away to another room for the night.

   Now the top layer of sand was carefully swept away, destroying what little remained of the pictures after CJ had trampled them. To comply with the directive of the Navajo gods, that images must be destroyed on the same day they are made, and great care was taken to ensure every bit of the images was removed. Finally, this top portion of sand was collected in plastic bags and taken away; but where it went, or what happened to it, I do not know. We swept up the rest of the sand that had borne no images and put it back in the buckets for reuse. Only when the room was completely clear of any trace of the images, and of sand or pollen, was a meal of traditional Navajo mutton stew and fry bread served in dishes on the floor. [25]

   That was the end of the first part of the ceremony. It was after midnight before Baa and I left, and it was not until 1:30 am that we reached home and could get to sleep.

✳ ✳ ✳

Early next morning Baa and I drove back to CJ's place, where Mr. and Mrs. Manuelito and several other people had spent the night, because it was too far to travel to their homes. Breakfast was cooked and put on the floor, including dishes of fried potatoes, fry bread, and a meat patty so ferociously

---

25 Traditional hogans had no furniture, so everything was placed on the floor, including dishes of food. Because this modern house had been transformed into a traditional sacred space for the ceremony, it was natural that food should be served and eaten on the floor in the old-fashioned way.

hot with chili I thought it was on fire. Then, after breakfast, we began the next part of the ceremony.

It opened with general prayers and then CJ was dismissed to the bedroom while more sand paintings were prepared. I fetched the buckets of sand and tipped them out on the floor, where once again the sand was shaped into a round, smooth, mound. Mr. Manuelito began to draw fresh images, one for each point of the compass. But these were not Lightning Beings, but images of ancient Navajo spirits.

"It needs a steady hand," someone said, as they all began to help build the images.

Now that I was expected to join in, I took some colored sand between my thumb and finger and did my best. The sand has to be released a few inches above the surface to get the best result, and it is a painstaking business in which each line of each image is literally built up grain by grain. Not surprisingly, Mr. Manuelito was far better at this than we were, and his images were much sharper and completed much faster than ours. It took more than an hour to produce the spirit beings, one for each of the four directions, and this time the directions were reversed, with north pointing south and so on. Again, the abalone and the glass were filled with bitter herb liquid, but they were not placed in the same position as the night before; but slightly to the right of the west cardinal point.

When all was ready CJ was brought in again, this time wearing only his undershorts. He was given white pollen to offer to the images, while the medicine man anointed the spirits using a feather dipped in the contents of the abalone shell. Again, CJ was placed in the center of the iikááh facing east, and for a second time the divine connection was made. Then, when CJ was seated, the medicine man began his chant in which he named each spirit using its Navajo name, and relating what it could do and what it represented, before calling on its power to help his patient. This time, it seemed to work.

It wasn't exactly "take up thy bed, and walk," but there was a definite and noticeable improvement in CJ's mobility. I had to assist him to the bedroom and to get some clothes on, but he was able to return to sit in a chair beside the sand painting under his own steam, and without any further assistance from me. Sitting only a few feet away from him, I could see the swelling that so bedeviled his hand had gone down considerably, and he seemed to be carrying himself better and to be moving more easily. I even saw his right foot tapping slightly to the rhythm of the chant. Overall, he looked better than I'd seen him at any time recently, and much better than the night before.

This second part of the ceremony lasted about four hours, but by the time it was over CJ had improved remarkably. Whereas up till now I had had to give him considerable physical support to walk even the few steps to his room, and had to help him dress and even eat; now he could get in and out of his chair unaided, he could use his arms more freely and could walk around unaided, and he told us the pain in his shoulders and arms had lessened considerably. I should have mentioned that in both sessions, his sore shoulders had been anointed using herb water from the abalone shell, and this had been done expressly to reduce his pain.

At the end of the ceremony Mr. Manuelito recited a list of actions CJ was not to perform for four days. Among them were that he was specifically banned from taking a shower, even though he was covered from head to toe in sand and pollen. This injunction was to prevent the good effects of the ceremony from being washed away. He was not to cut anything with a metal knife, he was not to sleep with his wife, and he was warned to show due respect for the powers invoked on his behalf. In the Navajo world everything comes in fours. There are four seasons, four original clans, four sacred mountains, four directions and four colors; and it would take four days for the cure for CJ to become effective.

* * *

So, there you have it: CJ looked better, he moved more freely, and by his own testament his pain had lessened considerably. Observationally, I could see that the ceremony had a beneficial effect on him—an effect that was obvious to us all. But the question was, how long would this effect last and would it be permanent? This was something I always wanted to know about the cases Blue Horse and I dealt with, but rarely was I able to find out. The best I could hope for was that the family of a patient, or the patient themselves, would phone Blue Horse to say how much better things were since we'd been round; but that happened in only a small number of cases. Occasionally, I'd run into someone we'd taken away curses for, or taken bad stuff out of, and that person would tell me how much better they felt and still felt. I don't know if it's significant, but I never encountered anyone who claimed we'd made them worse.

While it's always nice to know one is doing some good in the world, this kind of anecdotal evidence falls woefully short of the detailed medical follow ups I would dearly love to have made, had such a thing been possible. Unfortunately, the vast distances between one patient and another on the reservation, the many hours of driving, the natural shyness of the Navajo and, not least, that I am in no way medically qualified to conduct such a follow up study, made it impossible. But with CJ it was different. CJ was family and I was sure to find out his long-term progress in the end. Even so, it took far longer than I imagined.

With one thing and another, it was more than two years before I caught up with CJ again for long enough to talk to him about all this. We met again at a squaw dance [26] at Pueblo Pintado, a small settlement deep inside the reservation, and he appeared much healthier than I remembered him before the ceremony. He confirmed that he'd benefitted greatly from Lightning Way, and felt much better for it. He had his good days and his bad days, he said, and he still took pain killers, but generally he felt much better. The one thing he regretted was allowing himself to be struck by lightning in the first place.

"Two people warned me about the lightning before it ever happened," he confided. "There was a Spanish lady who read palms, and she took me aside one day and warned me about the lightning before it ever happened.

---

26 Some people seem to think there is something derogatory about this healing ceremony being called a "squaw dance". All I can say, is that is the name the Navajo use, and so long as they do, I can't call it anything else.

And a medicine man warned me as well. I should have been more careful," he added ruefully.

"But lightning struck your house," I reminded him. "What could you have done about it?"

But CJ just smiled in his engaging and enigmatic way, and gave me to understand that if only he had taken the precaution of having certain ceremonies done, the lightning strike and all that followed, would have been averted.

The Lightning Way and CJ's recovery was of personal interest to me because, years earlier, my house in London had been struck by lightning as I sat watching television while a storm raged overhead. Apart from the television, and a few other electrical devices that were blown out, there appeared to be little damage. But then, over a period of months, I progressively lost the use of my arms, until I could no longer raise them above shoulder height, nor could I reach behind me; and it was agonizingly painful to attempt to do so.

At that time I'd had no contact with the Navajo, in fact, I'd hardly heard of them, and it was not until several years later that I traveled to the United States. I certainly had no knowledge of the effects the Navajo attribute to lightning strikes, and so there could be no question of psychosomatic cross-cultural influence, yet the facts are plain enough. My home was struck by lightning and then, over a period of a few months, my arms ceased to work properly; exactly as happened to CJ, and exactly as Navajo medicine men say lightning can affect people. Coincidence? By now readers will have figured out that the clunky old machinery of coincidence is the least likely explanation for the many strange events I witnessed among the Navajo.

Not being in a position to benefit from Lightning Way myself, it took a year of expensive treatment from a leading therapist in Hampstead, before my arms worked again; and my left arm has never regained one hundred percent of its range.

* * *

Not long after the Lightning Way ceremony, I went with Blue Horse and Baa to visit a woman in Grants, a small town off 1-40 in New Mexico. She was a very jolly lady, who lived in a nice house, and gave me a string of dried peyote buttons that looked exactly like large beads on a necklace. She'd just returned from a place known to Indians as the The Garden. Little known to white people, The Garden lies within the few counties close to the Mexican border where peyote grows wild in the USA. Indians travel there from all over North America to buy medicine, or collect it from the wild, and it was one of those places I'd always wanted to go. Much later, and after much persuasion, I was able to get Blue Horse to take me there. [27]

This woman, Louise Benally, was a relative of some sort and had an eleven-year-old daughter, which made it all the more distressing when she told us she'd been diagnosed with breast cancer, and the surgeon wanted to operate immediately to remove her breast. Baa suggested she wait and try traditional methods to cure her tumor, and for the first time I found myself disagreeing with Baa and Blue Horse in public. I felt a breast cancer tumor was too dangerous to leave to develop, and I said so. Blue Horse treated her in the traditional way and sucked some bad stuff from her breast; but what happened after that I never found out, because almost immediately after this I had to return to England for a while.

To make sense of this story, I'll have to jump forward a few years to the fourth birthday party of my friend Erik Faria's son Easton, whose mother is Navajo. I'd wanted to go to a squaw dance near Chaco Canyon, but no one else wanted to go, and Baa said it would be over by the time we got there. So, instead, I went to Easton's party, which was being held at the home of his Navajo grandmother Sally, who lived at that time on the outskirts of Gallup.

The family made me very welcome and the barbeque was great, although I thought the heavy metal band playing live in the garden was a bit much for a four-year-old (by which I meant for me). As they weren't going to stop thrashing away on my account, I sought shelter by sneaking into

---

27 See below, Chapter Six.

the house in the hope of finding a quiet corner. But a few moments after entering, I was confronted by a woman who declared: "I know you. You're Blue Horse's assistant!"

I hadn't the slightest idea who she was, but it turned out this was Louise Benally, and she told me what happened after our first meeting in Grants four years earlier.

"I had to go back for a mammogram a few days after you'd seen me," she said. "When they looked at the results, I was completely clear—there was no cancer at all! The doctors couldn't believe what they were seeing. I've been free of cancer ever since, and there's no sign of it coming back."

While not one to underestimate Blue Horse's powers of healing, I didn't know what to make of this, and my first thought was that the original diagnosis might have been wrong. It was possible, but unlikely, because breast cancer is a well-known condition and it would be unusual for an experienced team to make a mistake. In any case, there must have been *something* in her breast to make the doctors want to operate. It was definitely cancer, according to Mrs. Benally, who told me she'd expected to lose a breast and knew that her life was on the line. Yet only a few days after being treated by Blue Horse, she assured me, there was no sign of cancer. Now, here she was four years later, and she was still clear of the disease and obviously right as rain.

A four-year remission for someone who has had a mastectomy and extensive chemotherapy or radiation treatment would be wonderful; but a four-year remission after the cancer apparently vanished spontaneously overnight seemed frankly miraculous. With all this in mind, I took steps to meet Mrs. Benally again, in order to check the facts and make sure I had understood correctly; when I did, it turned out that her story, while marvelous in its own way, was not quite as it seemed.

It is worth relating all this, because it is a good illustration of how careful one must be in this very sensitive area, where patients are desperate to be well again, but often don't fully understand what's happening to them. Working as a journalist in Britain, I often encountered this problem among patients—especially working-class patients—who did not understand the big words that doctors habitually use. As a result, they failed to understand what was wrong with them, or what was being done to help them; and I wondered if something of this sort had happened to Mrs. Benally.[28]

When we met again, she confirmed that she'd had a lump in her breast for about a year. Just before we first met the surgeon had warned her he might have to operate and when she went back to the hospital, she told me, she had indeed been operated on. But, when I questioned her a little more closely, I discovered that the "operation" had been a biopsy.

"They stuck a big needle in my lump," she told me, while confirming that she'd undergone no surgery other than that. She said she'd undergone radiation therapy, went for check-ups every six months, and still had to take a pill regularly; although she was unclear what the pill was for. She'd returned to see Blue Horse while I'd been away, and he'd worked on her some more in the sweat lodge (which I did not know about.) Only after all this did she have another mammogram, and it was only then that she had been told she was clear of cancer.

Naturally, I was delighted to find she was well and her cancer had gone, but the full story was rather different from the original. It was not that Mrs. Benally was trying to mislead anyone, far from it, she was simply delighted to be well again and excited to tell her story. But in her excitement, and doubtless not wanting to bore people with long and tangled tales, she gave a stripped-down version of the story that, while correct in its essentials, lacked many important details. Despite this, there seemed little doubt that she was now fit and healthy, and she assured me the doctors saw no sign of her cancer returning.

Again, I was in a situation where lacking proper medical records it was impossible to get a completely clear picture. However, as so often with

---

28 As an illustration, I always remember an elderly gentleman I met at a glaucoma clinic in one of London's most prestigious hospitals, who said he'd been treated there for five years without, he assured me, having any idea of what glaucoma was, or why he was being treated for it. In fact, his condition had been explained to him several times, but he had not understood what he was being told, and the real problem was that no one had bothered to check if he understood or not.

Navajo patients, Mrs. Benally had no doubts about attributing her recovery to the traditional treatment she'd received from Blue Horse. She made me aware of the enormous psychological boost and moral strength she had drawn from these traditional methods, and while it is not possible to assess exactly how much this may have contributed to her recovery, a positive attitude toward illness and a belief in being cured can do much good.

Patients determined to fight their diseases, and who remain mentally strong and resolute, usually do better than those who do not. When life-threatening crises occur, Navajos have the great advantage of being able to fall back on thousands of years of tradition; and the strength and comfort they draw from these traditions is quite remarkable. In the case of Mrs. Benally, it can plausibly be argued that the strength she drew from the traditional ways of her people, was of considerable benefit to her in this crisis, and may well have contributed to her recovery.

I am hardly alone in pointing out that our Western science-based medicine, so brilliantly successful in so many ways, is often criticized for lacking a spiritual element that many patients believe could help them in their time of trial. By contrast, Navajo medicine is replete with precisely this missing element.

IV

I am now living full-time with Blue Horse who is instructing me more closely in traditional ways. Recently we drove all the way to Albuquerque and found ourselves in a pleasant middle-class housing development. Not many Navajos live at addresses like that, at least, not the ones we visit; many of whom don't have addresses.

We get instructions like, "Go up the track fifteen miles. Turn north at the dead cow—we're the trailer about five miles up from there. You can't miss us." Wanna bet? I don't know if the spirits come to Blue Horse's aid with some kind of celestial address book, but I do know that he has an uncanny knack for finding places in the middle of nowhere; places I'm sure I wouldn't find in a month of Sundays.

This time we arrived at a beautifully appointed three-bedroom home in a smart street, whose owners were Samuel, a Blackfoot Indian and his wife Mary, who was Navajo. Samuel did complicated weaving in which he made big polygons in brilliant colors, something he said could take him years to complete. I drove Blue Horse to the house in his truck, but had to leave him there because I was due to attend class at the university. The professor had hardly begun when Blue Horse phoned, and I slipped outside to take the call. "There's a problem. I need you to come as quick as you can," he said, and it sounded urgent.

He didn't specify the problem, but what he said spooked me. I couldn't help wondering what kind of powerful witchcraft he was facing that would require my immediate attendance. I found it difficult to concentrate after his call, but stuck it out reasoning it wouldn't take long to join him once class ended. As soon as I could, I sped through the darkened streets to join him, only to find that his phone call had been a typically heavy-footed Blue Horse joke. He required my immediate assistance because an overabundance of food had been prepared—and there was only him to eat it!

By the time I arrived it was too late for food, and Blue Horse had already begun the divination. So, I slipped into my place on the floor to his right and waited to see how things would turn out. The couple were having the usual problems with jobs and money, but then Samuel told us he'd heard people moving about inside his home a few times. Once, the noise of someone inside the house was so loud he'd come downstairs armed with a club, but no one was there. He'd also heard a whistle, probably an eagle-bone whistle, being blown outside at night. The significance of this was that only a medicine man would possess an eagle-bone whistle, and only one who had sold out to the dark side would be blowing it unbidden around someone's home in the middle of the night.

"I realized this would have to be dealt with by traditional ways," Mary said, and she was right about that.

Near where we were sitting on the floor was a commercially produced rug printed with pictures of Lightning Beings and Corn Beings. Blue Horse disapproved. "Probably whoever made this rug saw a picture of a sand painting and made it from that," he declared huffily, and pointed out the many flaws in the pictures. Navajos deliberately leave vital details out of pictures of the Holy People, but Blue Horse attributed the mistakes in this rug to carelessness and lack of concern, rather than any attempt to disempower the pictures. He didn't think the white people who made these commercial rugs, knew enough about Navajo ways to even get things deliberately wrong.

Mary was clearly uneasy about the rug. "I thought maybe we shouldn't have bought it. Maybe we should have put it on the wall, not underfoot," she said.

"You don't have to throw it out, but maybe on the wall would be better," Blue Horse agreed. Because the ground is sacred to Navajos as their

Mother, something hung on a wall becomes of less spiritual import by virtue of not touching the earth.

As well as his weaving, Samuel made stone arrowheads and now, as he looked into the fire, Blue Horse told him that one of the people he'd given an arrowhead to, had placed it in the grave of a family member. This was serious witchcraft, and Blue Horse said he would have to go and remove the arrowhead. But I don't know when (or if) this will happen, because these things often fail to come to fruition. [29]

After a while Blue Horse stood up and led us out into the backyard, which was divided from the street only by a low wall. There he found a curse wrapped in deerskin under a plant the woman's aunt had given the couple. The plant, I noted, was dead. Once inside again, Blue Horse twice put red hot, glowing, charcoal into his mouth and blew his hot breath on the couple, before removing objects from them with his pipe. He sucked out bits of deer hoof, a piece of animal claw, and what looked like sheep grease from their bodies with his pipe.

After this, I drove him home, where we arrived at about 1:00 am. I was exhausted and quickly dropped onto the floor where I fell into a fitful sleep, only to be roused around 7:00 am by Blue Horse and Baa getting up.

* * *

Today was Blue Horse's birthday—at least, he said it was his birthday; but Blue Horse and his birthdays are at best semi-detached. He says he doesn't know how old he is, or when he was born, but then he does; or, at least, he picks a date from somewhere, but these seem to be fairly random. Today he said he was seventy, but I wouldn't bank on it, because last year he was seventy-two.

Anyway, Blue Horse and I went to the steam room at the public baths in Gallup for his birthday. Not as good as a sweat lodge, but I didn't have to cut yards of wood for the fire. In the afternoon, a woman came over to the house who had a drinking problem. She said she'd been drinking when

---

29 It didn't happen.

she didn't want to, and she feared she'd been cursed, and it was the curse that was forcing her to drink against her will.

This is a fairly common complaint among Navajos, that they are being forced to drink, or take drugs, or perform any variety of anti-social behaviors by witchcraft. It is a genuinely held belief, and it is surprising how often we found inside curses, items intended to engender precisely the behaviors the victims complained about. Jenny Pinto was a case in point, and as she sat fretfully explaining her predicament to us, she certainly didn't look like the kind of woman who would have a drink problem; at any rate, it didn't show physically. She was in her late thirties or early forties, a little overweight, possibly from the booze, but nicely dressed in a pink sweater and denim pants, not jeans. She had the air of an educated and competent woman, and it turned out that she was a school teacher in Gallup. The rub was that she'd just been cited for her fifth DWI offense. That's correct: five DWIs. Driving While Intoxicated. To get five DWIs in quick succession in Gallup, a town with a serious drink problem, you essentially have to drive around wasted all the time.

Blue Horse agreed to cedar for her, so while they continued talking, I got the fire going outside. Then, when all was ready, I carried in the charcoal on a long-handled shovel and, almost immediately after taking my place, I could see something in the fire that looked like a large spent bullet. Viewed from the side it looked flat, as if it had been flattened from hitting something hard after being fired. On the other hand, it looked too big to be a bullet. Only when Blue Horse pointed out that it was not a flattened bullet, but a stack of paper—in this case stacks of tickets for drunk driving—did it make sense. Mrs. Pinto was due to appear in court soon and she was facing a tough judge and a jail sentence, so it was no wonder she was worried. When I looked in the fire again, I saw an arrowhead pointing at her, something Blue Horse agreed was a dangerous sign. Long before the cedar was over, Blue Horse was sure that Mrs. Pinto had been cursed, and agreed to go to her home later that day and hunt out the evil.

We arrived at around five in the afternoon and found her waiting outside her trailer with the fire already burning. She was with her son, who was about fourteen years old, and it rapidly became apparent that the boy wanted nothing to do with these traditional proceedings. As soon as I'd brought in the charcoal, and Blue Horse had rolled the smoke, we should have been underway; except that Mrs. Pinto had the utmost difficulty persuading her son to take part in the cedar. He did not want anything to do with it, and he took part eventually, and grudgingly, only because his mother insisted that she needed his support.

Looking in the fire for clues, I saw what looked at first like a car, and then a packet of documents. There was a small owl—always a bad sign among the Navajo as it foretells death—and what may have been another watcher. Blue Horse leaned over the fire and, using a fire stick, pushed up a thin stick of charcoal about the length and thickness of my little finger. It stayed upright for a little while then broke in half, and half of it tumbled backward to the outside of the fire.

"I've been praying and praying on that stick," he explained. "That's what the problem is." That was all he said, and then he prepared to go outside taking Mrs. Pinto with him, and leaving me to guard the fire and the boy. Before going out Blue Horse gave Mrs. Pinto a stone arrowhead to hold in her left hand for protection, while giving me another, which was unusual when I stayed inside. As he went out, taking his whistle and drumstick with him, he told me to put a bit of cedar on the fire from time to time, but "not too much," he cautioned.

After they'd gone, the boy sat by the fireplace staring vacantly into the fire. He affected to be bored, and probably was, so to gain his attention I ran through a few things I was seeing in the fire, but nothing interested him. After a while, and at the exact place where the stick Blue Horse had been praying on had broken and fallen, there was a sharp "crack" and the charcoal collapsed, sending a round piece of charcoal with a cross etched into it tumbling to one side. This was the only part of the fire that moved during the time Blue Horse was outside, and I said to the boy that I thought this movement indicated that Blue Horse and his mother had found the curse. Pointing to the charcoal with the cross on it that had so suddenly appeared, I added that this probably meant the curse would have a cross on it.

Shortly after this Blue Horse and Jenny Pinto returned to say they'd found the curse, and I led the boy outside to watch it being opened. Inside we found a stick with a cross on the bottom of it, just like I'd seen in the fire. I thought at first the cross had been cut into the stick, but closer inspection showed that it was locoweed, which when it dries produces a crack in the shape of a cross at the cut end. Locoweed, also known as jimson weed, is an extremely powerful hallucinogen that grows wild everywhere in the Southwest,[30] and its inclusion in the curse was to create mental confusion in Mrs. Pinto. There was also an owl's feather, a symbol of death, so I had seen correctly when I saw the owl. Finally, the bundle contained a small container with the word BEER written on it. Blue Horse pointed inside to the fire, where he said this container could be seen, although from where I was standing I couldn't see it.

I told the boy to tell them what we had seen when the charcoal collapsed, which he did, and he now seemed rather more impressed.

"I didn't touch it, and you didn't touch it," I reminded him, and he had to admit this was so.

Blue Horse then sucked various bits out of Mrs. Pinto's shoulder, chest, and back, and when that was over, I put more cedar on the fire and Blue Horse told us to bless ourselves in the smoke. By now, such a change had come over the boy that he willingly blessed himself in the cedar smoke.

* * *

---

30 Locoweed, *Datura stramonium,* grows wild across North America and in parts of Europe. It is an extremely powerful hallucinogen that can induce poisoning even in small doses and is sometimes fatal. Traditionally, it played a part in Navajo medicine, but I was always told that only the most advanced medicine men could use it safely, and it was too dangerous for anyone else. In fact, in all my time among the Navajo I never encountered the use of locoweed except in curses, and it may be that those few medicine men who knew how to use it properly, passed on without leaving this knowledge behind.

A woman named Loretta drove from Phoenix seeking help for her cancer. She didn't have much confidence in her doctors, because after a long fight the doctors had assured her she'd been cured; but the cancer had returned. Now she didn't know what to believe, and hoped that traditional medicine could solve the problem. Her husband was in jail—she didn't say what for—but she seemed a decent enough woman herself and was accompanied by her mother, her children, and a few in-laws, many of whom were relations of Blue Horse. First, she told us about her fight with stomach cancer, "cancer of the stomach lining," as she told us.

"They told me I had to have this tube put into my stomach so they could feed me through it," she said. "But I don't want it, because when you have things like that they're always going wrong, and you're in and out of hospital all the time. They said that if I didn't have the tube, I'd last one to two years at most, but if I had the tube I could go on for a long time. But they told me I only had five years to live when she was born (pointing to her young daughter), and she's seven now."

Loretta said she'd already experienced a couple of episodes when she'd become numb on her left side and had experienced one fainting spell. Her gall bladder had been removed and she said she did not want any more surgery. Unsurprisingly, she was scared of dying and leaving her children behind—and who would not be?

I brought in the charcoal and then Blue Horse asked me to roll the smoke, the first time I'd done so for a cedar. So, I did—and it's another one of those things that's easier said than done—and lit it and passed it on to him. When I'd made the five-pointed star, the charcoal at first looked pretty innocuous. Then Blue Horse showed me where, on the arm of the star pointing towards Loretta, there was a patch of glowing and pulsating red. That, he said, was the inflammation caused by the cancer in her stomach, and it was on the left side of her stomach; which turned out to be correct.

More images began to appear when I brought in a second shovelful of charcoal and among them was a "watcher". The watcher sees all activity around a household and is considered particularly dangerous; and I could also see a man hiding under a hooded cloak, who had just one eye peering out,[31] and then another figure emerged. This new image, Blue Horse assured me, was a little doll someone had made of Loretta with the intention of making her ill. The idea is similar to the voodoo doll, but without pins stuck in it; and he told Loretta the doll had been hidden in the hollow handle of a broom. This broom, he said, had been left behind at a house she'd once rented, but it was still working on her and he offered to go and get it.

"But we don't live there anymore," Loretta objected, sounding confused.

"I'll manage," replied Blue Horse, sounding confident.

A strange hole appeared in the charcoal near the center of the star, that made it look as if something was missing. When I pointed this out, Blue Horse turned to the only man the family had brought with them, who was married to one of Loretta's relatives, and said it was about his brothers. Now we learned the man had four brothers who kept trying, but failing, to better themselves and this failure, Blue Horse said, was the black hole we were seeing. The emptiness into which their hopes, dreams, and efforts disappeared.

The man, who was in his early twenties, agreed with this diagnosis. "It seems that when one of us is doing well, the others don't," he said. "We don't seem to be able to do well together. When one goes up, the others go down." And Blue Horse said he could fix that, too.

Later, he took his pipe to the left side of Loretta's stomach and sucked out some bad stuff. He said it was snake, but it was so mangled that heaven only knows what it was. It looked like some kind of vegetable fiber, but what kind of vegetable, or what kind of fiber, I couldn't say. Loretta said that she felt better with it out, and I was dispatched to burn it after the cedar finished.

---

31 A Swedish friend I took to a cedar witnessed a similar hooded and cloaked one-eyed figure and suggested it might be Odin, the chief of the Norse Gods, who had only one eye and went about heavily cloaked to conceal his identity. It's a great idea, but there are plenty of traditional explanations for such a figure without invoking the Gods of the North. I sometimes see runes in the fire, but I put that down to my cultural background as runes would be meaningless to Navajos.

Before we broke up, arrangements were made for us to go to Phoenix on Friday to see if we can fix things there, but I don't know if we will go, because these arrangements often fall through.[32]

* * *

The next day, at least four people came for help, including a woman from Flagstaff, Arizona, whose eldest son had been stabbed to death eighteen months earlier. Now her younger son was fourteen and big enough, and strong enough, to exact the revenge burning within him. He'd put two youths associated with his brother's death in hospital with his knife, but the real killer was still loose as the police had no case against him. His mother was terrified for her remaining son's safety, and equally terrified he was about to earn himself a lifetime in prison.

A few days later we made the four-hundred-mile round-trip to Flagstaff to see them. But by the time we got there the fourteen-year-old was already in custody. I watched the fire while Blue Horse found some curses around the trailer home, and the family seemed very pleased. I hope their nightmare soon ends.

Unfortunately, at this time I was suffering from a bad bout of illness and only functioning on auto-pilot, so I wasn't taking much notice of what was going on, and was in no condition to make extensive notes. But the day after the Flagstaff trip I began to feel better, and as I sat at the kitchen table hugging a mug of hot coffee, Blue Horse told me how in the old days people killed and ate a yearling horse in the autumn to ward off colds and flu. It had to be a yearling because, so he said, they are particularly good and sweet to eat.

"Do people still do that?" I asked.

"Some people," he replied, rather mysteriously, but I wasn't sure I believed him. Not long before, on the day after Saint Valentine's Day, we were driving into Gallup when we saw a large number of people walking

---

32 We didn't go, but I'm not sure why.

along the hard shoulder of I-40. I even spotted a couple kissing on the central median between the east and westbound lanes.

"It's an old Navajo custom," Blue Horse explained when I mentioned this unusual phenomenon. "The day after Saint Valentine's Day, people walk along the side of I-40."

So many people were doing this, that for a moment he had me fooled. "You're making it up," I told him, once I'd had time to think about it, and he laughed and confessed that he was.

This left unanswered the question of why so many people were walking along the side of I-40 the day after Saint Valentine's Day? I never did find out. But the story about eating a yearling pony in the autumn was true or, at least, at one time it had been so; though it doesn't seem to be common these days.

* * *

I've more or less recovered from flu, or whatever it was. New Mexico is the repository of a number of exotic diseases including bubonic plague, the Black Death, which can be caught from fleas on prairie dogs. So, I always give myself a good look over when feeling really ill—just in case. Blue Horse said that when he was a boy they ate a lot of prairie dog, cooked in a hole in the ground with potatoes and wild carrots, but that it isn't so popular these days. Given the attendant risk of Black Death, I'm not surprised! Anyway, I've declared myself fit enough to start accompanying Blue Horse on his rounds again, and today we went to see a family who live near a little place called Counselor, which is north of Cuba, a small town in northern New Mexico.[33] They were a Navajo family named Curley, whose daughter Leah played for her school basketball team.

Leah turned out to be a five-foot-nine girl of seventeen, very athletic and good-looking, whose school was on course to play in the state finals at the Pit, the university stadium in Albuquerque—if they could win their next

---

33 There is a persistant urban legend that during the height of the Cold War in the 1970s, Cuba elected a mayor named Fidel Castro. So far as I can discover, it doesn't seem to be true; unfortunately.

game. So, it was vital that Leah played, but she was having trouble with her ankle, and the family thought there might be more to it than a simple injury.

It was a long, long, drive that took us deep into the reservation via Crownpoint to Pueblo Pintado. Blue Horse was insistent that we accomplish the entire drive—there and back—in daylight, which was a tall order. His desire to do so had little to do with evil forces, but a lot to do with leaving the paved road at Pueblo Pintado, and heading across country on one of the many dirt trails that crisscross Navajo territory. These trails are left over from the days when Indians traveled on horseback, up until the 1950s in this area, and for the most part are known only to Navajos. They are short cuts that take you across miles and miles of unpopulated countryside, and using them substantially reduces the journey time required if using the few paved roads in the area. Blue Horse and I took these trails often, but only during daylight if possible, because they are so rough and dangerous.

I've occasionally taken one of these back trails unaccompanied, if I've been the same way before and can be reasonably confident of finding the right track. But even in daylight they are a maze, and take you across an entirely empty landscape that offers no clue as to where you are, or even in which direction you are heading. There is no one to ask the way when you get lost—and note I say "when", not "if" you get lost—because the area is completely uninhabited. I've never attempted these trails at night unless accompanied by a Navajo, and to do so would be to invite disaster. Not only are they rough, with potholes big enough to smash the sturdiest axles, but much of the area is outside the range of mobile phones. Even if you get through to the police or AAA, you won't be able to tell them where you are, because you won't have the slightest idea. In any case, the chances of them coming out to you before daylight are about zero. Cattle, invisible at night, wander the unfenced range and people are killed and seriously injured every week by crashing into them. Hitting a 1,200lb. steer at thirty miles an hour is no joke, and neither is getting lost in the wilderness for the night. So, I strongly discourage visitors from taking these trails, unless you can find a Navajo guide to go with you.

Today our route took us into the Jicarilla Apache Reservation and then, not long after that, hidden behind a small hill, we found the family home. We could see that a considerable amount of building work was being carried out, and new foundations were being laid for a house extension. No one came to the door to answer our knock and so we waited, and after about ten minutes Mr. Curley turned up. He was a supervisor of some sort on the local oil field, which was presently enjoying a massive boom, and he also had a classic type-A personality. He was driving a huge white truck that was flying an oil-field warning pennant, and he didn't seem too pleased to find a white man on the team. He kept giving me lessons about Indians and their beliefs; as if I didn't know.

Thankfully, his wife and daughter Leah soon arrived and fed us good food and coffee. While we were eating and chatting to Leah and her mother, another daughter appeared. She'd been in the house all the time but, not surprisingly, had been reluctant to answer the door to two strange men while she was alone. It turned out that the family had four children, and this daughter was studying business at San Juan College in Farmington.

When the cedar started I fetched in the charcoal, rolled the smoke (I was getting quite good at it by now), and made the star while Blue Horse settled to divining. Soon, he stood up and led us all outside, where he began to seek directions by blowing his whistle to call his spirits to him. When the spirits come he hears an inner voice, he says, guiding him towards the hidden curse. What I see, is him taking sightings using his drumstick held straight up, or slightly twisted to left or right, as if he is taking imaginary bearings along imaginary lines. At least, I would say they were imaginary, if it wasn't for the fact that they almost always lead him to the curse.

Quickly, Blue Horse walked across the foundations for the house extension, and headed towards a steep outcrop of rock overlooking the home. After walking back and forth for a few minutes, while he again took more bearings, he led the way to the top of the outcrop. At the top we found a clump of yucca and in this yucca, he said, we would find the curse. But before examining the plant more closely, Blue Horse pointed out that the yucca had four upright shoots, all of which appeared to be dead.

"Four shoots, four children," Blue Horse said decisively, meaning that as these shoots were dead and blighted, it showed the intention was that the four children of the house should die just as the shoots had.

One of the oddities of desert yucca is that it can have long, stick-like, shoots coming out of it that have died, while the rest of the plant is apparently doing fine. Now Blue Horse knelt down and began to explore with his hands among this yucca's thick clumps of spiky green leaves. He quickly found a bundle wrapped up in loom thread and sisal that had been hidden in the yucca for so long that, just like the curse at the Carlton's house, part of the plant had grown up through it. Inside was a piece of wood with drawings on it, and a piece of stone that looked like an arrowhead. Blue Horse ordered me to "clear out that yucca patch" and went off immediately with Mr. and Mrs. Curley to hunt for another curse he said was nearby. With a long-handled spade Mr. Curley lent me, I chopped the yucca to pieces; cutting it off at the roots and scattering the debris.

While battling the yucca, which is a strong and stringy plant, I found hidden deep inside the leaves the remains of a plastic packet that had once contained a child's snack. Some kind of popcorn, I think, with a price of eighty-nine cents printed on it in faded figures. Inside was a stone, but as I lifted the bag and shook it, the "stone" fell to the ground where it crumbled into dust. When I looked closely, I saw that it was not a stone at all, but a clay ball that had been deliberately placed inside the packet. In all probability it had been rolled from river clay, or just dirt, mixed with urine from a corpse, and some evil device had probably been incised upon it; but what that device might have been we would now never know. Satisfied that I'd dealt with the yucca, I went in pursuit of Blue Horse, who was in the corral with Mr. and Mrs. Curley.

I arrived just in time to see him dig up a piece of bone that had been wrapped in aluminum foil. When examined the bone proved to have been shaped to resemble a tiny skull, and when we turned it over, we found a snake painted on the underside; again, it appeared to have been there for a long time. When I told Blue Horse about the plastic packet, he congratulated me. "You're getting good at this," he said. Then, when Mrs. Curley saw the bag, she commented: "They're not eighty-nine cents anymore—this must be twenty years old or more."

If Mrs. Curley was correct the bag dated from the 1990s, which was the decade in which her children were born. On this evidence, the popcorn bag—a product aimed at children—had protected a clay ball that was part of a curse aimed at her children. Readers from less arid climes than the American Southwest, may wonder how a cheap plastic bag could survive two decades in the open: the answer is—very easily. It's not uncommon in this part of the world for litter of all kinds to survive intact for years in the bone-dry environment. Particularly if, as in this case, it is protected from what little moisture there is by the thick leaves of a tough plant like the yucca. It was a pity the clay ball had shattered before we had time to examine it, but I collected the rest of the curses and burned them by the simple expedient of setting fire to a patch of dry sage and throwing everything on it. Then I went back to the house, where I found Blue Horse performing a general blessing for the family.

The Curleys told us they'd been convinced for a long time that they were cursed and had called in several medicine men, none of whom had been much good. Now they'd found the right man in Blue Horse, and they were so pleased they gave him a big wad of cash as a bonus on top of a good-sized donation. Mrs. Curley was so carried away she even gave *me* ten dollars which, as an apprentice I was not supposed to have, and which I was reluctant to accept.[34]

This caused Mr. Curley, who had been rumbling away in the background like a type-A volcano the entire afternoon, to erupt into yet another lesson about Indians. "A word of warning, a word of warning," he began. "When Indians give you something, always accept it. It doesn't matter how poor they are—always accept it and say thank you. That's a word of warning, a word of warning." So, I thanked Mrs. Curley and pocketed the money, and soon after this Blue Horse and I left for home along those same dangerous dirt tracks; but the business had taken so long it was already growing dark.

Earlier in the day Baa had set off to drive alone to Phoenix to join Blue Horse's daughter Fox. The two planned to drive together to San Diego,

---

34 I later worked out that my "income"—if that is the word for it—during my apprenticeship averaged about $5 a year, and almost all of it from unsolicited handouts like this one. Blue Horse would occasionally contribute to my fuel costs and once, and only once, gave me a few dollars as a tip. On the other hand, he gave me a roof over my head and fed me.

California, to attend the passing out parade of Fox's fiancé Ernie, who had completed his training as a US Marine. Blue Horse had not heard from Baa all day, which was unusual, and as we drove home he was already in a state of anxiety, when a coyote crossed our path heading north. This is a particularly bad sign, as coyotes always indicate trouble, and to the Navajo the north is the direction of cold, black, night. So, having a coyote cross our path heading north was an ill omen indeed.

Blue Horse told me that if he'd had a rifle he would have stopped and shot the animal. As he didn't, he drove on, became frantic, and began driving too fast in the dark along the dangerous dirt trails; one hand holding the wheel, and the other holding his phone, with which he made call after call to Baa. Because we were outside mobile phone coverage he wasn't able to contact her, and all he achieved was to make our drive far more dangerous than it already was. He nearly drove us off the road more than once, but he wouldn't let me drive, although I offered several times. Then, just as we reached Pueblo Pintado where the paved road resumed, Fox called to say the two women had met and all was well. With that, Blue Horse relaxed enough to let me drive (thank you Lord!) and we reached home safely at about 9:30 pm that night, having spent nearly twelve hours on this particular sortie.

This incident was a good example of how prophecies, or ill-omens, can become self-fulfilling. If, in his state of agitation, Blue Horse had driven us off the trail and we'd been injured or worse; most Navajos I know would have ascribed the crash to the coyote's malign influence. The real reasons would have been Blue Horse's agitation, his driving too fast through the dark using one hand, his concentration on his phone and not on the rough trail ahead, and his refusal to let me drive. It could be argued that it was the coyote that caused Blue Horse to panic, and that it did so with the intention of causing disaster, and to some that is perfectly plausible. But the truth is that long before he saw the coyote Blue Horse was already half-frantic because he hadn't heard from Baa. And he would have been in the same "two and eight" as we say in London—it rhymes with "in a state"—coyote or no coyote.

A day or so later, Blue Horse told me that the team Leah Curley played for had won their game, so all seems to have turned out well.

* * *

Shortly after this I had a long talk with Blue Horse, during which he provided some important insights into the qualities required of a medicine man. I'd been asking questions about the background of some of the cases we'd dealt with, and he began by cautioning me against this tendency of always wanting to know more.

"When people come to see you they're often short-tempered. They're upset and angry and frightened, too, some of them," he said. "You have to deal with what they tell you and what's in the fireplace. You can't start asking them questions about what it's all about, or they're going to tell you, 'That's none of your business!' That's what makes being a medicine man so hard. You don't know any more than what they're tellin' you, and sometimes I don't know what to pray for them. That makes it hard, too. But you can't ask too many questions—you have to let them tell you, and if they don't want to, you have to leave it at that. They're comin' to you for help, and you have to help them with what they give you. Maybe you see things in the fire and you can tell them what you see, and if they tell you more that's good and you can use that. But sometimes they don't.

"To be a medicine man you have to be tough. I don't mean tough like a strongman, a gangster, but you have to be tough in your mind. You have to have a strong mind to deal with all these people wanting things, wanting you to help them; and it's hard. But that's what a medicine man is for: to help people. When we gather here to help people, we don't know what's wrong with the person who's come. Often, they don't know either, their family doesn't know. But the fireplace knows, the fire knows, those charcoals know, that water knows, so we have to ask them humbly, prayerfully, to show us what they know, and they will show us. All we have to do is look and pray, and we will be shown."

* * *

V

I went with Blue Horse to a care home for elderly people on the east side of Gallup called the Red Rocks Care Center. The care home had recently built a hogan in its grounds, and it was a good hogan, well built, with a good earth floor and an oil-drum stove in the middle that made it "hot as hell"—as Blue Horse put it—even though a chill wind was blowing outside. Inside, on the wall above the seat of honor, was a plaque thanking a Mr. Dixon and a Mr. Begay for their work in building it.

The old people were holding a ceremony for a husband and wife who were having problems and who they believed had been cursed. It turned out that the couple's main problem was drink, and they were both pretty bad with the stuff. Their daughter was sponsoring the cedar for them, and the elderly residents had gathered in the hogan in the hope the curse could be lifted. But when I arrived all their attention switched to me, as everyone was astonished to see a *bilagaana* with the medicine man. Bilagaana means a white man in Navajo, and as it's unheard of for a medicine man to have one as an assistant, I usually come as a surprise even to young people. But these Navajo elders had never before seen a white man at a ceremony, probably never imagined such a thing could happen; let alone had they ever heard of a bilagaana being apprentice to a medicine man. Blue Horse advised me to explain to them that he was showing me traditional ways; which I did, and after that they warmed to me.

Naturally, Blue Horse made the most of having a white man as his assistant and bag carrier, and soon the bilagaana was running hither and thither carrying out all sorts of errands. I was greatly assisted in this by an old Navajo called Benny, a close neighbor of Blue Horse's, who lives on Baa's land at the back of their house and was there as a friend of the patients. Benny is an elderly gentleman, bowlegged from childhood privation, who seems happy enough and is pleasant company, although he speaks hardly a word of English. He's also the only person I know who still lives in an old-fashioned earth-and-timber hogan with a genuine earth floor. His hogan has no windows, and the only light comes through the hole in the roof, where the chimney of his wood-burning stove goes out.

Unlike modern homes, hogans were never meant for people to live *in*. Almost all traditional activities—weaving, sewing, cooking, eating, chopping wood, farming, butchering, preserving meat and corn and, in fact, just about any activity you can think of—was carried on outdoors.[35] The purpose of the hogan is to be a shelter in bad weather, a safe place to sleep at night, and a warm refuge in winter. It was never intended as a living space, in which people spend most of their days and nights, as so many do in their homes today.

Eventually, we settled down to the real business of the meeting, and Blue Horse began the cedar. This time I could see nothing in the fire, but after a while Blue Horse declared that he'd seen all he needed, and ordered Benny to get some ash to bring with him. Unfortunately, the only source of ash was the stove where the fire was burning. Benny tried to cool the ashes by spreading them on the earth floor, an old Navajo trick, but they were still too hot to put in a plastic bag. The couple's daughter eventually solved the problem by producing an empty cookie tin, which Benny half-filled with soft gray ash, although it was still so hot he had to juggle it from hand to hand. Then, accompanied by the daughter and one of the men, Blue Horse set off in search of the curse and leaving me in charge. I thought he would search the immediate vicinity of the hogan, or at least somewhere around the care home, but no; off he went in the daughter's truck and he was away for the better part of an hour, which is a long time in these situations.

---

35   This included dying. Traditionally, if a person died inside a hogan, it had to be burned for fear the ghost would linger there. Consequently, people were usually carried outside to breathe their last.

As is customary in his absence, I moved to sit in Blue Horse's place and watch over his implements. Once he had gone, everything became very relaxed, with people stretched out on the floor, people coming and going from the hogan, and people sitting around chatting at leisure. From time to time a nurse popped in to check on the "old lady" who was our patient and who, I learned, was actually only sixty-five, which is not particularly old these days.[36] I did notice that while the older staff at the home spoke some Navajo, they did not speak it well, and certainly not as a first language, while the younger ones hardly spoke Navajo at all. Another unfortunate testament to the retreat of the native language.

As I sat waiting, my attention kept being drawn to an odd-looking spot in the charcoal. I could see a sort of hollow about the size of my fist, which had within it a strange-looking object of about the same size. This strange object had in turn another strange object like a tube poking out of one end. I hadn't the slightest idea what it was, yet I couldn't help thinking it might be important. About half an hour after Blue Horse had gone, that particular part of the charcoal suddenly collapsed, at what would have been about the time Blue Horse found the curse. Then, after another thirty minutes, the man himself reappeared triumphantly waving the cookie tin.

He settled down in a well-illuminated spot just outside the door, and as we all gathered around, he took the curse from the cookie tin and described how he'd found it on a large public trash heap a few miles away. It was wrapped in what looked like Christmas tree tinsel, and he pulled away the tinsel to reveal a bundle a bit bigger than my fist, out of one end of which poked a tube. I told Blue Horse it looked very much like the object I'd seen in the fire while he was away, adding that in the fire it seemed to be hidden in a hollow of some sort.

"It was," he said. "It was inside a little cave in the side of a pile of ashes."

At this, the daughter who had accompanied Blue Horse nodded in agreement. Now, when I could see it properly, I saw that the "tube"

---

36 While almost all the names in this book have been changed to protect people's privacy, there were occasions, like this one, when I never knew the people's names to start with.

sticking out of the curse was the broken neck of a glass bottle with the bottle cap still screwed in place.

The glass was old and brittle and began to fracture the moment Blue Horse tried to take the curse apart. Fearing he might cut himself I warned him to be careful, but even as I spoke the glass shattered, and out fell a stone with an horrific face painted on one side in white relief: this face looked exceptionally evil—but there was more to follow. When Blue Horse managed to unscrew the cap from the bottle, we found that painted on the inside of the cap was a cross and the figure of a man. The daughter told me the top was from a bottle of cheap rot-gut liquor of the sort her parents only too frequently resorted to. There was a second stone inside the curse that had to be cleaned with water before we could see that a snake had been painted on one side.

* * *

The next morning we were up before 5:00am, well before dawn, and drove to the trailer of a woman with eight children whose husband had recently committed suicide. Donna's children were poorly dressed because, shortly before his demise, her husband had burned down their home with everyone's clothes inside it. I don't know if the dead husband had done this deliberately, or if he was crazy or drunk, or perhaps both. I asked Blue Horse, but he said he didn't know.

We'd gone to Donna's trailer the week before to remove some curses, and we returned this morning to perform morning prayers. This is the early-morning ceremony that is usually performed before the sun rises, and is intended not only to help and bless the family, but also to send the evil back to those who sent it. The whole family was there. Donna and all her eight children, including a baby, and they all watched quietly as Blue Horse performed a blessing inside the home. After this Blue Horse, Donna and her three eldest children and I, went outside and stood in the pale blue light of a cold dawn praying; while Blue Horse blew his whistle, and waved his eagle feather to waft the blessings of the rising sun over us.

Later, Donna gave us breakfast. There wasn't much because the poor woman has eight hungry mouths to feed, but we were grateful for what we were given.

* * *

Times can be rough for people everywhere and it's no different among the Navajo. But, occasionally, I gained insights into how extremely hard life can be for some people, from the youngest to the oldest. One of these came when I drove Blue Horse up to Farmington, near the north-east boundary of the reservation, to cedar for Billy Tohe and his wife Dolly. Billy was an old Navajo soldier who'd fought in Vietnam, and Dolly (possibly a corruption of the Navajo *doli* meaning a blue bird) taught at a nearby elementary school, although she had almost reached retirement.

They were kind and hospitable people who made coffee for us, and while we were sipping coffee and talking, Billy told us about the problems he wrestled with daily, and how they had all begun in Vietnam. This war ended for the United States in 1973, when US troops were withdrawn from the country, but for a combat veteran like Billy it never ended. He told us how he had been accidentally sprayed with Agent Orange, the chemical that US forces used to defoliate the jungle to make movement more difficult for the Vietnamese. The long-term damaging effects of Agent Orange on human beings are well documented and this, plus post-traumatic stress disorder from combat, had dogged him for the rest of his life. He still got blisters on his legs caused by Agent Orange, although it was more than forty years since he'd been sprayed, and his nerves had never recovered enough that he could hold a steady job. But that was not the half of it.

"We lost four children," Billy said, patting Dolly's arm to comfort her. "The chemical damaged my sperm and two of our children had no throats when they were born, and two had no colons. I suffered from post-traumatic stress disorder, and all the time if there was a sudden noise I'd jump, or if something was out of place, I'd jump; or I would have bad dreams. Since I got back from Vietnam, I've never slept more than four hours a night in all those years." Which meant poor Billy had not spent a peaceful night for more than forty-five years.

He'd first applied for compensation thirty-five years earlier, but only in the last year had the authorities agreed he had a case. He'd at last been offered help for his post-traumatic stress disorder and to this end had recently attended a long seminar in Denver, Colorado.

Billy said: "I'd been talking to this psychiatrist at the seminar, and nothing was happening for me, so I walked out; walked out into the corridor, and then the psychiatrist called me back. Somehow, I started crying, and I never cried in Vietnam and I never cried since I got back, but I started then. The psychiatrist started hugging me and he was crying too and we both stood there holding on to each other crying. He told me it was OK to cry and that's when I started to get better. I'm a lot better now."

He was also finally in line to receive some kind of disability pension. But it's impossible not to think that if he'd received the treatment he needed all those years ago, a well-motivated and intelligent man like Billy might have achieved much as a productive, tax paying member of society, instead of spending his life involuntarily on its margins.

What Dolly had to tell me was every bit as disturbing, particularly when one remembers that Farmington is a prosperous oil town. She teaches children up to ten years old, but some of the children come to school so hungry they are unable to concentrate on their lessons. So acute is the problem that for years she has kept bread and peanut butter and jam in her classroom cupboard, so she can make sandwiches for them. Other pupils in her class often slept outdoors, because they were so terrified of their violent parents who were high on drink and drugs inside the home.

Dolly told me: "Some of them say 'My dad is in jail. I don't know where my mom is. I don't want to learn, I don't want to be in school'. I tell them that wherever their mother and father are, I'm sure they love them, but they know it's not true. They're angry and want to run around hurting other children. Sometimes, when I've talked to them and fed them, they calm down a bit and they'll learn a little; but it's not easy for them or for me. And it's not just Navajo children. It's Hispanic and white children as well, all types of children, and all in about the same numbers."

The oldest of these children are ten years old. It's a frightening vision of the social dissonance building up in the USA, where dysfunctional parents, unable to cope in an increasingly technological and highly educated world, are creating a generation of children even less able to cope than themselves.

We cedared for Mr. and Mrs. Tohe, and Blue Horse found a curse that was unusual in being contained within a sea shell. It was a strange looking shell, white and circular like a snail's shell, but with little humps like horns sticking up from it. There was something jammed into the shell which I couldn't make out, but everyone said it was the representation of a snake. There was also a stone shaped roughly like an arrow head, with a sad face and four dots drawn on it, which Blue Horse said stood for the four directions. I asked if it might be the four Tohe children who died at birth, but Blue Horse said he thought not. Then he took a stone and smashed the arrow head and the shell, and as there was no way of burning either, the remains were placed in a paper bag with some ash and handed to me to throw into the Rio Grande when I got back to Albuquerque.

* * *

A few days later, early in the evening, a family came for a cedar. There was a woman in her mid-fifties, a slightly older man, and a younger man who was their son. I brought in the charcoal and took my place cross-legged on the floor as usual at Blue Horse's right hand. While he was talking to the family, I noticed something in the fire that was oddly shaped and dirty brown in color, which made it stand out from the rest of the black charcoal and gray ash. At first it looked like a flat top with two legs, that was lying sideways in the fire. I looked at it one way, and it looked like two legs dangling; then I looked at it another way, and it looked like a tooth with roots. Whatever it was, my gaze kept coming back to it, and the more I looked at it, the more I became convinced that I'd seen that shape somewhere before—if only I could remember where?

I was concentrating on this odd shape so much I wasn't listening to the conversation going on around me which, in any case, was all in Navajo. Then, after a while, the conversation reached a point where people began using technical terms, which are usually expressed in English. Then I heard the woman say "ENT clinic"—Ear, Nose and Throat clinic—and point to her ear. At that moment everything became clear: what I was seeing in the fire was the anvil bone of the inner ear. I'd seen drawings of it in anatomy books, and it's true that when viewed from a certain angle the anvil bone, technically called the incus, does indeed appear to have two short legs or roots. It is this little bone that when struck by vibrations from the malleus, another tiny bone in the inner ear, forms a vital connection necessary to allow us to hear. The woman was having trouble with her hearing and that's why she had come to seek help.

Blue Horse constantly reminds me that everything will be revealed in the fire, and time after time, what he points to in the fire looks pretty well like what we find. When I first started as his apprentice, I thought this was because there are so many shapes in the fire that something is always going to fit something else. But, actually, he doesn't point to any shape, only to those that are relevant; and often that relevance isn't apparent until the curse has been found and opened, and we have the full picture. It can't be an endlessly repeating series of coincidences, hundreds of coincidences? Surely not. With increasing regularity, I am myself seeing in the fire shapes that turn out to be significant, and this was a good example. I wasn't listening to the conversation, and even if I had been, I don't know the Navajo words for incus or malleus, or even if such words exist; so I couldn't have been the victim of some kind of auto-suggestion that made me see an incus bone in the fire. What explanation can I offer for this? There is one, but at this time I am not prepared to admit it.

However, there was no time for philosophizing, because we had a wedding to prepare!

Blue Horse's daughter Fox was at last to marry her longtime fiancé Ernie, the US marine. Ernie followed traditional ways, while at the same time being a Mormon, as was his family, and so the wedding was to be held at a Mormon temple. In fact, a lot of Navajos are Mormons, or Roman Catholics, or members of any number of religious sects, and I once met a young Navajo who had converted to Judaism. Many of these converts continue to follow traditional ways, and attend healing and peyote medicine ceremonies, as well as going to church. What regular church goers might find a confusing mix of conflicting religious views is not a problem to Navajos, who generally take the view that the more religions you have, the holier you are likely to be.

Fox had always dreamed of a white wedding—and she certainly got one. The reservation had been struck by a long period of drought, during which there had been no measurable precipitation for one hundred and fifty days. So, naturally, the heavens chose the night before Fox's wedding to dump more than a foot of snow on us. When I woke on the morning of the wedding and looked through the window, I thought we must have been magically transported to an Alpine ski resort during the night. The main I-40 freeway running east to west through Arizona and New Mexico was closed, and the back roads to Phoenix were blocked with more than three feet of snow. We had to take shovels and dig our way into the temple before the wedding could take place; yet, despite the freaky weather, a good time was had by all. The bride looked lovely in a beautiful long white wedding dress, while Ernie was smart and handsome in his marines' dress uniform. Blue Horse, the father of the bride, was resplendent in a new white Stetson and a calfskin jacket, and looked every inch the powerful medicine man he is.

Everything went off splendidly and the only problem was that we had intended to have barbequed steaks after the ceremony, but the snow made this impossible. So Baa, who is Fox's step-mother, had to cook the steaks in advance, and she did this standing outside in freezing temperatures, in more than a foot of snow, and with a light snow still falling. Further, she cooked them all on her own—and there were dozens of them—because all the other women were occupied with other tasks related to the wedding. Navajo tradition draws strong divisions between men's work and women's work, and cooking is women's work. As men, we are not allowed to cook nor take part in work that Navajo women consider to be exclusively their domain; and any man who tries to intrude into the women's world is likely to get the rough edge of their tongues. So, we did the men's work of gathering the wood and lighting the fire and fetching and carrying. But only Baa could cook, huddled in a borrowed, oversized, man's anorak against the still falling snow; though I did manage to find an umbrella and hold it over her to give her some protection. Afterwards, we took the steaks to the wedding and ate them cold.

We should have been better prepared, because three days earlier Blue Horse had warned me that it was going to snow. "I can smell it," he assured me. Naturally, I'd thought he meant an inch or two within a few hours, and when nothing happened I thought no more about it. Now, while the meteorologists were sure our blizzard was due to unusual weather patterns over the Pacific Ocean, Blue Horse had his own explanation. During their visit to San Diego for Ernie's passing out parade, Fox and Baa had filled a bottle with sea water and brought it home. When we'd had a sweat the previous weekend, Blue Horse had mixed the seawater with the water we poured on the hot stones, and now he attributed the blizzard to the use of the seawater. "This snow's coming up from California," he said, which indeed it was. "That's because we mixed the seawater from California with the water for our sweat."

One result of the blizzard was that the house was packed that night, because many guests couldn't get home. Altogether, about fifteen of us sardined into the little wooden house and with the exception of Blue Horse and Baa, who had a bed in the back room, we all—including the bride and groom—spent the night on the floor.

The next morning, still unable to go far because of the snow, we drove over to Ronny's father's house near Wide Ruin. Ronny is married to another of Baa's daughters, Cecelia, and his father had recently died; in all probability murdered over some gambling winnings. The FBI was still investigating, but it was difficult to get any information from them. So, the purpose of our visit was to cedar at the house to discover if any guidance could be obtained by this means.

It had snowed again overnight, but the morning dawned crisp and clear with the sun blazing from a cloudless sky of cobalt blue, making the snowdrifts sparkle as if studded with diamonds. The Southwest has many strange sights and one of the strangest, at least to me, is that of a large cactus covered in snow, with a cold, hungry and extremely fed up vulture perched on the top. We passed several as we drove along, the truck plunging through drifts three feet deep or more. At the wheel Blue Horse seemed to delight in driving as fast as he could, sending billows of snow flying in every direction, while the truck skidded so violently I feared it might turn over.

There were four of us in the little cab, packed in so tightly we couldn't even buckle our seat belts. Enormous drifts overhung the sides of the roads, and the junipers were so bowed under the weight of snow that some branches touched the ground, while others had snapped under the strain. When we arrived at the house, Blue Horse drove in through the paddock entrance at about 40 mph, and finally managed to get the truck stuck in a big drift. (And he wonders why I always volunteer to do the driving!)

When we'd finished shoving and shoveling the truck out of the drift, Ronny took the time to show me the extensive parcel of land he and his family held rights over. [37] Pointing to various landmarks he outlined a colossal spread, at least five miles long and nearly as wide, making a total of something more than twenty-square miles. At first I found it strange that the family should have so much land when, judging from the house and the ramshackle buildings around the paddock, Ronny's father had not been well off. Twenty-square miles of land should provide a reasonable amount of wealth even if, as was the case, it is not particularly good land. But, as so often with Navajo families, there was a catch; which was that nothing could be done with the land unless everyone in the family agreed—and they didn't.

Cecelia said she and Ronny wanted to build a hogan on one of the hills, and she pointed hopefully to a couple of hills nearby. Ronny wanted

---

[37] Navajos do not own land on the reservation, it belongs to the tribe, and is held in trust for the tribe by the US government. Individuals and families cannot buy or sell land, but they do retain the right to farm land they have controlled for generations.

to breed horses, someone else wanted to farm sheep, another to grow corn, and another to raise cattle, and so on. The family could agree on nothing, and so the land sat idle because of a facet of Navajo culture that holds that one person's opinion is as good as everyone else's. So long as one person objects, that person's objections cannot be overridden by the others.

To the Navajo this is a mechanism for maintaining the status quo and the harmony so vital to their world, although in these family squabbles harmony often seems to be in extremely short supply. My friend Magnus Akee, who holds a high position in the tribal government, once explained how the Navajo government possesses eminent domain, a legal term that means they have the right to overrule public objections against tribal developments. But in their entire history the tribal government has never used this right, he assured me, because of the deep cultural attachment to valuing all opinions as of equal worth.

Inside the house Ronny had lit a huge potbellied wood-burning iron stove that had US ARMY NO.1 stamped on its side. I don't know how old it was, but it looked like something Custer would have been familiar with. When we were about to start the cedar, Blue Horse told me to move up to complete the circle, but the stove was so blisteringly hot I couldn't. Sitting about two and a half yards away, the heat was so fierce it reddened the skin of my arm through my shirt and a thick woolen sweater with the sleeves rolled down.

During the cedar Ronny said that his father had possessed various sacred items as well as instruments for medicine, but had never told him what they were for. Among these sacred items were four bags of soil, one from each of the four sacred mountains that traditionally mark the eastern, southern, western and northern boundaries of Navajo territory; territory the Navajo believe was given to them by their gods.

The first of these mountains is Tsisnaasjini', Dawn or White Shell mountain, the sacred mountain of the east, known in English as Mount Blanca, in Colorado. The second is Tsoodzil, the Blue or Turquoise Mountain, the sacred mountain of the south, which in English is Mount Taylor, in New Mexico. Quaintly, Mount Taylor is today often thought to mark the *eastern* boundary of Navajo territory, but that is only from the point of view of people traveling from east to west along I-40. The third is Doko'oosliid, the Abalone Shell Mountain, the sacred mountain of the west, now the San Francisco Peaks, near Flagstaff, Arizona. The fourth is Dibé Nitsaa, Big Sheep Mountain, the Black Obsidian mountain, which marks the northern boundary of the Navajo world, and in English is called Mount Hesperus, also in Colorado. There are other sacred mountains, but these are the four that set the outer boundaries.

Viewed on a map, these four sacred mountains form an oblong that is slanted towards the northeast, and their positions are at first confusing to those trained in conventional map reading. The east mountain is definitely the furthest east, but looked at on a map, it is not obviously any further north than the north mountain; in fact, the two appear to be almost on a parallel. The west mountain is definitely the furthest west, but may actually be slightly further south than Mount Taylor, the south mountain. But this is to modern eyes, and it is important to remember that the Navajos who made these designations had no maps; instead, they had a vision from their gods who set the boundaries of their land for them. Once the mountains are viewed through Navajo eyes, with the east as the cardinal point and not the north, it all snaps into focus. Seen this way round the eastern mountain is to the east, the western mountain to the west, and the north and south mountains are both in their proper places.

All these mountains are hundreds of miles apart, with the distance between San Francisco Peaks in Arizona and Mount Blanca in Colorado at least three-hundred and eighty miles. While from San Francisco Peaks to Mount Taylor in New Mexico, is two hundred and eighty miles. These mountains cannot be seen from each other, and the fact that people without a written language, or maps, managed to use them accurately as boundary markers from at least the sixteenth century onwards, is a testament to their detailed knowledge of their environment. Sadly, today these four sacred mountains, the great pillars of the Navajo world, lie outside the boundaries of the reservation. Something that speaks vividly of the disruption the Navajo people have suffered since the coming of the white man a hundred and forty years ago.

As the cedar continued, Blue Horse began to urge Ronny to use his father's bags of soil in some kind of medicine ceremony or, at least, to take possession of them; but this Ronny was reluctant to do. Blue Horse pressed him to move back from Phoenix to the reservation and become a medicine man; although Ronny didn't seem too keen on this idea either. After a while, they went out alone, and when I looked through the open door I saw them conferring in the snow. Next, I heard Blue Horse blowing his whistle, so I knew they were hunting for a curse.

Later, they came back with it and when the curse was opened, among the other objects inside was a piece of material cut in such a way as to represent a strange, elongated, bug-eyed creature, like one of those creatures that live in the deepest parts of the ocean. Then, when I looked into the fire again, sure enough, there was the same strange shapeless creature with the big eyes that Blue Horse was now holding. It meant something to Ronny and with this, plus a shell his wife had seen, there was some strange connection with the sea; but what it was, and how it was connected to Ronny's father—which it certainly was—I don't know. I could not ask, and as Blue Horse chose not to tell me, that was how I had to leave it.

After we had driven home and were back at the house, Blue Horse took me aside to tell me I was learning well, and that he was surprised at how fast I was learning. Now it was time for me to learn more, he said, and for me to cedar for people myself. He said he would teach me more about the four sacred mountains, how to use a crystal properly, and how to gaze at the stars through the crystal. Most important of all, he would teach me how to hunt down the witch curses, and to suck things out of people in the way that he does.

I was not expecting this. These are among the deeper aspects of Navajo medicine and were something I'd never really contemplated learning, because I never thought I'd get the chance. I'd always regarded my position as apprentice as a privilege that gave me a position from where I could observe the many fascinating aspects of Navajo medicine and culture. But I'd never thought of myself as a *real* apprentice in the sense of undergoing a long period of learning that would result in me becoming a fully-fledged medicine man in my own right. And the reason I didn't think I would ever become a real medicine man, is that I did not think the Navajos would let me.

While certain aspects of Navajo medicine have become more visible to outsiders of recent times, there is still a strong and insular segment of society that does not want outsiders involved in any way. They think the best way to preserve their secrets is to keep them absolutely secret, except among those Navajos—and only Navajos—suitably qualified and sanctified to know them. I don't want to argue the point, but I do want to emphasise that there is nothing in this book that reveals any of those secrets. Now, to my astonishment, Blue Horse seemed to be suggesting that it was time for me to begin the long journey that would lead me into the deeper levels of Navajo knowledge. Although I didn't know it at the time, this was going to cause problems.

VI

It has taken a long time, but I've finally persuaded Blue Horse to take me to The Garden. This is the place in Texas where Indians go to collect peyote, and it means driving all the way to Rio Grande City and back. We planned it as a family outing, partly because it would be more enjoyable that way, and partly because it would give me more cover hidden among a minivan full of Navajos. I had good reasons to travel inconspicuously, as I shall explain; but then, one by one, everybody dropped out, until only Blue Horse and I remained. Then Blue Horse started to have second thoughts.

We postponed our trip to The Garden several times, and eventually got underway late in the year with winter closing in fast. The distance there and back is more than two thousand miles, which we covered in only sixty hours; hauling home three-hundred and fifty pounds of fresh peyote, and driving anything up to sixteen hours a day. It is perfectly legal for a Navajo medicine man to possess and transport peyote, but I was on edge during the entire journey because the law says nothing about a white man driving the truck—even if he is the apprentice. I knew this, because before we left I consulted the law: the 1994 Amendments signed by President Bill Clinton, to the 1978 American Indian Religious Freedom Act. The amendments state:

> *"Notwithstanding any other provision of law, the use, possession, or transportation of peyote by an Indian for bona fide traditional ceremonial purposes in connection with the practice of a traditional Indian religion is lawful, and shall not be prohibited by the United States or any State."*

That was clear enough, but would the law protect a non-Indian like me? My friend the Navajo medicine man Emerson Jackson, who was also a former president of the Native American Church, summed up the dilemma rather succinctly: "If you get stopped and the officer's an Indian, you won't have a problem. But if the officer's a white man, you could have a big problem." Big problems were something I could do without.

I always believed that because I was not the owner of the peyote, but merely the driver of the truck, I was not acting illegally. But police and border patrol officers can't be expected to have an intimate knowledge of relatively obscure corners of the legal code. What worried me was that if the officers were unsure of the law—and especially as the Thanksgiving holiday was looming as we set off—then faced with a white guy from England driving three-hundred and fifty pounds of peyote medicine along the Mexican border; they might decide the easiest thing to do was to put me and Blue Horse behind bars, and let the court sort out matters after the holiday. That would leave us languishing in a Texas border jail for a week, or more, and neither of us wanted that.

The idea that I could hide among a minivan full of Navajos emboldened me, as I could pass myself off as a mere passenger, but when it became apparent that Blue Horse and I would have to go alone, I decided to go anyway. Few white men get the chance to go to The Garden, and few indeed go in the company of a powerful native medicine man. It was now or never, because I was unlikely to get a second chance.

In order to buy peyote Blue Horse had to obtain papers from the head of his local branch of the Native American Church, certifying that it was for religious use only. These papers also confirmed him as a full-blood Navajo and included his tribal roll number, an individual number given to every registered member of the tribe. This paper work is an administrative device intended to give the federal authorities some oversight of the sale and distribution of peyote; and the Indian negotiators, of whom Emerson Jackson had been one, had to make this concession in 1994 to get the amendments through Congress. It remains illegal to resell peyote even when it has been bought from a licensed dealer, and it can be given away only for religious use. Blue Horse had been president of the NAC branch himself, but it wasn't his turn this year and the current president lived the best part of a day's drive away. So, between shuttling papers across the reservation, hiring a vehicle suitable for the trip, and one thing and another, I was a busy man during the build-up to our journey.

Even so, right up to the last minute it was never certain we would actually go. Various problems besetting the family delayed our departure for a week, as Blue Horse felt his authority was needed at home. Baa decided only an hour before departure that she was not going and so, when Blue Horse and I finally got under way, we traveled *a deux*.

It was a couple of days before the Thanksgiving weekend—the big annual holiday as precious to Americans as Christmas—and we knew the roads would be crowded. This was not entirely a bad thing in my view, as extra traffic offered a little extra cover. First, we drove for three hours to Clines Corners, New Mexico, then turned south. Shortly after this, Blue Horse performed a protection ceremony inside the car in which he took yellow corn pollen—or "corn powder," as the Navajos call it—and anointed the inside of the Jeep. We were traveling at about eighty mph when he reached for his *jish* medicine bag and took the powder from a small rawhide bag. He prayed for a short while before taking his eagle feather and wafting a blessing; then he dabbed the yellow pollen all over the dashboard, the steering wheel, and me. The idea is that the pollen forms a barrier that goes ahead to protect the travelers during their journey, in the same way as a crucifix is often dangled from the rear-view mirror.

Whether it was the pollen or not, we had a relatively uneventful journey until we reached Roswell, New Mexico, home of the alleged Roswell incident of 1947, when an alien spacecraft is supposed to have crashed nearby. This is a claim supported by some extremely dodgy film and multitudes of conspiracy theorists; but when you're a small, isolated, town in the middle of nowhere, anything that boosts the local economy is worth a shot; and Roswell has taken its shot well.

We had just passed through the town and were continuing south towards Texas, when Blue Horse took a call from Baa, who said that someone had tried to break into their house. The house is isolated, Baa was alone with her baby granddaughter Santae, and the only other person staying with her was Santae's mother Fox, who was at work until 10:00 pm. This was a serious problem and we began to discuss turning back. Then, while we were talking, a large bird was caught in the headlights as it rose from the roadside and flew into the night. I thought it was an owl, and as owls are a bad sign among Navajos, I thought Blue Horse would make us turn back. He surprised me by saying the bird was not an owl but a hawk, and he was probably right. However, ornithology didn't solve the problem of two women and a baby, alone in an isolated house with a criminal on the prowl. We'd already driven for hours and couldn't possibly get back until well after midnight; even so, I thought we would have to try, although it meant abandoning the trip. Then, at the last moment, Blue Horse managed to contact Ronny, who agreed to go to the house and stay there until we returned; so we pressed on.

Not long after this, as we were approaching Carlsbad, a real owl flew directly across our path. The evil surrounding its appearance was mitigated slightly by the fact that it was flying east—toward the rising sun. If it had been flying north, I feel sure Blue Horse would have turned back, because even with Ronny on his way to the house, he was still afraid for Baa, Fox, and the baby. I told him it was OK to go back, but he shook his head and confided that the holy nature of our journey to The Garden, would be certain to attract the attention of the *ch'iint'ii*, evil spirits who would try to stop us. He put down much of the domestic trouble before we left, the attempted break-in, and the owl, to attempts by these spirits to thwart our journey to the sacred medicine. To be on the safe side, and to bolster our position against the evil ones, he carried out another protection ceremony as we drove on through the night.

We stopped at Fort Stockton, Texas, and found a motel. I didn't sleep well, and we were up and away by 6:00 am the next morning, although it was a while before we realized we'd crossed a time zone, and it was actually 7:30 am local time. Before we set out, Blue Horse conducted one more blessing ceremony in the dawn light. He took a beautiful little pouch of white doe hide, decorated with a circular pattern made of many beads of green and black. Putting a few pinches of protective pollen inside the little pouch, he hung it from the rear-view mirror of the car.

We were already some miles south of Fort Stockton, when the golden disk of the sun finally topped the horizon and the first rays fell upon us. We blessed ourselves Indian fashion in those first rays, by wafting the goodness and radiance toward us with outstretched hands as we drove along. This meant me taking both hands off the wheel, but we were already way beyond the town, and out here in the countryside there was already so little traffic on the road it hardly seemed to matter.

From Fort Stockton we drove south towards Del Rio, and as we approached the Rio Grande and the border with Mexico, and began to run parallel with both, it was notable how sparsely populated this part of the country is. For more than a hundred miles I saw no sign of human habitation, apart from two tiny towns that seemed to consist of barely a dozen buildings each. Approximately twenty vehicles passed us going in the opposite direction and none at all overtook us. I didn't see a single vehicle on the road ahead of us, nor did any join the road ahead, or cross over it. This area was so remote that at one point we couldn't find a radio station to tune to. All I saw was brush and sand, and sand and brush, and more brush and more sand, and a yawning emptiness that stretched forever in every direction.

This had once been Comanche country, and for the first time I understood why the United States found it so difficult to come to grips with the Comanche; who gave them a good hammering for more than forty years, before finally succumbing to disease and superior numbers. The countryside was as vast as the ocean, and as equally capable of swallowing tribes, as armies, without a trace. It was hard to believe that anywhere on this crowded planet could still be so empty, so when we stopped for gas I bought a local area map—only to discover that for this part of Texas the map is almost completely blank, because there is nothing to put on it!

We stopped for food and more fuel in Del Rio, and it was when we got south of the town that things began to heat up. First, I was pulled over for speeding. The officer was an older reservist whose real motive for stopping us was that Blue Horse might be an illegal Mexican immigrant. The officer turned out to be a very polite gentleman of the old school, and I escaped with a written warning, meaning I would not be prosecuted. But later we were stopped twice by the border patrol and our licenses were checked and the vehicle was searched.

Then, around two in the afternoon, I had my first view of the upland area that is The Garden, and was surprised to see how lush and green it was. I'd always been led to believe that the peyote cactus, *Lophophora williamsii,* grows in the desert, but this land was verdant; with thick green bushes and undergrowth, and long, waving, green grass—hence the name The Garden, I suppose. Before we arrived, I'd had no difficulty in imagining what it would be like to walk slowly through an empty desert searching for peyote cactus to harvest; but I'd never thought of searching for it among long, thick, grass and bushes. Blue Horse explained that it didn't matter where the little cactus grew, because it would unfailingly reveal itself to believers, while remaining stubbornly hidden from unbelievers, no matter how diligently they searched.

"If you believe in the medicine, you'll find it. If you don't believe in the medicine, you won't find it," he explained. "If you believe, you can stand in a field where at first you see nothin'. Then, maybe you see one little medicine bud. Then one by one, they start to come out like stars in the sky, and soon you're surrounded by them. At night, they glow, and you can see them in the dark."

He estimated it would take us a day to gather three hundred pounds of medicine, and by "a day" he meant the Navajo reckoning from sun-up to sunset, about twelve hours, or twenty-four man-hours altogether. That equates to just over twelve pounds per man per hour, which sounded over-optimistic to me; though later I learned this was about right; although doubtless it meant back-breaking work toiling under a relentless sun.

By now these kinds of calculations were academic, because it was obvious there would be no time for us to gather our own peyote. First, we'd promised to get home in time for the family's Thanksgiving dinner. Then there was the attempted burglary, and the fact that Ronny couldn't stay at the house forever. Finally, I'd just discovered we'd arrived at the height of the Texas deer hunting season, which made wandering around in the bushes suddenly seem a lot less attractive. Instead, we would have to buy from a *peyotero*; one of a dwindling band of collectors licensed to harvest peyote by the state of Texas. Then, just as we'd decided this, and without any warning, Blue Horse suddenly developed extremely cold feet and tried to back out of the entire enterprise.

I'd been shooting some video with the peyote pampas in the background, while Blue Horse talked to camera about the importance of peyote in native religion—great anthropology, by the way—when he suddenly asked me to stop recording.

"You don't understand," he complained, almost tearfully, when I'd put the camera down. "A lot of people back in the tribe gonna be real mad if they find out I've been bringin' you down here. They don't want no white man here. They don't think no white man should come down here in this sacred place. It's OK by me and my family. We know you believe in the medicine, but these people can make big trouble for me. Maybe even take away my certificate as a medicine man if they find out. Then I can't do nothin'. Can't do medicine. Can't make a livin' anymore. Them peyote people, them collectors, gonna be real spooked if they see a white man. They're not gonna sell nothin', they're gonna be scared you're a drug dealer. Even with the right papers I've got, they'll be scared they're gonna get into trouble if they sell to a drug dealer by mistake!"

Wherever Indians gather, at least in the Southwest, a lone white face tends to be equated with either a drug dealer or a bootlegger, and I've had plenty of experience of this. The only exception being when I was once mistaken for a bishop. Even so, it was hard to know what to make of this sudden outburst. He'd briefly mentioned these kinds of objections before we'd left, but he hadn't put any great emphasis on them. I suppose his fears resurfaced now because of the looming reality of buying a considerable amount of medicine and trucking it home.

It took almost an hour to calm him down and reassure him, and the price was my agreement to stay out of the way when he went to buy peyote. The mechanics of buying peyote and, if possible, of collecting it, was something I'd wanted to witness first-hand; and to me it was the most important part of the trip, because these undertakings have rarely been properly researched or recorded. Now, I would not be able to, but I had to concede because Blue Horse made it clear that if I didn't, there would be no purchase and we would go home empty handed.

When we finally reached Rio Grande City, at about 3:30 in the afternoon, the next stage of the drama unfolded. The peyoteros live mostly in or around Rio Grande City, and some stick up boards outside their homes to advertise their services. Even so, they don't make themselves readily available to outsiders; so, if you want to buy peyote, you need to know someone who knows someone. Because we had originally intended to gather our own medicine, Blue Horse hadn't brought any peyoteros' phone numbers with him, and as it was some years since he'd been to The Garden, he couldn't remember where to find one either. The usual drill is to phone the peyotero on arrival and wait until he comes to find you, but without a number to call, it looked for a moment as if we'd driven more than a thousand miles for nothing. Then Blue Horse had an inspiration and phoned his sister, and his sister had the phone number of a Mr. Rodriguez whom she could recommend.

Mr. Rodriguez told us to meet him at a gas station on Main Street. We didn't have to wait long before he arrived driving a red pickup truck; when he saw me his jaw did indeed drop, just as Blue Horse had predicted.

As I watched Blue Horse walk over to Mr. Rodriguez's truck and talk to him through the window, I fully expected to be told to stay at the garage while they went off to get the medicine. But when he came back, to my surprise, Blue Horse said I could go along. So, with Blue Horse driving—something which apparently made Mr. Rodriguez more confident that Blue Horse was in charge—and me keeping my fingers crossed because Blue

Horse was not insured for the vehicle, we set off for Mr. Rodriguez's small holding.

"Don't say nothin'! Don't open your mouth," Blue Horse kept repeating as we drove along. He seemed to think my English accent would make things worse by sounding exotic and foreign, and he was probably right. He was in a highly agitated state.

"I know how to behave. I'll stay out of the way. I won't say a thing," I assured him.

When we stopped, I found myself in a yard looking at a corral with some fine horses. I don't know much about horses, but Mr. Rodriguez's yearlings looked like quality animals to me and Blue Horse, who does know a thing or two about horses, readily concurred when I asked him. So, while he and Mr. Rodriguez went into a huddle near one of the outbuildings to examine the medicine and agree on a price, I amused myself by feeding handfuls of hay to the horses.

In the end it was all done quickly and smoothly, and soon I was loading sacks of medicine into the back of the Jeep. Mr. Rodriguez got his money and signed Blue Horse's papers, I threw a blanket over the sacks to hide them, and we immediately started for home: it was as simple as that. Despite all the buildup, and Blue Horse's nervousness, the whole business took less time than it takes to order a meal in a busy restaurant, and was about as dramatic.

It was already dark when we ran into our first border patrol checkpoint about twenty miles south of Laredo. It was one of those rolling checkpoints, that move from place to place to be as unpredictable as possible, and the officer in charge seemed to know what he was doing. He demanded my documents, looked at my passport, looked at me, and then shone his flashlight into the back of the Jeep. The windows were tinted, and I'd covered the peyote sacks with a blanket, so he couldn't have seen much; then he turned to Blue Horse, who handed him his driver's license.

"Where've you been?" the officer demanded.

"Laredo," I said, pretending he'd said "Where are you going?" I didn't want to tell him we'd been in Rio Grande City in case he put two and two together.

"What you been doin'?" he demanded, looking grim and shining his flashlight into the car again.

"Medicine," Blue Horse said, beginning to pull his NAC papers from their envelope, but the officer didn't look at the proffered papers and simply waved us on. I wasn't sure he understood that by "medicine" we were talking about peyote, or if he thought I was taking Blue Horse to the hospital in Laredo. Blue Horse, however, was quite sure.

"See," he said triumphantly. "You got to say the right words. You always say the white man's word. You always say 'peyote,' so everybody's gonna be suspicious. But if you say 'medicine' like an Indian, they gonna let you through."

He may have been right, but it felt like a close call to me, and as we drove on I decided we were definitely going home via San Antonio, which would take longer, but would lead us away from the border and its patrols. But by this time it was getting late and we were tired, so we stayed the night in Laredo.

* * *

Paranoia is that instinct most useful when struggling to obey the Eleventh Commandment: Thou Shalt Not Get Caught. Stops by the border patrol, by a traffic cop, a Jeep full of medicine, and the thought of a day's more driving along the border, were enough to send my paranoia into overdrive. Over the years my paranoia and I have developed practical techniques to keep us out of harm's way, and one of these is that— contrary to popular opinion—the safest time to move anything you don't want anyone to know about, is in broad daylight at peak traffic times. With proportionally more vehicles on the roads the police have proportionally more cars, accidents, and incidents to deal with, and so officers are more thinly spread than at other times. It follows that my paranoia would dictate that for a safe passage through Laredo, and away from the border towards San Antonio, the best plan was to hide among the peak morning traffic.

So, shortly before 8:00 am the next morning, I eased the big Jeep out of the motel car park and into heavy traffic, and we set off along the expressway toward San Antonio. Before starting Blue Horse had performed yet another protection ceremony in our hotel room, and he assured me that his prayers were strong and we had nothing to fear. Yet despite our precautions—both practical and spiritual—only three miles further on we ran into another bloody roadblock! This one looked serious, and European style it divided traffic into cars, vans, and trucks, and there were lots of officers milling around the entry points. There was also a lot of traffic, the queues were building fast, and to keep the public on their side, I knew the officers would have to process everyone through as fast as they could: then I saw the sniffer dogs.

There were two dogs at each stop point, and the sight of the dogs made my heart jump for joy. Their presence meant the officers didn't have time to indulge in searches, and were relying on the dogs to tell them if anything illegal was aboard a vehicle. Sniffer dogs are trained to sniff out the most common drugs, such as marijuana, cocaine, and heroin, and they are not trained to sniff out peyote—which is perfectly legal in the right hands—so I knew the dogs would not bother us. With no signal from the dogs, I reckoned the officers would wave us straight through. But when we reached the head of the line, and I held up my British passport and US driver's license for inspection, the officer showed no interest in my documents; but a lot of interest in Blue Horse. "You Mexican?" He demanded.

I'd told Blue Horse not to show anyone the official papers for the medicine unless we were definitely going to be searched. So he was in the process of pulling only his driver's license from his pocket, when the officer suddenly demanded to know if he was Mexican. Stung by this, which was the third or fourth time he'd been accused of being a Mexican by policemen and border officials during this trip, he reacted strongly. Bringing his right palm up sharply, he slapped the center of his chest with a noisy thump, and looking the officer straight in the eye, replied loudly and proudly, "Navajo! Navajo Indian!"

It took a moment to sink in, but then the officer nodded admiringly and repeated, "Navajo. Navajo, eh?" And without another word, and without bothering to look at Blue Horse's license, or my papers, he waved us through. I wasn't sure if we'd had a close call or not, but after this second brush with the authorities, Blue Horse was more sure than ever that our successful progress was all down to him. Looking extremely smug, he assured me: "My protection prayers are strong. I told you, you'll be OK."

"Yeah," I said. "You did."

If my precautions and paranoia seem like over-kill, all I can say is that at the time it didn't seem that way. I genuinely feared we might be detained, even though I beleived I was on the right side of the law. But none of us were lawyers, so we couldn't be sure. I had to balance that uncertainty against a reality; that if I didn't make this trip to The Garden, I'd probably never get another chance to go. Blue Horse was aging, his appetite for long, tiring, excursions was diminishing, and he'd told me several times this would be his last trip. If it was, I didn't want it to end in jail.

Having negotiated what I hoped would prove to be the last road block, we turned off the highway and parked at a roadside café, where I could see the Jeep from inside while we ate breakfast. I wanted to know if anyone had followed us, and kept a wary eye out through the café window in case anyone was taking an unhealthy interest in our vehicle. Nobody was or, if they were, I couldn't see them—how's that for paranoia!

After this, the most dramatic incident during the rest of the journey came when Blue Horse decided to hold another blessing ceremony for the medicine as we sailed past San Antonio at eighty mph. We didn't have time to stop to hold this ceremony, so he decided to perform it on the move, and while I was concentrating on the road ahead the car suddenly filled with smoke. Spluttering, it took me a few moments to realize the smoke was accompanied by the strong smell of Indian tobacco, meaning the car was not on fire as I'd first feared. Instead, Blue Horse had rolled a smoke and was blowing tobacco smoke over the sacks of peyote, and all around the vehicle as a blessing and protection.

"There goes my no-smoking contract with the car-rental company," I thought, as clouds of smoke engulfed the inside of the Jeep.

But Blue Horse was unconcerned, as he took the eagle feather from his jish and, pouring cold water into his little silver cup, handed me the smoke while he commenced praying. He prayed for fully fifteen minutes, while I held the smoke in one hand, drove with the other, and intermittently puffed up clouds of smoke. When he'd finished his prayers, Blue Horse dipped the tip of the eagle feather into the silver cup and blessed the medicine, the vehicle, and both of us with the holy water. When he'd finished, I checked the speedometer and we were still traveling at more than eighty mph yet, despite this, he constantly urged me to go faster.

"We gotta get home for Thanksgiving!" he cried over and again.

"I don't know what you've got to celebrate," I told him. "All Thanksgiving means to Indians is that some white man turned up and stole all your land."

"We celebrate because we know we're gonna get it back again," Blue Horse replied, rather wittily.

It was a long drive home, over countryside often so flat, on roads so straight, that once again there were times when only the curvature of the earth prevented me from seeing forever. It was not until we were almost home that Blue Horse suddenly, and quite unexpectedly, imparted the most important piece of information from the entire trip. He told me that once Mr. Rodriguez had recovered from the shock of seeing me, he was so intrigued to hear that I'd come all the way from England to learn about medicine, that he wanted to show me around his ranch, where the peyote grows and is harvested.

"He says he's gonna show you round his ranch. He'll show you all about how they get the medicine, how they dry it and grind it up, and where it grows," Blue Horse said, as if such invitations were so common as to be hardly worth mentioning. "He wants me to run a medicine meeting for him down there in February. Maybe you can come along with me then, give me a hand with everything. You can take a look round then." This was exactly what I'd hoped to do, so I was extremely pleased.

We arrived home at 2:00 in the morning, by which time we were completely exhausted. Though we'd been away for less than three days, we returned to find that winter had arrived on the reservation. It had been a heatstroke-inducing eighty-seven degrees Fahrenheit in Rio Grande City, but at home it had been snowing. The temperature in the high desert, where we live at six to seven thousand feet or more above sea level, had dropped to between minus ten and minus twelve degrees at night, while during the day it hovered at only a degree or so below freezing.

One of the few things peyote cactus cannot tolerate is freezing, and if it does freeze it turns to mush. So, despite our tiredness, before we could sleep we had to get the sacks out of the vehicle and inside the house where they would be safe from the cold. I'd driven for sixteen hours and was looking forward to the luxury of the sofa, but Ronny was lying on it snoring loudly, so I had to abandon the idea. After getting the sacks inside, I lay down in a little space between them on the bare floor and slept. I was so tired I could have slept on a prickly pear cactus—several prickly pears, in fact.

The next morning, while we were sitting around recovering from the journey Quin, one of Blue Horse's young granddaughters, noticed ants in one of the sacks of medicine. Fearful the ants might spread through the house, or eat the medicine, the women decided to sort it into clean boxes immediately. Ronny and I carried the sacks outside and tipped them out in the back of a pick-up for the women to sort. Normally, this sorting would be done exclusively by the women, but because Ronny and I were already there, the women said we could stay and watch. The biggest of the cacti were approximately the size of large grapefruits, something that caused considerable surprise, because peyote cacti of that size are rare today. The biggest ones were entrusted into Ronny's care, as the only Navajo male present, and as he held them in his hands and admired them, Ronny told me a strange story.

"Long time ago, so they say, when the earth was created, the medicine was the first thing on the earth. The earth was hot then, my father said, and the medicine was the first living thing to grow on the surface. Because it was created first, that's why it knows everything; because it was here first and saw it all happen. That's why, when you pray with it, when you ask it things, it knows and it tells you—that's what my father said."

I'd never heard the medicine explained in this way before, but Ronny seemed convinced by his explanation, and it is a good one. Later, Ronny gave the biggest plants to Blue Horse, who reverentially placed them in a glass display cabinet, where they would be the envy of all his friends and neighbors; and he assured me they would be fine for a couple of months before starting to dry out. It turned out the ants had been in only one sack, and the rest of the medicine was mercifully free of them. So, after the women had sorted all the plants of various sizes into clean cardboard boxes, Ronny and I carried the boxes back into the house again, so they could be stored safely.

    I wanted to return to Rio Grande City to visit Mr. Rodriguez and learn more about the collection and processing of the medicine. But, it was not to be. My attempts to arrange a visit only provoked a fog of rather unlikely excuses, and the medicine meeting Blue Horse was supposed to run for him did not happen either. So, in the end, I never did get my tour of the growing fields and harvesting methods used to collect the peyote cactus. Nevertheless, it was a memorable visit, and one I will always feel privileged to have made.

VII

When I next flew to England I didn't think it would be almost a year before I would see Blue Horse again. During this time, I experienced the death of both my parents and the death of a long and dear relationship. I also had to sell my parents' house and my own house, and sort out endless legal difficulties related to my parents' estate. When it was all over, I found myself entirely alone: I had no one, needed no one, and was beholden to no one.

What followed was a conscious decision to destroy my former life, and to this end I divested myself of all my possessions. What could be sold, I sold. What could not be sold, went to the dump. What could not be dumped was burned, and what would not burn, I smashed with an ax. All previous correspondence, all computer files and discs, and all reminders of days gone by; the accumulations and detritus of a lifetime, was systematically destroyed.

When it was over, I owned nothing except two sets of clothing and two pairs of track shoes, one set of which I was wearing. I retained only my grandfather's watch and a silver box my children had given me with their photographs in it. At last, I was free. Free from the baggage that had weighed me down for half a lifetime, until it had become almost too heavy to bear. I was elated. The old life was dead, and I could embark on a new one without a backward glance.

Light as Ariel I landed at the Sunport, Albuquerque's airport, with no home, no job, no nothing; only to discover that among the many things I no longer possessed was any money. I stuck my plastic into a cash machine to find my account rolling its eyes like a steer in a slaughter house. There was just enough to cover a couple of nights in a cheap motel, and I had to walk three miles to get there—good thing I had no luggage! All my money had been tied up in legal issues in England, and I left London when I did because I was assured my legal problems were over, and by the time I crossed the Atlantic cash would be in my US accounts. Brethren, put not thy trust in lawyers. Or accountants, or any denizens of the finance industry.

When I reached my motel room it still had blood on the bathroom walls from the last occupants' syringes. Fortunately, I had the good sense to phone my friend Erik, who had a spare room which he invited me to use while I sorted myself out. It took a month, during which I signed up for a degree course in anthropology; then, thankfully, everything came good. Money dropped into my bank, and the first thing I did was to buy a car and drive to see Blue Horse. I bought another used Nissan Xterra, a bit less used than the first one, because they handled the rough Navajo tracks well, and I found them generally more useful than New Mexico's ubiquitous pick-up trucks.

I'd kept in contact with Blue Horse from England and not many weeks had slipped by without us talking by phone. Now, when I arrived once more at his small wooden house, it was to find that nothing had changed during my absence. The signed copy of my little book *Meeting the Medicine Men*, about our first encounters, that I'd presented him with before I went away, was in exactly the same spot on top of the television where he'd placed it before I left twelve months previously. True, Blue Horse couldn't read,[38] but I thought Baa might read some of it to him. It turned out she'd tried, but when he discovered that not every line of every paragraph on every page was about him, he quickly lost interest.

Blue Horse and Báa were pleased to see me and asked me to stay for a few days. Blue Horse said he'd missed his apprentice and immediately

---

38 He can read simple stuff, road signs for instance, and can sign his name and write numbers. But I've never known him read even a short newspaper report. Given his obvious high intelligence and abilities, I often wonder if dyslexia, undetected and probably unknown in the little time he spent in school in the late 1940s, was the real reason for his illiteracy.

announced that I was going back to work. "There's a lady needs help," he explained.

"What's the matter with her?"

"Dunno," said Blue Horse. "Find out when we get there."

I'd hoped to ease myself gently back into the exceedingly deep waters of Navajo sorcery and witchcraft, but it was not to be. As it turned out, this was for the best, because that night Blue Horse put on one of the most dazzling demonstrations of a medicine man's powers I was ever to see. An unworldly display that seemed to draw from the deepest roots of human existence, as they were before the rise of civilization cramped and corralled us. Baffling, primitive, dramatic, it broke the illusion of the ordinariness of life, and I was left wondering that if one man could do such things: perhaps, if only we dared, so could we all.

It was September, heavy rainstorms were sweeping the area, and many small Navajo farmers had lost their winter corn and squash. As we drove out that evening dark storm clouds were gathering. Flashes of lightning flickered along the horizon, and the Puerco River was running at record heights. Usually little more than a trickle, the river was now a surging mass of thick, brown, silt-laden water sixty yards wide, rushing, roaring, and foaming through the desert. Any more rain threatened a flood of Biblical proportions.

"Our gods are angry with us," observed Blue Horse, looking out of the car's rain-streaked window. It was a joke: I think.

We drove along the Devil's Highway and for ten miles were followed by a cop. I stuck to every speed limit, obeyed every traffic signal and drove like the Virgin Mary, until the officer grew bored and sheered away, leaving us alone. After another thirty minutes or so, we turned on to one of the many tribal trackways that crisscross the reservation and began heading northeast. As I've mentioned before, these tracks are rough and difficult to follow at the best of times. Now, after the heavy rain, the one we needed had pretty well washed out, and with thick black storm clouds obscuring the dying sun, we were soon surrounded by an all-enveloping gloom that made navigation almost impossible.

Blue Horse had been traversing these tracks since boyhood, but even he was having trouble tonight. Several times we had to stop the car, get out, and hunt around for the way, our search illuminated solely by lightning from the storms raging around us. It's not uncommon in these high-desert areas to have several massive thunder storms raging all around; yet have no drop of rain fall nearby because there is no storm overhead. It was a small mercy, for the way was perilous enough without having to drive through a downpour. Then, after a while, the rain began, and was soon so heavy that it bounced a yard high as it hit the ground; until it seemed to be "raining from both heaven and earth", as the Arabs say.

I had no idea where we were, or where we were going, and it was pointless to ask, as I would have been no wiser even if Blue Horse had told me. As we made our way through the downpour the windshield wipers could hardly cope, and for ten miles we crept along at little more than walking pace. Eventually, my headlights picked out the shadowy outline of a lone pickup truck parked at the side of the track facing in our direction. It was one of those huge, super-powerful diesels, with the dual rear wheels so beloved by farmers in these off-road areas. My first thought was that it must have broken down, but as we came alongside, the driver's window rolled down and, ignoring the torrential rain, a smiley-faced boy of about twelve stuck his head out and waved to us. As he was alone in the vehicle, my next thought was to wonder who on earth had abandoned a child in the wilderness on a night like this?

"That's them," said Blue Horse.

"What?"

"Follow that truck."

I watched in astonishment as the boy took the wheel of this enormous vehicle—my Xterra would have gone easily in the back—slipped it into gear, and set off; but there was nothing to do but turn around and follow him. He was an extremely good driver, I'll give him that, and led us unerringly down miles of treacherous and narrow trails. The trails kept branching off, and all I could do was follow the truck through the storm, until we found ourselves in the paddock of a small farm. Grouped around the paddock were several dilapidated old cars and a trailer in which the family lived. The place had the usual chorus of yapping dogs, now dripping wet, and even more resentful of intruders than usual.

When the boy climbed down from his truck, he was so small I had to ask how he reached the pedals to drive. "Easy," he replied nonchalantly. "I drive standing up. It's the only way I can see through the windshield."

By now it was almost dark. The rain had eased off and the moon had risen, its pale globe flickering fitfully between the storm clouds that scudded across the sky in a rising wind. Looking around, I had no doubt that, wherever we were, it was far from anywhere I'd been before. The boy led us sloshing through thick, red, Navajo mud to a hogan at the side of the paddock where he opened the door for us. A pale light came through the doorway and the boy indicated for us to enter; then he walked away through the rain and disappeared into the darkness; and I never saw him again.

Inside, the hogan was warm and dry. Brightly lit by two oil lamps, it was heated by a small wood fire burning in the oil-drum stove in the middle of the earth floor. Sitting on the floor, their backs resting against the wooden walls, were members of the family. Present were our patient—I will call her Ella, but for reasons that will become obvious this was not her name—her husband Jim, her mother, her father, a couple of aunts, and two other relatives from the extended family; all of whom lived together in the trailer at the farm. They all looked fairly elderly, except for Ella and her husband, but looks can be deceptive among people who have spent a lifetime working outdoors on a small Navajo farm.

Blue Horse had told me on the way over that Ella had been extremely reluctant to see him, and only pressure from her mother and aunts had forced her to do so.

"She don't want to see no traditional healer," Blue Horse said.

"But why?" I asked. It was unusual for traditional Navajos to react against bringing in a traditional medicine man.

"We're gonna find out," he replied, but said no more.

After a while, Blue Horse and I took our places near the center of the hogan, and the family formed a circle for the divination. One of the men took a couple of shovelfuls of charcoal from the stove and placed them in front of us; then Blue Horse rolled the smoke and when it had been lit, he passed it to Ella and encouraged her to smoke and talk about what was bothering her. With some reluctance she began to tell us, but in English, because her Navajo was poor.

My guess was that in normal times Ella was of a fairly cheery disposition; but these were obviously not normal times. She said she was in her mid-thirties, had several children, and that as well as working on the farm, she and her husband Jim had jobs in Gallup. As Navajo families go they were quite well off, she said, and were always able to pay their bills. But now Ella could not work, the bills were piling up, and she and her husband were fighting about money and much else besides. The reason she could not work was that she'd recently suffered a stillbirth. She was in pain, and the small local clinic had told her some of the afterbirth was still inside her, had become infected, and needed to be removed. But she felt unable to face traveling to a big hospital in Albuquerque, a journey of 200 miles each way, with all the time and expense that would entail. Meanwhile, the rows over money, the still birth, and the whole fraught situation was affecting her family, including her mother, who had begun to suffer from violent internal pains of her own. Because Ella had given birth successfully on other occasions the family, particularly the women, ascribed the stillbirth to witchcraft and they wanted Blue Horse to root out the cause. This would usually be something a woman would welcome; which made it hard to explain Ella's reluctance to see him, and her obvious nervousness now he was here.

Her husband Jim also struck me as probably a jolly type in normal circumstances, but when it came to his turn to talk he confirmed his wife's version of events, and that their fighting was affecting the children and the family. Add to this the pains Ella's mother was unaccountably suffering, plus the fact that her father had recently gone deaf, and the story added up to a whole lot of trouble and woe for the family.

While the smoke was going around, and the talk was going on, I'd taken the opportunity to observe the charcoal, and what I saw was highly unusual. Something was lying on top of the coals at exactly the point where I would usually bury the remains of the smoke. I generally see well in the fire, but this time the more I looked, the more convinced I became that something it was trying to block me from seeing what the coals wanted to show me. It wasn't that I was out of practice, or anything like that, it was that something, somehow, was deliberately blocking me. This was confirmed when the smoke came back to me: as I prepared to bury it in the hot coals as usual, Blue Horse stretched out a hand to stop me.

"Scrape the ash off the smoke, *chischille*," [39] he ordered. "Scrape the ash off and put the end here by my other instruments."

This was the only time in our long association that such a thing happened. It was an ominous turn of events and I knew from this, and from other tiny clues in his general demeanor, that Blue Horse had seen something unusually troubling in the charcoal. When I had done as he bid, he took some crushed cedar from his white doeskin bag and sprinkled it on the coals, sending a cloud of aromatic blue smoke soaring into the rafters. Then he stood up and gave me a fire stick to hold in my left hand for protection and, pausing only to tell Ella and Jim to collect a bag of fine ash and bring it to him, he took his whistle and his drumstick and headed out through the door.

Outside the wind had risen still further. It was completely dark now except for a little intermittent light from the moon, as it dodged between the storm clouds, and occasional flashes of lightning on the horizon. Standing facing east, the direction of the dawn and the rising sun, Blue Horse blew his whistle and said some prayers. Shortly after this, Ella and Jim emerged from the hogan to join us, carrying the bag of wood ash which I took charge of.

Jim had scarcely handed the bag to me before Blue Horse ordered: "Charles, go that way a bit and draw a circle. You've done it before."

Actually, I hadn't. I had no idea what he wanted, and as I walked out into the darkness all I could do was hope for the best. Fortunately, Blue Horse continued to shout instructions. Yelling above the wind: "Keep going, keep going! That's it. About there. Draw a circle in the dust, but don't close it completely! Leave a doorway in it."

---

39 Chischille means "curls" or, when applied to a white man, "curly hair".

Using the fire stick, I drew as precise a circle as I could about ten yards in diameter. It was difficult to see much in the dark, and to make things worse the strengthening wind was blowing twigs, grass, old tin cans, and damp bits of paper all over the place. While I was drawing the circle, Blue Horse continued to walk back and forth blowing his whistle. He, Ella and Jim were no more than fifty yards away, but I could hardly make them out thought the dark and the dust and debris kicked up by the wind.

When I'd finished the circle I rejoined them, and Blue Horse led us to a mound where the family dumped waste ashes from the stove. The mound was little used during the summer months, and the wind had covered it with a thick layer of sand that made it almost invisible. Yet Blue Horse went straight to it, and after casting around for a while he called for a shovel, which Jim duly fetched.

"Dig here," Blue Horse commanded him, pointing to a spot about three yards from where we stood. "Two shallow shovelfuls. Don't go too deep."

Jim piled the diggings in a little heap near our feet, and then Blue Horse knelt down and began to search in the pile. After a few seconds, he held up a curse wrapped in deer hide, which he threw into the bag of ash I held open for him. Next, I was dispatched to place the bag in the center of the circle I'd drawn in the dust; a circle which the stiff wind was now rapidly wiping out.

"Make sure you go in through the doorway, Charles!" he yelled after me, his voice sounding urgent. "Don't break the circle whatever you do!"

People who live in well-lit cities have no idea how dark it can be at night in places where there are no streetlights or, as in the case of this isolated farm, no electric lights of any kind. The night takes on an inky, impenetrable, blackness that surrounds like a wall and must be experienced to be understood. Now, with only the fitful and uncertain light of the moon to guide me, I had trouble finding the circle in the dark—let alone its entrance. I found it eventually, and placed the bag with the curse safely within it, in as sheltered a spot as I could under a half-dead sage bush. Then I made my way back to Blue Horse's side, although with difficulty.

By this time I'd had enough of stumbling about blindly in the dark and the wind and asked for a flashlight, which Jim obligingly went to fetch from the trailer; leaving Blue Horse, Ella, and me standing alone in the rising gale and the pale moon. A moment later the moon disappeared behind a cloud and plunged us into inky blackness.

Despite the fact that I knew something unusual was going on, I was completely unprepared for what happened next. Shrouded by the dark, and with her husband safely out of the way, Blue Horse turned to Ella and I heard him say: "The little boy you lost is with us. His spirit is here." And he pointed to a patch of ground a few yards away. "Did you know it was a little boy?"

I was close enough that I could see Ella slowly and silently shake her head, as Blue Horse continued: "The reason you lost him was that you were unsure about him. You weren't sure if he was your husband's baby or somebody else's, were you? It was your fear that caused you to lose your baby."

I saw Ella reel in shock. For a moment the moon came out, and the one brief look at her face it afforded was enough to confirm the truth of what Blue Horse had said. She was thunderstruck—and what woman would not be in such circumstances—frightened and horrified. Looking around anxiously to make sure her husband was not near, she said in a flat monotone, "I killed my baby." And she stood silently, shaking her head and looking at the ground. A second later we heard the trailer door bang shut, and we knew her husband was on his way with the flashlight.

Quickly dropping his voice and pointing toward where the curse was contained within the circle, Blue Horse spoke sternly, but reassuringly, to Ella. "Someone made you do it. But don't worry, *sitsi'*, my daughter. I'm gonna fix it for you. I'm gonna make it so everything will be all right for you, and no one will ever know."

What Blue Horse meant by "someone made you do it" was that someone had cursed Ella, so that she would fall for another man and have his baby; with all the repercussions that would have in this small, isolated, family community. It should also be noted how swiftly Blue Horse acted to assure her that, whatever she had done, he could overcome the evil and fix it for her, so that *"no one will ever know"*. Now she understood that, provided she had the good sense to keep quiet, the secret was hers.

We fell silent as her husband approached and Ella did her best to regain a little composure. Mercifully, the moon disappeared again, hiding her distress, but as a precaution I took the flashlight from Jim to make sure he couldn't shine it on his wife. Then, guided by the flashlight, Blue Horse led us back to a spot near the hogan door, where he blew his whistle before praying and beginning his hand trembling. The hand trembling led us to the side of the family's trailer, where Blue Horse began a new search while I held the flashlight for him.

"I'm looking for an upturned stone or rock," he explained. "There's one here somewhere."

Our search took us to one end side of the trailer, where I cast about with the flashlight without seeing anything obvious, until Blue Horse suddenly shouted: "That's it!" And pointed to a small mound about the size and shape of an upturned washing-up bowl.

"It's just a dust pile," Jim observed, sounding disappointed, but Blue Horse was certain.

"Kick it and see what's there," he ordered

In the desert "dust piles" are not always piles of soft dust. Some form naturally, then bake in the sun until they become so rock hard they can last for years. This one was so old and so hard, that it took several savage kicks from Jim's heavy work boots to break it into a few large pieces. Blue Horse seized the biggest, raised it above his head and dashed it to the ground, where it broke open and out fell a second curse.

"There it is," he said, bending down to pick it up and drop it into a second bag of ash I'd acquired.

Satisfied, he raised his whistle and drumstick to eye level and began squinting along them taking bearings. He took several bearings that seemed to provide an intersection of lines between the points where we had found the two curses. Then, having assured himself, he led us to a small tree growing about twenty yards from the trailer. In the dark I couldn't tell what species of tree it was, but it was a typical desert specimen. Thin, and not more than eight or nine feet tall, its trunk was no thicker than a man's calf, and at about five feet above the ground it forked into two meager branches.

"Look at this," Blue Horse said, pointing. I focused the flashlight's powerful beam at the spot he indicated and there, carved into one of the branches at just above head height, was a face with two eyes: and the eyes were focused on one of the trailer windows.

"Where's your mother's room?" Blue Horse asked Ella.

"It's that one," she said, pointing to the window the eyes were focused upon. "And that other curse in the dust pile was right under mother's window, too!"

Blue Horse permitted himself a nod of silent satisfaction and then, telling Jim he required an ax, he waited until the man had departed into the darkness before he felt he could express himself safely.

"This is going to be difficult with a lady present," he said, looking from Ella to me and back again. "But look here, where the tree forks, you can see *'atsxil*, a woman's private parts."

I looked, Ella looked, and damn me—he was right. Where the trunk forked was what looked like a vagina, with hair and all. The fork was a woman's open legs, viewed from on top in reverse. Pointing at the face carved in the trunk, and then at the vagina, Blue Horse told Ella: "All this is aimed at your mother. It's to make her go crazy over a man and break up your family. How would it be if you were havin' some other man's baby, and your mother was also havin' an affair with someone?"

The look on poor Ella's face showed she could imagine it only too well. And while I didn't think Ella's prematurely aged and overweight mother looked the *femme fatale* type, witchcraft or no witchcraft, long experience with human beings told me you can never be certain. But then, a few seconds later, Blue Horse offered further explanation.

"This didn't work on your mother," he told Ella, indicating the tree. "The pains she is having inside, that's the urge the curse made her feel for men. But she's a good woman and it couldn't send her that way, so when it couldn't make her do what she didn't want to, that's when it turned to pain."

At this moment husband Jim reappeared with an ax, and we fell silent while Blue Horse took the ax and quickly cut away the face. It took several heavy blows to remove it, because it had been gouged deep into the wood. He cut it from the tree in one piece, so the face was preserved and could be placed in the sanitizing ash inside the bag, along with the other curse. Then he axed the vagina away. While he was doing this, I distinctly heard, carried on the storm wind, the sound of a medicine man's whistle being blown in the distance. Not just once or twice, but several times. Neither Ella nor her husband seemed to hear it, but Blue Horse and I did, and we knew it could mean only one thing: the witchmen knew we were at work undoing their evil, and out in the darkness and the storm, they were making medicine to stop us.

Once the tree had been dealt with, Blue Horse led us back to the ash pile, where he intended to open and examine the curses. Despite the atrocious conditions, we had to unwrap the curses outdoors so as not to introduce the evil into the hogan. But first I had to retrieve the other curse from the circle drawn in the sand. By now the moon had disappeared again, the wind had risen almost to a gale, and the air was so thick with sand and dust that the flashlight was nearly useless. The result was that I had great difficulty finding the circle, even though it was no more than fifty yards away. On every step of the way I was being hit by flying twigs, pieces of waste paper, tin cans, and even a metal bucket that came rolling across the ground in the wind and gave me a painful rap on the shin.

At times like this, one can easily imagine that the witchmen we heard whistling had, by some dark power, brought on the storm to frustrate our every move; and at one point, as I stumbled about blindly, I almost despaired of ever finding the circle and its hidden curse. Then, at the very moment I was wondering if the wind had not already blown the curse away where I would never find it, I caught a glimpse of one corner of the paper bag fluttering in the wind. It was at the outermost limit of the flashlight's now limited beam, but it was enough to guide me in.

All the time Blue Horse was screaming at me through the storm to enter and exit only by the door in the circle but, unfortunately, the circle had practically disappeared by now. The best I could do was to retrieved the bag by going through where I *thought* the entrance had been, and carry it back to him. I was only just in time. A few minutes later and the gale rose to new heights which would have blown the curse—the one specifically aimed at Ella and that had caused the pregnancy, the still birth, and the trouble with her husband—away across the desert. Into whose hands it might have blown it, is not something I wish to speculate about.

Seeking shelter in the lee of the hogan, I held the flashlight steady, as Blue Horse dealt first with the curse aimed at Ella and her husband. It was a big one, about eight or nine inches long, and bound in stiff deer hide. So stiff that he called for a pair of pliers to open it, but we didn't have any, so instead he used the large black obsidian spearhead he'd given Jim to hold for protection. Stone blades made of obsidian, a volcanic glass that breaks to the last molecule, can be hundreds of times sharper than surgical steel if properly chipped. Now, using the obsidian spearhead as a knife, Blue Horse cut through the tough hide in an instant.

Inside we found a bundle of hair—most probably Ella's—a crudely made stone arrowhead, and a stick of wood of about a finger's length and breadth, that had been split in half before being bound back together with rawhide. When Blue Horse cut the rawhide and separated the two halves, we saw the image of a man had been drawn on one half, and the image of a woman on the other.

"See? This is to split you two up," Blue Horse said, holding out the two halves to Ella and her husband. "Once the stick was one, like a man and wife, then they split it in two so you'd be divided. See, there you are on the two halves, Ella on one half and Jim on the other. That's the way they work. Then there's the arrowhead. Something broken, something sharp—that's what they curse with."

But there was something else that we almost overlooked: a tightly wrapped piece of paper that turned out to be a dollar bill. "*Beeso*," I said in Navajo when I saw it, meaning money. Blue Horse called for water, and when it was brought he carefully unwrapped the dollar bill and washed it. Now we saw that while this was undoubtedly a dollar bill and the design was visible, the color had somehow been bleached out of it until the paper was almost white.

"You've been fighting about money," Blue Horse reminded them, but they needed no reminding. "This is why," he said, holding up the dollar bill. "See how the color's faded out of it? In the same way, all the money will fade out of your lives, right down to the last dollar."

After this we opened the second curse, the one aimed at Ella's mother and then, after briefly examining the wooden face he'd hacked from the tree, Blue Horse returned everything to the safety of the ashes and gave the bag back to me. I placed it safely under a big stone to stop it blowing away, and then we all went back inside the hogan, where Blue Horse used his hollow tube to suck an enormous amount of bad stuff from both Ella and her husband. Among the things he removed was what looked like a long black worm from Jim's neck. This proved to be particularly difficult to find and remove. Later, Blue Horse told me he knew it was there only because: "When we were outside, I could hear it singing to me."

By the time Blue Horse had done some medicine to protect the family from further cursing, and had blessed everyone and the hogan, farm and trailer, it was after midnight. As we drove away, storms were still raging all around, and vivid flashes of lightning illuminated our way, while thunder crashed directly over our heads bringing with it more torrential rain. Pointing to the heavens, I yelled above the din: "Is this because the witchmen are cursing against us? I heard the whistles."

"Maybe," he yelled back. "Maybe they have other things waiting for us."

He would not elaborate on what those other things might be, so I turned to the question of how he knew of Ella's infidelity, and how the guilt of it had perhaps contributed to her stillbirth; something which in modern medical terms may not make sense, but within the Navajo context is understandable.

Not for the first time, he looked at me and heaved a tolerant sigh. "Chizchille, you've got your satellites, your computers, your phones that tell you where you are all the time, and your hi-tech and your spies who can listen to everyone's thoughts. But we don't have that. All we got is what our ancestors give us. We got the fireplace. We got the water and the fire, we got the earth and the sky, and nothin' more. But if we trust it, if we believe in it, if we look into it, the fireplace will show us everythin' we need to know. I've told you all this before. Why do you keep asking?" He was tired and more than a little irritable.

"I saw something in the fire, too," I told him. "But I didn't know what it was, it seemed to be trying to block me from seeing what I needed to know. I knew it meant something big, and then you told me not to put the smoke in the fire. Could you really see all that about Ella and everything?"

"I could see," he replied. "And if you stopped asking these damn fool questions, you'd see as well."

I took that last remark with more than a pinch of salt, but as he had now pulled his trademark white Stetson over his eyes, it was clear I wasn't going find out more. Somehow, despite the storm, the drumming of the rain on the car, and the innumerable bumps in the road, he went to sleep. Leaving me to find my way home through a storm so severe it flooded parts of Gallup and closed I-40.

* * *

Ever since that night I have been struck by how certain Blue Horse had to be—how certain *anyone* would have to be—to say what he said that night to Ella, a woman he had never met before. If he'd been wrong, all she had to do was to start screaming and the men from the farm would have come running with their guns, and it would have been very much the worse for us. But he was right; so how did he do it?

First of all, it was not a guess. No sane man could say out loud guesses that a married woman had been carrying another man's baby. Not in London, not in New York and certainly not among the Navajo. Not only that, but Ella knew only too well that he spoke the truth. So, it was not a guess: Blue Horse knew the truth. Second, I saw something in the fire that I knew to be unusual and significant, and while I couldn't read it because something was blocking me, this didn't stop Blue Horse. Third, while perhaps more than usually dramatic, what happened that night was in no other way exceptional and Blue Horse repeatedly, and successfully, performed many similar feats of divination during the years I accompanied him.

It was as a result of nights like this, and many other such incidents, that I found myself inhabiting a parallel world in which everything I once believed or, more precisely, once emphatically did not believe, was being challenged. In our sophisticated western world we don't believe in witches and witchcraft anymore. Why would we? We are all exceptionally clever, well-educated, successful, cosmopolitan products of our age and we don't have time for such old fashioned phooey.

For several years I was the night news editor of the London Evening Standard, the world's biggest selling evening newspaper, where I was responsible for news gathering world-wide; and you had better believe me when I say that in such a position one has no time for fairy stories. Yet despite my years of ruthlessly separating fact from fiction, I was having trouble facing the powerful challenges, not so much to my *belief* as to my *disbelief,* that were coming daily from the evidence of my own eyes. In this strange parallel world, almost a parallel universe, events I would once have dismissed as fairy tales no longer seemed like fiction. Yet so tenacious, so steely strong, was the strait jacket of my upbringing, education and professional background, I found it impossible to perform the *volte-face* necessary to abandon my *disbelief* and accept Navajo *belief.*

As may be imagined, this was an extremely uncomfortable position to be in. But how could I go to dinner in Hampstead or Manhattan, and tell them I was studying witchcraft because I believed in it? They'd think I was nuts. Yet to the Navajo, to be studying with Blue Horse and not believing in witchcraft, was equally nuts.

When struggling to find explanations for the strange events recounted here, I generally ignore anthropology, archeology, religion, legend, prophets and seers, and turn instead to hard science, particularly to physics; and not only because I have the good fortune to be married to one of the world's outstanding women physicists. I turn to physics because it routinely deals with unseen and unknown forces, and unknown dimensions of time and space.

Readers are encouraged to research this more deeply for themselves but, put simply, the highly advanced mathematical models the world's greatest physicists use to explain the universe, do not work easily. In order to get them to work better, it's necessary to add extra dimensions—up to twenty-two extra dimensions—on top of the observable three of width, depth and height, with which we are all familiar. In physics time must also be considered as a dimension, but this does not help much. To make the models work more easily—and even then they are far from perfect—not only time and the twenty-two extra dimensions have to be included, but it may be necessary to add a number of unseen and undetected forces supposedly at work within the universe. When all this is done, the math works better, but the plain fact is that no one has any idea whether the unknown dimensions and unknown forces that have been added, exist or not. Or, if they do, how they might be detected. What it comes down to is that a scientific theory, may be based on data that have no known physical existence.

Similarly, the events I observed in the company of Blue Horse are far easier to explain if one also accepts unknown forces that have no obvious physical existence—in this context these would be occult and spiritual forces—and that they affect the unfortunates who have been cursed by Navajo witches, and influence the outcome of Blue Horse's endeavors to lift these curses. He certainly believes this, few Navajos I know would doubt it, and my "model" of Navajo traditional medicine works a lot better if we admit that such forces exist. So, why don't I come straight out and say: "I believe unknown occult forces explain my observations?" The answer is, that I have no idea how I could prove such an assertion; no idea of what such forces consist of, if they do exist, or how they could be measured.

Another problem is that while it is respectable in physics to postulate any number of weird and wacky unknown forces, I do not feel I can do the same. While in this book I have given many examples of witches

125

and witchcraft, I have endeavored to report factually and accurately what I observed and experienced, without attempting to draw unsubstantiated conclusions. There is no doubt there are Navajo witches, and no doubt they make and plant curses intended to do people harm; the evidence is simply overwhelming. But while this is proof of people at work, it is not proof of occult forces at work. The evidence provided by curse victims as to their sufferings, and of their recovery after Blue Horse has lifted the curses, is honestly given and deserves due consideration. But I cannot say this is evidence of unknown forces from beyond our physical realm. It may be, it may not.

At this point in my journey with Blue Horse, while I found the evidence for witches and witchcraft clear enough, I still could not bring myself to believe that witchcraft really had an effect on anyone; which was strange given that I live in a society where a large section of the population believes in the power of prayer. If I was ever to get out of the uncomfortable no-man's land, the dissonant parallel world I was forcing myself to inhabit, something would have to give: the question was becoming urgent. But when, where, and how, was this to be achieved?

VIII

After a demanding day, it seemed like I'd hardly lain down on the floor to sleep, when I was awakened by Blue Horse crashing around making coffee at about 4:30 in the morning. He never does anything quietly, and how he gets by on so little sleep I'll never know. We were due at a squaw dance and I just had time to shower and grab a couple of cups of Blue Horse's industrial-strength coffee, before we left in separate vehicles. But at least the coffee meant I was awake enough to appreciate the glory of a truly spectacular dawn.

There are no skies like the skies of New Mexico, and whether at morning or evening, the celestial display is likely to be, well; celestial. On this morning, the newborn sun came up from behind a hill like a pulsating powerhouse of spectacular nuclear explosions, which is exactly what it is. As it pumped itself up above the horizon in a vast, blazing red, white and gold ball, for a few minutes its early light brought out the many and varied colors of the desert. From the most delicate blues and pale greens among the bands of shale, to the darkest black of the now solid basalt rock, that was blasted to the surface eons ago from New Mexico's many volcanoes. Within minutes our star had ascended enough that its rays were simply blinding; so bright they bleached all color out of the landscape and seared it in a merciless white light. But in those few moments, when it first lifted above the horizon, and for just long enough for a man to stop and bless himself in its rays, it revealed the true beauty of the planet we are privileged to inhabit.

I arrived at Pueblo Pintado to find a lot of people—more than a hundred—attending at least five patients who had come for healing. A squaw dance is a healing ceremony that can involve a number of patients with varying illnesses and conditions and generally goes on for three and a half days. It is one of a number of ceremonies that in the old days people—by which I mean white people—knew as a Navajo Sing, although the Navajos never used such a term. At this one, each of the five patients had a personal hearth in which food was cooked for them, with each hearth presided over by the patient's relatives. Temporary shelters consisting mainly of plywood and plastic sheeting had been thrown up all around the site, and inside these were tables where families could eat. Slightly to one side was an old-fashioned army field kitchen, where most of the cooking was done for the guests, and the hogan where the patients gathered was at the opposite end of the field where the ceremony was being held. When I got close, I could see the walls of the hogan were made of plastic sheeting, although the plastic had been covered with a sort of tarred cloth, which from a distance made the structure look more permanent than it was; and effect that was not accidental.

The field kitchen apart, cooking was being done using traditional trenches. For large-scale communal cooking Navajos cut a trench about two feet deep, four feet wide, and ten feet long, and use the extracted earth to throw up a barrier on the windward side. Wood is burned in the trench from logs placed vertically, not horizontally, in the corners so they burn slowly upward. The charcoal from these logs is spread throughout the trench, but the cooking does not take place in the trench. Instead, the hot charcoal is shoveled out and spread on the ground immediately in front of it. Then large metal grills, approximately half the size of a single bedstead are placed over the charcoal, and the women cook on these. In this way, they do not cook over the open fire and can maintain better control over the temperature of the dishes. Hot coals can be shoveled away to prevent overheating, or shoveled together to increase the heat. It's simple, ingenious, and the food is delicious.

Of course, when I arrived, everyone started looking at me wondering what this white man was doing here. But, when they saw me link up with Blue Horse and Baa, they must have reckoned I was OK, and I was made welcome and fed traditional mutton stew with chili and fry bread for breakfast. Navajos are by nature polite, hospitable and kind, so if you are fortunate enough to be invited to an important ceremony, follow these simple rules: don't take photographs, don't get in the way, and save your stupid questions until it's all over. But do make sure you're invited, because inviting yourself is bound to lead to difficulties.

After breakfast the warriors appeared on horseback, and rode round and round the hogan, whooping and firing their rifles into the air. This is a traditional event at a squaw dance, when on the last day of the ceremony the men saddle up and ride at breakneck speed around the hogan, firing their weapons to scare away the evil spirits that cause illness. These men were mounted on lively horses and rode faster and faster, firing all the time; urging their mounts in ever-tighter circles, until I was convinced the horses must topple over. But the warriors were skillful, and after some fancy riding and shooting, they galloped away again in a cloud of dust and gun smoke.

Blue Horse had brought with him an old-fashioned 0.44 Winchester rifle, one of the short-barreled ones you still see sometimes in cowboy movies, that fires ammo approximately the size of my thumb. He calls it his "buffalo gun", although whether he's ever fired it at any buffalos, I wouldn't know. He'd chosen this particular weapon because, he said, "for a squaw dance you need a big, deep, sound." I couldn't see Blue Horse while the warriors were riding and shooting—he'd disappeared around the other side of the hogan—but I could certainly hear him. Every time he loosed off a shot from the Winchester, which was often, a deep *boom!* rolled across the reservation; they must have been able to hear him for miles around. When the fusillade came to an end, a lot of food and presents in the form of cloth, popcorn, sweets and pop were taken into the hogan.

Shortly afterward, a group of people who at a squaw dance are known as the "visitors", and who were camped separately and fed at a separate kitchen, gathered around the hogan. They were led by a man banging a small skin drum of a type I'd never seen before. It was looped round his neck with a skin loop, and he beat it with a drumstick of a type I had also never seen before. The stick was short and thin and formed into a complete loop at the top—not unlike the way a shepherd's crook loops over, but going all the way around and then back around its own loop a bit more. The sound was soft but compelling, and the visitors, more than 100 of them, gathered around the hogan entrance in an excited crowd, singing and chanting to the rhythm of the drum.

Everyone was excited, and as their excitement grew more people, particularly children, came running to join them from the main camp, and soon people began to throw presents from the hogan. And I do mean throw—they were not passed out gently—and before long, sweets, potato chips, cloth, and goodness knows what else, were sailing through the air to be caught by the outstretched hands of the crowd; many of whom carried plastic bags to keep their goodies in.

I'd brought four big packs of Seven-Up and Coke to give away, but I thought that chucking heavy cans of Coke around might to lead to injury, so I handed them to the eager hands shooting out from all directions. So many hands, that in a journey of less than twenty yards, I gave away more than half the Coke and Seven-Up. Then I ducked inside the hogan, where I found the medicine man in the seat of honor on the west side, the drummers to his right, and various people, including the patients, seated around the walls.

There were four drummers grouped on the men's side, that is to say, on the south side of the hogan and the rest of the space was packed with patients, officials, families and friends. Baa, who had gone into the hogan for some last-minute healing, was sitting wrapped in a traditional woman's blanket on what would normally be the men's side and nearest the door. This is an unusual place for a woman, but I suppose she was sitting there because she'd come late and it was the only place left for her. The hogan was packed not only with people, but piled high with sweets, pop, bolts of cloth and food, all of which were to be given away as gifts. Later, I saw people with as many as ten or more big pieces of cloth wrapped around them, dragging heavy sacks of gifts back to their cars.

When things quietened down a little, I went to sit in my car with Baa's son CJ, who I'd run into again. I hadn't seen him since we'd held the Lightning Way ceremony for him, and he told me more about the results, which he said had benefited him a good deal. He certainly seemed much better.[40] After getting so little sleep during the night, I slept for a couple of hours in the car, and when I awoke the squaw dance was pretty well over, except that more food was being offered. I wasn't hungry, so I waited until Blue Horse and Baa had eaten to follow to them out. I should add that while inside the hogan, people gave money to the drummers. About a dollar each seemed to be the going rate, and I gave mine in quarters (silver, *beeshłagii* in Navajo), which Blue Horse said was the traditional and most appropriate way, and the way in which he usually donated.

We'd traveled separately to the squaw dance because Blue Horse and Baa had intended to drive into Gallup to pick up some supplies when it was over. In the end, I went to Gallup and picked up the supplies and they went home, and when I arrived back at the house, I was in for a big surprise: Blue Horse and Baa were convinced that a skin walker was banging on their back wall.

Navajos almost universally believe in skin walkers, as do many non-Navajos who live near the reservation, and these creatures are greatly feared. They are human shape-shifters who are believed to be capable of transforming themselves into swiftly moving animals, often deer or coyotes, wolves or owls, or even bears, in order to travel around quickly. Skin walkers are often medicine men who have sold out to the evil forces of the dark side, and the danger is that you may be going for help to a medicine man who is also a skin walker intent on doing you harm. But shape-shifters don't have to be medicine men, or even medicine women, and one of the elements that makes them more than usually frightening and dangerous, is that they could be anybody; even the closest members of your family, and you would never know. If all that was not terrifying enough, skin walkers

---

40 For more on this, refer to the Lightning Way in Chapter Three, above, where I included what CJ said about how the ceremony had benefited him.

rob graves to take pieces of the corpse to make spells, and will even drain the urine from a freshly buried body to make powerful curses.

Interestingly, while the skin walker's choice of animals is intended to enable it to travel fast, this choice does not seem to include horses. The obvious conclusion is that the Navajo belief in skin walkers predates the tribe's adoption of the horse sometime in the first half of the eighteenth century. Shape-shifting is not an idea confined to the Navajo, or even North American Indians, it is a world-wide phenomenon. Europe once had a lively tradition of shape-shifting but, with the exception of the werewolf, like so much of the European supernatural tradition it is now largely forgotten

I had heard many stories about skin walkers by now, and been present on at least two occasions when skin walkers were said by the Navajos accompanying me to have manifested themselves, although I saw nothing for certain on either occasion. This, then, was the first time I'd encountered one in circumstances over which I felt I had at least some control. That is to say, in broad daylight, where I could see what was going on around me, and in the company of people like Blue Horse and Baa, who I trusted and whose word I believed.

I looked around the outside of the house and couldn't see any sign of a skin walker—or anyone else—although inside again, I did hear knocking on the outside of the house, and a little while later heard a rifle shot fired in the distance. Blue Horse was convinced it was a skin walker knocking on the wall, and I certainly heard *something* knocking, but at first Baa was more worried it might be a burglar. So, the next time she and Blue Horse said they heard knocking, I went outside again to see for myself.

The knocking this time was coming from the back wall of the house, but as the house had no back entrance, the best I could do was to run out through the front door and round to the back of the house as fast as possible. I failed to apprehend the mystery knocker but, nothing daunted, made a search of the area, even going deep into the trees and surrounding bushes, but found nothing.

After I'd repeated this performance several times to no avail, Blue Horse and Baa called the police. It had never occurred to me that one could call the police in such circumstances but, apparently, Navajos often call the Navajo police to complain of skin walkers. It took some time, but eventually a uniformed woman officer pulled up in a patrol car and took a look around outside. Blue Horse and I went with her, but we didn't find anything. The policewoman told us: "I was called to the people over there—indicating the nearest neighbors—about half an hour ago. They saw something and took a shot at it, but they didn't hit it." That must have been the shot I'd heard earlier.

After she'd gone, I asked Blue Horse if by "it", the officer had meant a skin walker. "Oh yes," he confirmed. "That's what she was talking about." I wanted to be sure because few Navajos, not even uniformed police officers, will usually allow the words "skin walker" to pass their lips even in English, let alone in Navajo, for fear that by merely uttering the name, they might attract these greatly feared creatures to themselves. People generally refer to them as "it" or "those who go around", or some suitable circumlocution to avoid actually speaking the words. People are genuinely terrified of them, and the police respond because they believe in skin walkers too. Not only that, but our neighbors had been bothered by knocking on their walls in exactly the same way—which we, of course, didn't know until the policewoman told us—and had seen something worth taking a shot at; an action the police officer obviously thought was amply justified.

It is worth remembering that in big cities, people who think they're being haunted also sometimes call the police. A poltergeist is allegedly a ghost, or spirit, that throws things around the room and causes chaos. At the *Daily Mirror* newspaper in London some hard-bitten and not easily fooled journalists had a shock one day when a poltergeist caused chaos in the newsroom. At a loss what to do, they called Scotland Yard, which obligingly sent a couple of detectives to investigate.

Then there was the case of the Enfield haunting in North London between 1977 and 1979, now made famous by books and the film *The Conjuring 2*. Children, furniture, and much else besides, were regularly flung around the rooms to the terror of the family who occupied the house. My former colleague, the newspaper photographer Graham Morris, was convinced this was a genuine haunting. Not a man easily bamboozled, Morris witnessed a good deal of what happened in the house, and his conviction was only strengthened when he was hit in the face and badly bruised by a flying brick of Lego—a piece he was sure could not have been thrown by anyone in the room.

The family in the Enfield haunting, the tough journalists at the *Daily Mirror*, and the Navajo people of the Southwest, far-flung though they be, are united in finding the presence of a police officer reassuring in such circumstances. I have no idea what the police are supposed to do about errant spirits and demonic entities, and I'm sure the officers don't have a clue either; it's difficult enough dealing with crime in this world, without extending the long arm of the law into the next. Even so, Blue Horse and Baa were grateful the officer came out to them, and were much reassured.

Shortly after this strange event, a friend of Blue Horse's named Notah Clah, who lived in the far north east of the reservation, told me how his aunt had made a dramatic death bed confession that she herself was a skin walker, and had been the cause of almost all the evils that had befallen the family. I knew Notah well, he was an extremely steady and deep-thinking man, who held strong religious convictions, and I can think of no reason why he should want to make up the events he related to me. While I was already aware that his first wife had committed suicide, I didn't know that he attributed her death to witching and a skin walker until he told me this story. A story that demonstrates why these entities are held to be so dangerous, how deeply they are embedded in Navajo life and culture, and why Navajos fear them so much.

I should explain that on a previous occasion Notah had told me his wife suffered terrible abuse as a child, including sexual abuse, and that it was her inability to come to terms with this, or to seek traditional methods of protection from evil, that led to her eventual suicide. From a Navajo point of view, these are not necessarily separate occurrences, but a sequence in which the abuse, the skin walker, and the refusal to seek protection, are all linked in a deadly chain of witchcraft and cursing that eventually results in death. Unusually, when telling me his story, Notah used the English term "skin walker" which, as I have said, is a term Navajos will rarely, if ever, allow to cross their lips. The reason he did so, I think, was that we were in a holy place when he talked about this, so he probably felt protected and, also, speaking the words in English is not so bad as saying the same thing in Navajo. But, most likely, it was because he was talking to a white man from England, and to make sure I understood, he chose not to use any of the usual circumlocutions in English. I would have understood whatever form of words he had chosen, but I fully appreciate why he wanted to be sure.

Notah began: "One day, my late wife and I were looking out of the window and we saw a skin walker. It was a strange, wizened-looking creature that ran into our sweat lodge. I went to get protection (a ceremony performed by a medicine man to ward off evil), and the medicine man said there was something in the sweat, so we went there and we found some really bad stuff hidden right in among the stones. It was very bad. But my wife wouldn't go to get protection. I asked her five times, but she wouldn't go. That's why she died, because she didn't get the protection.

"On another occasion, when my aunt lay dying, she confessed that she was a skin walker and admitted to all the bad things she'd done. Skin walkers sometimes confess on their death beds in the hope of escaping punishment in the next world, but what she said came as a great surprise to me because I'd never suspected her. There was a lot of incest and cursing in the family, and she told me now that she'd cursed me, but I'd no idea she'd been doing all these things, and neither had anyone else. After she died, we had to set to and try to undo the evil my aunt had done, and it was difficult because the evil had to be sent to the north. Many of the people who'd done the witching, or asked for it to be done, had also died, but even when they're dead the evil goes on working, so you have to send it to the north, because that's where evil ones go; and so you send the evil they left here back to them in the north."

Navajo dead travel to the west, the land of the setting sun, but bad people go to the north, which is viewed as a kind of cold black hell. But that wasn't all. Notah was an important member of a branch of the Native

American Church, and he told me how a young man for whom he and the other church members had once entertained high hopes, had sold himself to the dark side.

"We let him run NAC meetings and he seemed really good, but then things began to happen. I gave him twelve feathers to make a prayer fan for me, but when he gave it back, there were only eleven. (The implication here is not so much that one feather has been stolen—although feathers for fans are expensive—but that because of its close personal connection, the feather could be used for cursing Notah). Another time, stuff of mine disappeared right after a meeting. My gourd and my whistle disappeared, and some other stuff, and it later turned out this man had taken it. He was trying to get rid of me so he could take over the church, so he conspired with a skin walker, and they sent a beautiful woman to me to try to lure me away. She was a white woman, a beautiful woman, and she wanted me to go away to Ohio with her. I didn't realize they'd sent her to me, and I asked her to marry me, but she wouldn't; not so long as I stayed here and remained with the church, because they wanted me out of the way.

"A year later, she asked me to marry her, and again she wanted me to move away to Ohio. Again, I refused, and then everything broke up and I went to see a medicine man. He made the skin walker's face appear in the fire, just like Blue Horse can make faces appear in the fire, and that's the first time I knew my neighbor was a skin walker. Then he made the young man's face appear, the one we had such high hopes about in the church, and I could see he was conspiring with the skin walker. Then he made a woman's face appear, and it was the face of the woman I loved. That was when the medicine man told me they had sent her to lure me away to Ohio, so that they could take over the church as a cover for their evil, and have the land I have here in New Mexico, but the medicine protected me.

"None of what happened was the white lady's fault. They witched her to do these things and she would have known nothing about their plans. Five years later she called me out of the blue and said, 'Do you know who this is?' I said, 'Yes, I know'. We're friends now and that's good, but the medicine man sent back the evil to that young man and now he's in jail.

He was convicted of rape, and he'll be there for a long time. You see, we can send the evil back to where it came from, and it will rebound on these people ten times stronger than it was when they sent it to us."

* * *

A woman came from Phoenix to ask Blue Horse for help. A lot of bad things had happened to her and, in essence, she was convinced she was being haunted by a skin walker. She said that she often woke up feeling "itchy down there," pointing to her genitals. "Like I've been doing it, except I haven't," she said. The implication being that the skin walker was having sex with her while she was asleep, and she believed the haunting was related to her falling out with some Navajo people at work, who in retaliation had cursed her.

This was an interesting experience for me, because I saw two things in the fire that turned out to be true. I distinctly saw a car crash. Then, while I was looking at it, CJ brought in some fresh charcoal and piled it on top. This covered up the car crash, so I guessed the crash had taken place some time ago, which turned out to be correct. The woman said that sometimes she felt so stressed, she felt sure she was going to have a heart attack; and while she was talking about this, I could see something in the fire that really puzzled me. It was an odd-looking, oblong-shaped object, with a faint blue metal tinge to it. I was sure it was connected to the woman, and connected in some way to the heart problem she was telling us about, but for the life of me I couldn't figure out what the object was. I was on the point of asking about it, when Blue Horse decided it was time to do some healing and the opportunity was lost.

He told the woman that her problems had to do with yucca, of which he could see plenty in the fire (as could I), and he took his pipe and began to suck, and soon he pulled from her the longest piece of yucca fiber I've ever seen taken from a patient. It was about nine inches long, or perhaps more.

"Do you know why it's so long?" Blue Horse asked her, as we sat looking at it in some awe.

"Because it was wrapped around my heart?" she replied, uncertainly.

"That's right. It was to give you a heart attack, and this is what you can feel tightening around your heart when you get so stressed," Blue Horse said.

The cedar was almost over before I had a chance to ask about the strange object. I'd begun to think that it might be a child's toy of some sort, and when I first asked our patient she looked blank. So I began to describe it carefully, but it was not until I mentioned the metallic tinge that she suddenly gasped and blurted out: "I found a Leatherman's tool under the bed!" At last, I realized that what I was seeing was a Leatherman multipurpose tool, which explained why it had a metallic tinge.[41]

This tool has an extremely sharp blade, and could have been hidden under her bed only with the intention that the blade would stab her ritually through the heart. In this world of witchcraft and evil, in which Blue Horse and I were so deeply engaged, there was no chance the tool could have been left there by accident. She knew that very well, and understood perfectly that it had been placed there to harm her. She also knew that it could have been placed under her bed only by someone very close to her, or by a shape-shifting entity like a skin walker; which did not preclude the person close to her, and the skin walker, being one and the same. Now, perhaps, you are beginning to understand, just a little, why Navajos find these creatures so utterly terrifying.

* * *

Before leaving this topic of skin walkers, I want to recount a personal episode that demonstrates how events can conspire in such a way, as to cause anyone to wonder if one might be after you. But first I should put my cards on the table. My starting point for all skin walker discussions is my friend the late Emerson Jackson, who was an acute observer of the world, and whose sound judgment and good opinions I valued highly.

---

41 A Leatherman is an American multipurpose tool. A similar idea to a Swiss army knife, but better in my opinion.

Once, when we were out on a remote part of the reservation, the subject of skin walkers came up, and because we were alone, I ventured to ask if he believed they were real.

"What? That a man can turn himself into a deer, or an owl, or a wolf?" Emerson scoffed. "No, I don't believe that." Then, he dropped his voice, and added: "But you and me are probably the only two people for a hundred miles around who don't believe it, so maybe we'd better keep quiet."

For better, or for worse, the following is the story of a strange incident that happened to me when I was living in Farmington, on the north-east edge of the Navajo reservation in northern New Mexico. The town's main function is to supply labor and services to the nearby oil and gas field, but I was staying there because I'd been doing some work with traditional Navajos on that part of the reservation.

Driving between the reservation and Farmington was like driving from one world to another and back every day. One was tough, demanding, raw, invigorating and sparsely populated, while the other was tough, demanding, raw and had bars, shopping malls, paved roads, hamburger joints, traffic lights and a population of forty-five thousand. While I had my guard up against witching, cursing, and evil entities while on the reservation, it went down when I turned into the quiet little street off 20th Street, where I rented a small furnished ground-floor apartment. It was so small that guests had to sleep in a cupboard (which admittedly was quite a large cupboard, but that's another story.)

I make the point about dropping my guard, because I was vaguely aware that I'd upset a powerful medicine man who lived not far from Chinle and the Canyon de Chelly, which are in the heartlands of the reservation. What I did to upset him I don't know—it certainly wasn't deliberate—but for whatever reason he'd taken against me. Such men are believed capable of sending skin walkers after those they believe have offended them, or they may be skin walkers themselves.

One defining feature of skin walkers is that they bang on the doors and walls of your dwelling. Traditionally, that would be the walls and doors of a hogan, but skin walkers, like everything else, move with the times, and the people I'd spent the day with had told me how one of their relations had been troubled by a skin walker in the big city of Albuquerque. It had repeatedly banged on the door of the man's upstairs apartment in a modern high-rise block, and had kept him awake for nights on end.

I was tired and went to bed early, and was just drifting off to sleep when I was startled awake again by a loud banging on my door. Immediately prior to this, through the gathering clouds of sleep I'd heard, or thought I'd heard, someone walk by my window; hardly an unusual occurrence on the ground floor of a block of rented homes. As I didn't know anyone in the town, I thought perhaps my neighbor, whom I'd scarcely met, had come on some errand. My second thought was to stay where I was in the hope he would go away. There was no further knocking and thinking my neighbor had gone, after several minutes I rolled over and drifted off to sleep. How long for I don't know, but I was awakened with a start by another loud burst of knocking. Four hard raps: *knock-knock-knock-knock!* It was astonishing how loud and hard those knocks were; much harder and louder than the average neighbor might be expected to knock on the door of someone he scarcely knew.

Wide awake now, I cocked an ear waiting to see if whoever it was would knock again—in which case I would have to get up and answer the door. But no more knocking came. So, I turned over once more and had just begun to drift off—when I was wrenched back to consciousness by another loud series of knocks on the door. By now I was beginning to become slightly alarmed. It was midnight and Farmington has a fairly high crime rate; so I reckoned it was unlikely anyone knocking on my door at that time of night would have my best interests at heart. With that in mind I stayed in bed, the knocking ceased, and I began to drift off once more. Sleep was coming more slowly now, because one ear was permanently on alert and, sure enough, just as I was about to fall asleep: KNOCK-KNOCK! This time two hard raps at the door startled me back to consciousness.

It was about now that the term "skin walker" first entered my mind. I knew they came and banged on your door, but I had no idea they could bang so loud. Nor had I ever thought a skin walker might follow me back to a modern apartment in a modern town with street lights, cars, traffic lights, restaurants, cinemas and the whole panoply of modern life. Ancient evil amid conspicuous modernity seemed as incongruous as it was unlikely; nevertheless, something, or someone, was knocking on my door. Then there was the matter of the doorbell, which was clearly illuminated at night. If someone was genuinely trying to attract my attention, surely that someone would ring the bell as well as knock on the door? Why I didn't just get up and open the door, I can't tell you. Most likely it was because I was tired, and hoped that whoever was knocking would go away and leave me in peace. So, I lay where I was, but the knocking continued at regular intervals, so regular, that I began to notice they occurred every fifteen minutes: loud, unmistakable and scary.

It is at times like this—alone in the middle of the night, in a town on the edge of a place where strange things undoubtedly happen—that one gets thrown back on basics. In this case basics meant: could I really believe that man can turn himself into a bear, or an owl, or some other animal, and come knocking on my door in the middle of the night? The answer, of course, was no—but that did not stop the knocking, and while the knocking went on, there was no possibility of sleep. I knew that no prankster would spend several hours knocking on my door to no result; my neighbor must long ago have gone to bed, and so I didn't know what to make of it. Then, after yet another burst of loud knocks, I'd finally had enough.

Slipping silently out of bed and walking noiselessly across the room to the door; without a sound, I slipped back the lock and stood motionless behind the door. One hand on the doorknob was ready to instantly throw it open, the other was with fist cocked and ready to fire. It was with keen anticipation that I awaited the next knock; then I would be through the door like lightning to confront whoever, or whatever, was on the other side, and the mystery would be solved.

But after waiting nearly an hour, no knock had come; which was extraordinary given that the knocking had been coming approximately every fifteen minutes for five hours. So, I gave up and went back to bed and…

you guessed it...no sooner was I in bed than KNOCK-KNOCK-KNOCK! Three raps this time, but they were the loudest yet.

Furious, I leaped out of bed, ran to the door, threw it open, and instantly came to a dead halt. There in front of me, stopping all further progress, was not a skin walker, but the metal mesh of the outer screen door, and it was firmly shut and bolted from the inside. Baffled, I slowly closed the door, sat on the sofa, and tried to think. I'd forgotten about the screen door, which I'd automatically locked before going to bed. The screen was made of light but strong metal, with not enough space between the interwoven strips for anyone to get a finger through, much less a hand. No one could have been knocking on the wooden front door, because no one could get past the screen to knock on it. Yet, it was knocking on my front door that I had repeatedly heard.

This was a real puzzle and, reluctant to go back to bed, I sat on the sofa behind the door and pondered. Then I had another uncomfortable thought. I'd once met with the chief exorcist of the Roman Catholic Church in England, who told me that almost all the cases of demonic possession referred to him were really cases of drug or alcohol abuse, or mental illness. But there were a few, he assured me, that were cases of genuine demonic possession. This was perhaps not the best moment to be remembering that if there were genuine cases of demonic possession, there must be genuine demons; and if there were genuine demons, there might be genuine skin walkers, and if there were genuine skin walkers, one of them might be knocking on my door!

I told myself to calm down. By now it was nearly 4:00 am, and as I sat on the sofa in silence, it was the silence that gave me the clue that unlocked the mystery. The sofa was near the door at the opposite end of the room from the bed, and it began to dawn on me that while I'd been sitting on the sofa thinking, there had been no knocking. Similarly, when I'd waited behind the door in ambush for an hour, no knock had come. Had the creature sensed my presence and backed off until I was once again in bed, or was something else going on? To test the idea, I walked back across the room and threw myself on the bed.

Within a few minutes, I heard another series of hard knocks apparently on the door. I went back to the sofa and waited: and all knocking ceased. My theory was beginning to harden into a certainty. It had rained heavily in recent days, rare in these parts, and I think that what had happened was that the damp had penetrated into the wooden beams holding up the floor of my apartment. As a result, the beams warped, and the banging I heard was the beams straightening themselves as they dried out in the warmth of the night. If they were drying at a uniform rate, which would be a reasonable assumption, then the bangs they generated would come at regular intervals; in this case about every fifteen minutes. But why did the noise stop when I went to the other end of the room?

The reason, I think, is the extra weight I placed on the beams when I walked to that end of the room, was just enough to jam them and stop them from moving. This would account for why the banging stopped whenever I walked to that end of the room, and restarted when I walked back and climbed into bed again. The knocking continued for three successive nights, but became progressively weaker until, on the third night, it was barely audible, and after that it stopped for good.

Do I really think warped wooden beams are a satisfactory explanation for this strange event? Well … it's plausible; I'll say no more than that. Blue Horse had his own explanation, of course. The skin walker was real, he said, and had been sent to get me, but because I was not afraid it had failed.

"They feed on fear," he told me cheerfully, after I'd recounted the story. "It wanted to scare you, eat your fear, and grow big and strong so it could kill you. But you weren't scared, so it starved and got weaker every night, and that's why it went away again."

That incident had its worrying moments, but there was another in which I really did convince myself, at least for a short while, that unknown occult forces were ranged against me; and with rather less excuse than in the case above, I'm a little ashamed to admit. In many ways, this second incident was far more dangerous, although it ended in pure farce.

It occurred after Blue Horse and I had been called out to deal with a witching up north in Arizona. While we were driving home in the dark it began to snow heavily, just as we were heading over a pass in the hills not far from Window Rock, the Navajo tribal capital. Soon it was blowing a blizzard and I could hardly see a thing. Blue Horse's advice was to "follow the white line up the middle of the road", which might have been sound enough in the days when there were half a dozen cars on the reservation; but now was completely crazy, especially as some oncoming vehicles were doing the same thing!

It was the night of the 23rd of May, which is late in the year for snow, let alone for a serious snowstorm. I'd been up against witchcraft all day and tired, hungry and irritable, it somehow became possible—on a high pass, in the dark, in a whirling blizzard—to believe that a malevolent witch had conjured up the storm to kill me. It provided an interesting insight into the human mind (in this case mine), that for almost all its hundreds of thousands of years of existence, so far as we know, never had cause to doubt for a moment that witches and witchcraft are real. Our present state of disbelief is, in fact, an historical aberration, and if my experience that night is anything to go by, it may be less than a couple of brain cells deep.

Unlike most Europeans and Americans, I'm surrounded by people who have no doubts about the existence of witches and witchcraft. People who in circumstances such as this storm would say, truly believing it, that if my car had gone off the road and Blue Horse and I had been killed, that we were the victims of a vengeful witch. People who honestly believe that storms can be conjured Prospero-like from the air, and that the lives of many good men and women have been ended in exactly this way by witches and witchcraft. Usually, I brush off these kinds of thoughts but, for reasons I can't explain, for a few minutes that night, as the blizzard increased to a whiteout and I could see nothing but a blinding wall of whirling snowflakes; I came to believe it too.

The storm quickly took on an evil intensity that grew with each passing second, until the blizzard reached a point where I could see nothing but a solid wall of snow. It was so thick that the beams of my headlights bounced off it, reflecting the light back into my eyes and blinding me. Switching to dipped headlights made little difference and blinded, disoriented, and with a feeling of desperation rising within me, there came a moment in this maelstrom, when I somehow convinced myself that witches were trying to kill me. It came on fast, without any warning: one moment I was my normal self, the next I was convinced I was the victim of witchcraft.

"I'm pulling off the road," I told Blue Horse. "I can't see a thing."

"You don't have to pull off. Keep going straight ahead," he advised, knowing the pass a lot better than I did, and not understanding the source of my distress.

Blinded, terrified that I might run into an equally blinded driver coming the other way, and now sure of a witchcraft plot to murder me; I was so far beyond the rational that for a moment I thought Blue Horse might be a witch too.

"I'm not going on. I'll be killed," I told him, slowing the car to a crawl. A few seconds later, seeing through a tiny gap in the all-enveloping snow a narrow path leading off the road to the right, I turned onto it and gratefully came to a halt.

"What's the matter?" asked Blue Horse, looking puzzled. He had not the slightest idea what was wrong with me, and to him the storm didn't look so bad.

"The witches," I said, pointing to the whirling storm around us. "Someone's trying to get me killed." And the "someone" in this case did not exempt my friend, teacher, and the medicine man whose apprentice I was, who was sitting beside me without the slightest idea what I was going on about.

Before he could say anything, an indeterminate object of huge mass loomed out of the storm and came to a towering halt only inches behind my car. If I'd had a gun, I would have reached for it at that moment, but I had not, and a second later my Nissan was bathed in a fierce glare that came flooding through the rear window and filled the interior with a harsh white light: it was accompanied by the angry honking of a car horn.

"You're blocking his driveway," Blue Horse observed laconically.

In that moment, everything snapped back to normal. Witches were no longer necessary to explain that on a high pass, I had been caught in a late-spring snowstorm, and mistakenly pulled off the road into someone's driveway. That someone knew the road a lot better than I did, and had turned off his lights to avoid the kind of blinding white-out I'd experienced. Now, further progress toward his warm hearth, warm food and shelter, was being blocked by some idiot parked in his driveway and so, not unnaturally, he was flashing his headlights and honking his horn. Without another word, I pulled over, and a big dual-wheeled truck that towered over my Nissan, drove quickly by without a word or a wave from the man behind the wheel.

"Can we go home now?" Blue Horse asked quietly.

"Sure," I said, feeling somewhat deflated.

Reversing the Xterra back onto the road, I drove slowly and carefully home through the snow. No longer attributing acts of nature to acts of witchcraft, and chastened by the knowledge that I could so easily become the victim of irrational thoughts, I tried to view the incident as a handy lesson. Yes, there are Navajo witches. Yes, they practice witchcraft: but can they conjure snow storms and aim them at those whom they wish to destroy? I had no proof of that. But I did have proof that a man with a lot of experience in this area could be convinced against his will—if only for a few minutes—that such a thing is possible.

IX

Today a man came to sweat with us who is a Cheyenne. The sweat lodge is Blue Horse's favorite recreation and he has a Sioux sweat, built after the fashion of the Sioux or Lakota tribe, which today this is the design probably most widely used among the tribes. The Sioux sweat has the stones placed in a hole in the center of the lodge, while the stones in a traditional Navajo sweat are on the left, the south side, as you go in. While there are variations in design, and variations in the sacred attributions of the sweat lodges among the different tribes, so far as I know, they all have their entrances facing east towards the rising sun. Today, I found this is not true of the Cheyenne, and our visitor explained why.

He said that "after the war with the soldiers," the Cheyenne decided to change the opening of their sweat lodges to the west. The reason was that so many of their people had died in the fighting, and so many spirits had journeyed west to the setting sun; the survivors wanted the spirits to be able to see into the sweat lodge, so they could see there were still Cheyenne in the world, and they still maintained their traditional ways. The elderly gentleman who told us this, said he'd heard the story from his grandfather. At a guess, his grandfather was born around 1900, about twenty years after the fighting with the United States ended, and he would have heard the story of the Cheyenne's battles from survivors who had witnessed them. Later, I spent a little time among the Northern Cheyenne in Lame Deer, Montana, where I found their sweat lodges did indeed open to the west.

The flight of the Northern Cheyenne from Oklahoma in 1878, under their chiefs Little Wolf and Morning Star, also known as Dull Knife, during which they fought their way home twelve hundred miles across hostile territory to Montana, is one of the most extraordinary feats of courage and endurance in the annals of human history. Largely ignored by American historians, and even by Hollywood, it deserves to be far better known than it is.

The next day, a woman came asking for a cedar. She was quite old and could hardly walk, and she had to be assisted into the house by her son, who was no spring chicken himself. I was ready to help Blue Horse, but the son wanted to do everything himself, so I sat back and let him. Then, after the divination, Blue Horse tried to suck some bad stuff from the woman's knee, but she experienced severe pain when he pressed his pipe to the joint. When he attempted to take some stuff from her chest, the pain was so great that she fainted and slid off her chair onto the floor.

I wanted to lay her down on the floor to recover, but Blue Horse and her son had other ideas. Blue Horse lifted her half upright so that her knees were resting on the floor then, while Baa and the woman's son held her torso upright, he fanned her vigorously with his medicine fan and blew rapid blasts on his whistle. After a short while, during which the woman's condition didn't seem to change much, Blue Horse suddenly shouted out loud "*Aoo!*" meaning "Yes!" in Navajo. As if on a signal, the woman awoke from her fainting spell and was, with some difficulty, helped back into the chair. A few minutes later, she declared herself to be feeling much better, and was soon well enough to walk from the house to her car without assistance. Her progress was slow, but she was walking noticeably better than when she'd arrived.

This turned out to be the start of an unusually busy day. I don't think we ever carried out so many cedars, or so quickly; it was one after another, as one patient went out and another came in. At one time, there were four trucks lined up outside the door, each filled with people wanting help. In one of these was Colindra Slowtalk, who came with her father from a tiny settlement deep inside the reservation in Arizona. Mr. Slowtalk said he'd once grown corn for a living, but conditions had become drier of recent years, and there was no longer enough moisture for his crop to mature.

For several years, he complained, whenever he tried to grow corn, it rarely grew above knee height. He didn't blame global warming, he blamed the bilagaana, "who makes everything go wrong".

Colindra worked as a technician for a big chemical company in Phoenix and was having trouble at work. She felt people were trying to get her fired, and she was also having trouble with her boyfriend. She had one child, she said, and told us she was a hand trembler in her own right. Colindra and her family all spoke Navajo, so at first I didn't understand a lot of what was going on. Then Blue Horse announced we were going over to the Slowtalk house that evening to find and remove some curses.

But it took time to deal with all the other demands for help we were getting at the house; so it was well into the evening by the time we reached the Slowtalk home. It didn't help that now was the time of the great Navajo mud. Twice a year, in spring and fall, parts of the reservation turn into giant mud patches. Navajo mud is unlike other mud. Thick, red and glutinous, it gets everywhere and when it dries it sets hard as concrete, particularly on your car. It will ruin your shoes in thirty seconds flat and if you slip over in it, the only remedy is to strip and throw all your clothes in the washer; because it will be impossible to scrape it off. The only descriptions of mud I've read that come even close to the Navajo version, are those written by German generals fighting in Russia during the Second World War. I always found it hard to believe a tank could be stopped by something so simple as mud, let alone an entire tank army: But I don't anymore!

Tires lose all traction in this gruesome mire and spin around aimlessly spraying mud in all directions, while the vehicle pirouettes in an endless circle. The driver has no control of either steering or brakes, and experienced Navajos take their hands off the wheel if their car gains traction, and let it find its own way through the ruts: all the while praying that it doesn't sink in over the axles.

After the ground around the house had been chewed up by all the other vehicles, I had to get my car out of Blue Horse's paddock and onto the nearest paved road. Normally, this takes about thirty seconds; this time it took more than thirty minutes. At one point my little Xterra went round and round in circles backwards, and I seriously thought we'd have to abandon the trip. It is no exaggeration to say that after thirty minutes of struggle, I'd hardly moved ten yards from Blue Horse's front door: and those ten yards were in the wrong direction. Eventually, I did manage to drive out through a back way we rarely use; and though there was more trouble on the big hill, we eventually made it to Colindra's place where her mother had food waiting for us.

After we'd eaten, Colindra went to move her car and managed to drive about three yards before it stuck fast in the mud, broadside across her parents' driveway. As the driveway was shared with neighbors, we had to move the car, but it defied all our efforts. Eventually, with the help of the neighbors, we did manage to get it to firmer ground and, gratefully, went inside to start the cedar. Then, when we were seated on the floor around the fireplace, Colindra produced a medicine bag of her own, and her hand began to tremble over everything, fluttering wildly like a small bird.

Hand trembling is a specialty of Navajo women, and the only time I've seen it done by a man is when Blue Horse does it; and he typically does it in a fairly controlled manner. By contrast, Colindra's hand seemed uncontrollable, and her thin arms and long slim fingers, only served to emphasize the almost manic fluttering movements of her hand.

After a while, Blue Horse detected a curse hidden in Colindra's car. So, we all trooped outside again and, as it was pitch black and the moon had not yet risen, Blue Horse called for a flashlight to search Colindra's car. The curse was hidden under the plastic trim on the floor of the driver's side, and when we took it apart it consisted of a piece of snakeskin wrapped around an arrowhead of black obsidian. This arrowhead looked far better made than the crude efforts we usually encounter, and had thin thread Navajo woolen thread rapped around the tang to bind the snake skin: it looked like an expert job and, unlike many of the curses we find, this one looked freshly made.

But closer inspection showed the arrowhead was not made of stone after all, but had been cut from a piece of deer's hoof, which is black and shiny like obsidian. It looked good on first inspection because it had been carved with a knife, which is a lot easier than chipping a stone, but it was a cheap imitation of the real thing. Deer hoof is not good, and is frequently included in curses, but it has nowhere near the power to curse as a stone arrow head properly made. It was puzzling that, despite this, the curse had obviously been put together by an expert, and at first Blue Horse wondered if whoever had paid to have Colindra cursed, had been the victim of a professional trick by the witchman.

"You can't trust anybody these days," was his comment, which made me laugh out loud.

Then I heard him muttering to himself, and he looked around, and up and down the street, but it was too dark to see much.

"What's the matter?" I asked

At first he just shrugged, so I didn't pay much attention, and after putting the curse into my bag of wood ash I thought we were finished for the night. Blue Horse, however, was not satisfied, and he wanted to go to the top of a nearby hill to say prayers. So, Colindra, Mr. Slowtalk, Blue Horse and I climbed into my car, and with me driving we were soon making our way up a narrow dirt track that took us to the top of the hill. There we turned left, and for a mile or so traveled on another narrow track that ran along the hilltop, until Blue Horse told me to pull off the track and stop, and then we all got out.

We'd stopped in a little pull-off where the car could not be seen by anyone driving along the track. From where we were, we could see over most of the surrounding countryside or, at least, we would have been able to if there had been any moon. A faint breeze was blowing and there was not a cloud in the sky as we stood in the dark under the blazing stars. But their light was so faint it was not possible to see more than a few yards in any direction; and when Blue Horse lined us up to say prayers, although he couldn't have been more than six yards from me, I couldn't see him at all. He prayed for the family under the open sky and the stars, and then blew his medicine man's whistle and blessed us all with his eagle feather.

With the prayers over, we were returning to the car when headlights suddenly appeared in the distance, coming toward us fast along the track. At this, the Navajos, including Blue Horse, panicked. (I didn't, but only because I little appreciated the danger, and at first had no idea what was happening.)

"It's them!" Mr. Slowtalk cried. "It's the people doing this to us. They're coming to see what we're up to!"

"Quick," Blue Horse ordered. "Get in the car!"

I scrambled into the driver's seat, and everyone piled in as Blue Horse urged: "Drive, Charles. Drive like hell!"

The suspect car was coming straight toward us from the direction we'd been traveling towards. To get away, I needed to turn around and out-race them, but there was nowhere to turn on such a narrow dirt road, and no time either. Instead, I pressed the accelerator hard, and drove straight towards the on-coming vehicle. The track was just wide enough for two cars to pass side by side but, hemmed in by the dark and with the other car's headlights aimed straight at us, there was little room for error and every possibility of a massive crash of metal.

"They must've had someone up there listening to us," I heard Mr. Slowtalk say from the back seat, and he sounded about as panicky as a man can get.

"Don't stop for them whatever you do, Charles," Blue Horse yelled. "Keep going and drive like hell!"

It is not unknown for witchmen to look into their own fires to see when good medicine men are undoing their evil, and I'd been present on another occasion when the witchman turned up to see what was going on, and had caused similar panic. Now it looked like we were heading for a high-speed showdown. With only seconds to go before our vehicles must meet, Colindra was sobbing loudly in the passenger seat beside me. She had her head on her knees, covered with her hands, in what the airline industry calls the "crash position": I rather wished I could have done the same. Then, at the last moment, the other car swerved slightly to the right: or I did. Or we both did. I couldn't be sure which it was. For a fraction of a second my headlights lit up a blue-colored car, covered in the red mud of the reservation, and with two Navajo men sitting in the front. But that was all I saw, as our two vehicles flashed by each other at a combined speed that must have been close to ninety miles an hour. A suicidally high speed given the narrowness of the track, the darkness, and the treacherous mud.

The other car had only a single rear light, and I watched for a few seconds as it receded in my mirror. I kept driving at about forty miles an hour, which was as fast as I dared, and then I heard Colindra say: "They've stopped. They've stopped exactly where we were praying." She was looking back through the rear window.

"They want to know what we've been doing," Mr. Slowtalk said.

They were all looking through the back window now, but when I looked in the rear-view mirror I could see nothing, probably because the car had driven off the track at the same place we had been. We drove on for a while until Mr. Slowtalk had recovered himself enough to direct me back to his house using a different route.

I've never been able to understand what that car was doing on top of the hill. Colindra and her father assured me that hardly one vehicle a week used the same track, which led nowhere except along the top of the hill; and there was no reason for anyone to be up there, least of all at that time of the night. Blue Horse, Colindra and her father, all agreed on this, and also that the car had pulled in at the place where we had been praying. They were equally sure as to why: the two men I glimpsed as our cars roared by each other were witchmen, and they knew what we were up to.

I had my doubts about this line of reasoning, figuring it could have been just one of those weird things. Then, as I drove him home, Blue Horse began to explain.

"That curse we found in the girl's car was made to look bad," he told me as we drove along. "Like the guy didn't know what he was doing, or wasn't doing it properly. But it didn't look right, and I thought maybe there was more to it. That's why I wanted to go up the hill and pray about it, protect them people if there was some trap. But they were waiting for us, see? They knew what we was gonna do."

"How could they know?"

"Same way we do. They have their fireplace too. We're gonna have to be real careful. Specially you."

I asked him why especially me? And then, in one devastating burst, he told me of the secret doubts he'd been harboring about me for a long time.

"People been talking about you," he said. "When you first come here, you brought lots of protection. White men are real difficult to witch because they don't believe this stuff, but now you're becomin' one of us. You're losing the protection you got just from being a white man. Now you're more like a native; now they can see where you're weak, and they're gonna go for it."

"Where I'm weak?" I asked, not understanding.

"You ain't scared."

"Not being scared is being weak?" I didn't understand and, in any case, I was nowhere near so certain as he seemed to be that I wasn't scared. It's hard to be in tight spots like the one we'd just been through and not feel a little fear.

"Not being scared is not understanding what's going on around here," Blue Horse scolded me, sounding extremely tense and serious. "You think you're above it all. You think because you're clever, an educated man, none of this can touch you. But I'm tellin' you, you can't mess with the stuff we mess with and not be scared. No one can, not if you understand it, and that's where you're weak. After all this time, you still don't understand what you're gettin' into; you don't understand its power, and you don't care. They know that, and that's what they'll work on. They'll set a trap for you, just like tonight, and you'll walk right into it because you ain't scared; and by the time you scared man, it's gonna be too late!"

I was flabbergasted and confused.

"But when I wasn't scared of the skin walker in Farmington you said that was good," I protested. "You said it couldn't get me because I wasn't sacred and it couldn't feed on my fear."

"It's two different things," he replied. "The evil of the witchman and the evil of them goin' around ain't the same."

"But you told me that witchmen can turn themselves into skin walkers!"

"Some witchmen can," he cautioned. "And some bad medicine men can. But not all of them. When a witchman goes around he's not a witchman no more, and when he turns back again, he's not goin' around no more. Remember, people who ain't witchmen or medicine men can be goin' around too. You have to understand the difference."

Then he gave me detailed instructions on how to shoot a skin walker should another one come after me: or "when" it came after me, as he put it.

"The only way you can kill one is with a silver bullet. People will tell you all different things, but a silver bullet is the only one can kill those goin' around. Most people don't have no silver bullet, so you need to tip your bullets with wood ash. Load your gun with hollow-point ammo. Put a bit of fine ash in the hollows and melt some wax to drip in and seal up the hollow, that way the ash will keep in. You can't kill one with that kind of bullet, but you can hurt them bad, and then they got to go away and mend. From now on, never go out except you're carrying a gun loaded the right way, 'cos they're cooking up bad stuff for you man, I'm tellin' you."

Rightly, or wrongly, I ignored this dangerous advice. I wasn't sure it was legal, but I was damn sure I didn't want a loaded pistol permanently stuck in my waistband. And if people were going to cast spells against me, or curse me, I still didn't think it would do me much harm. What worried me a lot more was Blue Horse's criticism that I'd not fully entered into his world. I knew he was right, and that I did see myself as separated by mental distance from the events in which I took part. Despite all I'd been through, everything I'd experienced and taken part in, at heart I remained an observer. And there was a good reason for this.

This observer status was extremely important to me, because an observer sets out to record the truth without fear or favor; and this is the traditional position of the reporter. The reporter should be an observer, he may in some circumstances have to become a participant in events, but the reporter should never become a partisan, someone who writes propaganda for one side or the other. If he does, the reporter loses all objectivity and becomes one of *them*, when he ought to be the representative of all of *you*. [42] I didn't think my recording of what I observed among the Navajo people

---

42 Which is how I see myself, relaying to readers details of events they are unable to witness for themselves. This position of observer neutrality is, of course, an ideal and in reality, in the rough and tumble of events, journalists may well become participants and even partisans; although I would encourage them to avoid the latter as much as possible.

would benefit from me becoming a hand-trembler, or a road-man qualified to run peyote medicine ceremonies, or by acquiring spirit guides for myself, even if such things were actually possible. Acquiring the knowledge of such matters: yes. Becoming one: no. For if I did, I would have moved from observer, to participant, to partisan. Instead of doing my best to explore this extraordinary world of Navajo medicine and magic, and returning to honestly describe whatever I had discovered, I would have abandoned my outsider's view. With it would go my objectivity and that, I believed, would not only damage my ability to record events dispassionately, but destroy my credibility as a witness.

However, there was no denying that I had become a participant in Navajo medicine, as this book amply demonstrates. Blue Horse's complaint was that having become a participant, I still strove to remain aloof as an observer, when what he needed was a proper apprentice. One who not only understood all the ritual and Navajo lore that went with the divination, healing, and seeking out of witch curses, and the many other matters we undertook, but one who believed in it all. He couldn't teach me the deeper, more learned parts of Navajo medicine, until I was ready to believe in them; and it was clear to him that I was not. The major symptom of my lack of belief being that I was not scared of events that ought—by any reasonable measure—to terrify the living daylights out of anyone.

It was not that I was unaware of the depths of Navajo learning, in fact, I was only too aware—but I feared that if I took the steps now being demanded, it would lead me towards becoming *hataałii*. The word is usually translated as "singer", but it more closely resembles "chanter", one who chants, and it is from the word chant that we get out word "enchantment". In ancient times Europeans were enchanted by those among us who made magic through magic chants, and it was through these chants that enchantments were cast. Among the Navajo *hataałii* designates a fully-fledged shaman and medicine man like Blue Horse, and it would be next to impossible for a non-Navajo to achieve such a status; if only because almost all those who could teach me would be vehemently opposed to allowing a white man to do any such thing. Worse,

I knew that if I even began to move in that direction, I might soon find myself bound by such strict rules of secrecy that I would not be allowed to write anything more; and that, I felt, would be a tragedy.

Blue Horse knew all this perfectly well, and I began to wonder if he was bringing it up because he wanted me to quit, so he could find a Navajo apprentice. But when I put it to him straight, he said he didn't want me to quit. I was a good apprentice, he said, and he wanted to teach me more "when I was ready," which was not terribly helpful, but it was the best I could get out of him.

While I was in no doubt that Blue Horse was telling me the truth about the growing danger, at least as he saw it, it was more difficult to know how much danger that really represented. Try as I might, I couldn't feel scared. With hindsight, given all I'd learned about Navajo witchcraft, I should have been smarter; but it never occurred to me that if the witchmen couldn't get me, they might target someone close to me. Again, with my experience, I should have thought of that, and because I didn't it resulted in a tragedy.

While all this was going on, and I was revolving in my mind these conflicting thoughts and issues, there began to be a definite increase in the number of incidents where I felt there was a threat. We began to hear counter-whistling more frequently, coming out of the dark from places where no one should have been. On more than one occasion, when I'd been left alone to guard the fireplace and the instruments, someone—usually a member of the patient's extended family—unexpectedly entered the room and was surprised to find me. I had the impression they were hoping to find Blue Horse's sacred instruments unguarded and vulnerable to cursing. A couple of times when we left someone's home taking with us curses we'd found, I thought we were followed, but I couldn't be sure.[43] And I'd definitely seen the two men in the car that night, who apparently drove to the very spot where we'd been praying.

---

[43] It is not always possible, or even desirable, to destroy curses on the spot. Some are better dealt with by being thrown into running water, and these I usually tossed into the Rio Grande from a road bridge in Albuquerque.

As I remarked earlier, paranoia is an instinct that has kept me safe—or, at least, one step ahead of perdition—for many years. But what I was experiencing now was not paranoia. I wasn't worried about counter-whistling or witchmen, what worried me was doing the right thing. I felt that before long I would have to decide if I was in or out: was I going to be a real apprentice to Blue Horse, take the plunge, and go deeper and deeper into the world of Navajo medicine man; or was I not? On the other hand, perhaps I was already in over my head. After all he had done for me, all the kindness, the hospitality, the teaching, Blue Horse deserved an honest answer: and I had to be sure that, whatever I decided, I would be true to my word.

* * *

Today I drove Blue Horse to Black Mesa, Arizona, to the home of a Mrs. Begay. In the end we never met her, but we did eventually locate her family and were able to cedar for them. The most noticeable thing about Black Mesa is how isolated it is. In all the time I'd been going back and forth across this reservation, I'd never come across places where people spoke no English. There are plenty of monolingual old gentlemen and ladies, and any number of Navajos who speak little English; but until today I'd never been in a community where a significant number of people didn't seem to speak English at all.[44]

Black Mesa is a coal mining area not far from Kayenta and Monument Valley, and at the time of our visit the mine was getting ready to close. Its only customer was a coal-fired power plant that generates electricity for the reservation, and the power plant was due to close for environmental pollution reasons. These reasons didn't seem to take into account the devastating effect closure would have on the Navajo miners, for whom the mine was the only source of income in a generally impoverished area. Not surprisingly, people were nervous about the closure and anxious about the

---

44 This obviously does not apply to everyone in Black Mesa, but it did seem to apply to the older people in the isolated communities we visited that day.

future, and this may have made them more than usually reluctant to speak to outsiders like me.

The area is mostly juniper forest crisscrossed by dirt roads that go deep into the woods, but exactly where they go, is known only to those who use them. Other Navajos consider this area isolated and it took about three hours to drive Blue Horse up there. When we arrived we couldn't find the place we were looking for, and it took another two hours to find the house, during which time Blue Horse often urged me to turn back. He quickly gets discouraged in circumstances like this but, eventually, I did find the isolated farm. It was miles down a dirt track, that itself was a spur off a dirt road, that in turn was miles from the nearest slab of pavement.

We were greeted by an elderly woman who came out to welcome us, and I replied: "*Ya'at'eeh, shi ma*"—hello, mother—which is perfectly correct Navajo. At this she looked at me suspiciously, before turning to Blue Horse to say in Navajo, probably not realizing I could understand: "I never thought I'd have to call him *shi yaz*"—my son—"Is he really Navajo?"

Before I could say anything, Blue Horse weighed in. "Oh yes," he said, lying through his teeth. "He's Navajo, all right. They all look a bit like that over the other side of the reservation." The old woman continued to eye me suspiciously, but said no more and nodded for us to come in. I suppose this meant she'd never traveled as far as the other side of the reservation, or she'd have known differently.

I never found out what was wrong with the people we cedared for that day, except that Blue Horse discovered and removed a curse. Inside the house, the grandmother and grandfather spoke no English. Their son could, but chose not to and then, when the grandchildren arrived, the same depressing pattern emerged that I have witnessed over and again: the grandchildren spoke less Navajo than I do—which is saying quite something.

One of the men present had worked in the coal mine for, I think he said, twenty-seven years. He was coughing badly, and may have been suffering from black lung, pneumoconiosis, caused by coal dust getting into his lungs. He asked us to go to his house because he thought he'd been cursed, but I don't know his name because he too spoke no English. His foreman was Navajo, all his fellow miners were Navajo and at home he spoke Navajo, so he had no need of the English language. By now it was getting late, after 6:30 in the evening, and we were tired and still had hours of driving before we could get home, but Blue Horse agreed to go.

We followed the old coal miner down several dirt tracks leading ever deeper into the juniper forest, until we arrived at a collection of shacks that lacked both electricity and running water. Here, nobody spoke English, Blue Horse assured me, which I rapidly discovered to be true. Not only no English, but they couldn't understand my attempts at Navajo either. Inside the old man's dilapidated shack, the only form of lighting was an old-fashioned oil lamp on a bare wooden table. Cattle wandered around outside, and chickens pecked at the dry earth, while on a slight ridge overlooking the shacks was an old-fashioned, wood-and-earth, hogan. The hogan's roof had fallen in and I guessed it was probably abandoned in the 1960s, or perhaps a little later, because the old miner told Blue Horse it belonged to his parents. I think that's what he said, although it could have been his aunt and uncle; in either case, he'd been brought up in it.

There wasn't time to light a fire for charcoal, and so Blue Horse had told me to bring a bag of fine wood ash with me. Now he instructed me to take just one handful of the ash, put it on the floor, and shape it into a mound. When I'd finished, there were lots of tiny pieces of black charcoal mixed in among the mound of gray ash, and it was into this mixture that Blue Horse now looked most carefully. I'd never seen him do anything like this before, and as soon as he was satisfied with what he saw, he went outside and blew his whistle. After a short time he came in again and prayed, before taking the old man outside while I guarded the instruments. Soon they came back with a curse, and after it had been treated with ash and the evil neutralized, it was consigned to the back of my car, along with one from the first witching that had also been given into my custody.

The old miner was most grateful and thanked us effusively before we drove away. Then, as we were trying to find our way back to a road, Blue Horse told me the curse had been placed by the miner's ex-wife, who wanted to take his shack away from him. In that moment I felt really, truly, ineffably sorry for the old man. His home was humble enough. No water or electricity, just a little rickety shack that didn't even look weather proof, huddled among a collection of other shacks in a mining settlement deep in the middle of nowhere. Yet someone hated him enough to want to curse it away from him: what a tragedy.

We eventually found a road, and later a restaurant a few miles from Kayenta. After we'd eaten, I drove nonstop to arrive home at 11:30 that night after a more than twelve-hour day. I was so exhausted that as soon as the door closed, I threw myself on the floor and went to sleep.

When I awoke the next morning, it was to find a family from Gallup had come seeking help. They had a lot of problems, not the least of which was that their soldier son had been injured by a roadside bomb in Afghanistan. Usually, we do the cedar inside the house, but this time Blue Horse said to do it outside which, because of the strong wind blowing, I thought was a mistake.

I got the fire going, and when everything was ready everyone came out of the house and sat in a circle, and I placed the charcoal in front of Blue Horse. While he was talking to the family the lively wind blew a continuous plume of fine ash from the fire, which in time formed a thin, bluish-white covering on the earth all around him. I watched as he quite deliberately, but without saying anything, pressed his open hand into the ash leaving the clear imprint of his palm and fingers. Then he drew a series of zigzag lines in the ash just below the imprint of his wrist. To anyone but me it would have appeared that he was merely doodling, but I could tell he was up to something, although I had no idea what. All the time he was doing this, the conversation continued quite normally until, without any warning, the soldier's mother began to tell of her distress that her son had failed a nerve test. Among his many injuries was one to his wrist, and this nerve test was supposed to show if he was ever likely to recover the use of his wrist and hand. His mother was saying that because he had failed the nerve test, she feared he would never be able to use his hand again.

The poor woman was in tears by the time she'd finished speaking, but Blue Horse gently told her to dry her eyes. Pointing to the handprint in the ash, and the zigzag-like cut marks at the wrist, he assured her: "It's here. I saw it in the fire. Don't worry, everything will be alright with your son's hand." To say that the woman was astonished would be to put it mildly.

One of the other young men in the family was having trouble with a woman. I'm not sure if she was his wife, or his girlfriend, but they'd had a baby together and now the woman had left him and taken the baby with her. What was worrying the young man was whether the baby was his. If it was, then he wanted to shoulder his responsibilities, if it wasn't, then he wanted to know the truth. Blue Horse took him away from the fire and down the slope until they disappeared behind the sweat lodge. When they came back, the young man looked much happier. "That's sorted that out," he said beaming, and he looked at Blue Horse with considerable admiration.

What had happened was that Blue Horse had taken him to pray at the pit where we light big wood fires to heat the stones for the sweat. These fires are laid out in a special ritual way, and in the ashes in the pit Blue Horse had shown him something that convinced him he was the baby's father. The pit is surrounded by a half-moon of stones that have been used to heat the sweat lodge, and which over the years have become too broken and too small for further use. Instead of being thrown away, they are carefully placed together to form a crescent half-moon, which itself is the shape of the altar used in many peyote medicine ceremonies.[45] The sweat, and the place where the stones are heated, are places of holiness through their continued use as places of prayer and healing, and the half-moon underlines this holiness. Blue Horse had used it as a place of divination to show the young man what he needed to know; but what exactly he saw, or how he was shown it, I have no idea. This may, in fact, belong to those deeper levels of Navajo knowledge that I had not yet decided whether I wanted to enter.

* * *

---

45 The half-moon ceremony is the most common form of the peyote medicine ceremony, and is characterized by a large half-moon shaped altar that is built of damp sand before the ceremony begins. Among the Navajo the altar is often a small round mound on which a large peyote button, known as the grandfather button, is placed. This mound represents the Navajo Nation, and apparently came into use in preference to the half-moon at about the time of the Second World War, when so many Navajo soldiers went abroad for the first time.

Not long after this I returned to Albuquerque; and I'd been there exactly two hours before Blue Horse called shortly before 6:00 pm, and asked me to meet him at McDonald's in Sky City, the casino run by the Acoma Pueblo in New Mexico. He needed my help, he said, and as he was already well on his way and passing through Grants, I would have to hurry if I was to link up with him.

I made it, just, and we left his truck in the Acoma parking lot and drove in my car for a few miles before turning off I-40 to the south and crossing a railway line. It was at this point I realized we were not going to Acoma at all, but to another pueblo, the nearby Laguna Pueblo, and shortly after we arrived at a neat, single-story home that belonged to an elderly Laguna couple, Mr. and Mrs. Lux.

A woman came out of the house to greet us speaking unusually precise Navajo; so precise that I suspected Navajo was not her first language. This woman, who was in her late forties or early fifties, was astonishingly beautiful. Her body was slim and graceful, she had dark skin, jet-black hair and bright shining eyes, and she radiated an aura of feminine power, grace and elegance that had to be experienced to be believed. I thought I might be having a vision, except that she ignored me entirely, and instead engaged Blue Horse in a conversation that might best be described as conducted in relentless Navajo.

Usually, when Navajos speak to each other in their own language, as with speakers of any language, there are gaps and pauses, ums and ahs, words are elided and some are indistinct, phrases are left unfinished and sentences incomplete; and often there are a few words of English thrown in here and there. But this time, though I detected an accent, the delivery was perfect, the diction exact, the grammar precise, and I had the impression this speaker was deliberately refraining from using English terms, even where Navajos might have done so.

It turned out that this stunning lady was May Lux, daughter-in-law of the Laguna couple whose house we were now outside. The secret of her well-expressed language was revealed when Blue Horse explained that she was not Navajo at all, but from Zuni Pueblo, and had learned Navajo when she lived on the reservation for a while. The Zuni and Navajo languages are two of the most difficult languages in the world, and English isn't easy either. To speak English, Navajo and Zuni with the fluidity May proved to possess is one heck of an achievement, and she is probably one of the few people in the world to be fully conversant in all three.

Inside the house May introduced us to her parents-in-law, and at this point things became linguistically complicated. Mr. and Mrs. Lux both spoke English, but their preferred language was their native Keres. The Keres language is spoken on only seven pueblos in the Southwest United States, and is what language experts call an "isolate,"—as is the Zuni language—which means it has no known connection to any other language. Mr. and Mrs. Lux did not speak Navajo, and Blue Horse did not speak Keres, but he didn't want to perform the ceremony in the only common language of English (he never does if he can avoid it). Eventually, it was decided that Blue Horse would conduct the ceremony in Navajo, May would translate from Navajo into English, and Mrs. Lux would translate into Keres any parts her husband found difficult to follow in English. All of which left me feeling badly under-gunned in the language department.

Mr. Lux told us he was in poor health, and he looked thin and unwell, but his voice was strong and he gave the impression of a man of character. His wife was a tiny woman, not quite five feet tall, who was undergoing kidney dialysis and greatly disliked it—and who can blame her. The couple had been married for more than sixty years, they said, and clearly doted on each other. "This man has been so wonderful to me all my life," Mrs. Lux said, stroking her husband's arm in the most affectionate manner. The couple said they wanted help to get well again, and Blue Horse decided to perform a ceremony called Enemy Way for them.

I was surprised when he said this, because to perform Enemy Way takes five days. When I queried it, Blue Horse replied that I was correct that the Enemy Way *could* take five days but, he said, he had a shorter version for use in circumstances such as these. "My version is like a shotgun, while the other one is like shooting at the problem with a BB gun for five days," he declared.

Enemy Way can be used for a number of problems, including exorcising ghosts, bad dreams and continual nightmares. For these reasons, medicine men often use Enemy Way to treat Navajo soldiers returning from the wars, who may be suffering from combat stress or post-traumatic stress syndrome.

Blue Horse had brought with him twelve fresh yucca leaves, each one strong and green, and with the white base of the leaf still visible. These he'd gathered in the first rays of the dawn sun, from four different yucca plants growing wild in the desert. He had taken three leaves from each of the four different plants, each of which faced a different cardinal direction: east, south, west, and north; and he'd had trouble finding plants with exactly the right leaves, he said, because they needed to be strong, yet pliable enough that they could be bent and knotted without breaking.

I watched in fascination as he began to bend the leaves, one at a time, around the small silver cup he uses to hold water during ceremonies. Slowly, he wound and then unwound each leaf around the cup to make it pliable, then tied each one into a loose knot, a bit like a love knot, until each leaf had been formed into a double circle. Working slowly and methodically, he placed the knotted leaves carefully, one by one, on a small rectangle of woven Navajo rug he'd placed on the floor in front of him. He used twelve leaves, he said, because there are twelve months in the year, and he took three each from four plants because of the four directions.

Up until now things had been quite restrained, with Mr. and Mrs. Lux watching and listening quietly, while May and Blue Horse spoke in Navajo, which May then translated into English for her parents-in-law and, of course, for me. Then, when Blue Horse was almost finished bending his leaves, May's husband brought in the charcoal for the divination and things suddenly sprang to life. Blue Horse advising his patients to talk to the fire, and at this Mr. Lux said he would first have to welcome the fire into his home, as was the way of the Laguna people.

"But I can't do that in English," he declared. "I want to do it in my own language."

So, he began to speak in Keres, a language I'd never heard before. It was much softer than Navajo, a free-flowing speech of gently rising and falling cadences that seemed devoid of the harsh, guttural, tones of Navajo. As he spoke, the old man held out his arms toward the fire as if to embrace it, while the gentleness of his words, the warmth of his expression and his whole demeanor, gave the impression that he was welcoming into his home an old and dearly loved friend. He didn't speak for long, maybe for three or four minutes, but during that time I probably heard more Keres spoken than most people will hear in a lifetime. Many pueblos are reluctant to share their languages, even with experts who want to study and preserve them, and some pueblos refuse to have their languages written down. This has begun to change a little recently but few people, even experts, have the privilege of hearing a language like Keres spoken freely, and at length, by a native speaker in his own home.

After the fire had been welcomed, Mr. and Mrs. Lux were encouraged to talk to it, and tell it their troubles. Mr. Lux said he had worked on the railway, and been fit and healthy all his life until now, in his old age, he was becoming unwell. He had grown thin, and his pants no longer fit. He said he could not sleep, and his bowels ached. Worse, he heard a voice telling him to do bad things to himself—by which he meant suicide—which he did not want to do, but the voice kept insisting that there was no hope, and it would be better that way.

"I want to get well again," he declared. "I want to be able to do things and feel good again."

I don't know how old Mr. Lux was, but as he'd been married for sixty years, he was probably in his eighties. Now, Blue Horse told him the Navajo believed a man's allotted lifespan was not the three score years and ten that it says in the Bible, but one hundred and two years. This was not an arbitrary figure, and it is the same number as the pieces of wood a fire chief usually reckons will keep the fire blazing brightly throughout an all-night medicine ceremony. He later assured me that it was a good age for Navajos to aim for, citing that his father had lived to be one hundred and two and his mother to be one hundred and six. "I'm just a kid," he concluded.

"So, you have plenty of life left to live yet," Blue Horse assured Mr. Lux. "And I'm going to make it so you feel good again and enjoy it."

When it was her turn to talk, Mrs. Lux told a similar tale of slow decline into dependency and low mobility. She walked with a stick and told us: "Because my husband worked on the railway, they gave us a free pass to go anywhere by train when he retired. We used to go all the way to California to see our children and relatives, but now I can't even climb up the steps to get on board." She laughed, but she obviously felt this deeply and told us she had to go to the hospital twice a week for dialysis. "And it tires me out," she said, sounding flustrated. "I feel so tired when they're doing the dialysis: I just want to get well again."

I lit the fire lighter stick, and Blue Horse rolled the smoke for everyone to bless themselves in the usual way. After smoking a little himself, he passed it on but, being Laguna, our patients had no idea of what to do with it; let alone how to bless themselves in the tobacco smoke Navajo style. Mrs. Lux, it turned out, had never smoked a cigarette of any kind in her long life.

"I don't know how to do this," she said, looking at the smoke rather apprehensively.

"Just take a puff of it, Mother," May advised her gently, and she did.

When the smoke reached May, she knew exactly what to do, and did it in the exact correct manner that you rarely see. Someone at some time had trained her to perfection in the ritual and, to be honest, that evening she gave us something of a lesson in the correct etiquette. Holding the smoke straight out in front of her with both hands, and keeping it rigidly in the same exact position, she blew the tobacco smoke first to Mother Earth from below her hands, then to Father Sky from above her hands, and then blew smoke to the directions. When he carries out ceremonies, Blue Horse does not usually bother about etiquette as such, insisting only that people who take part are respectful, and do what they are supposed to do in the right sequence. But I've never seen anyone use the smoke in such a stately and sacred manner as May did that night: it was a wonder to behold.

After the smoke had gone around, Blue Horse began a long prayer in Navajo and when he'd finished, May translated the prayer for her parents. To summarize, Blue Horse said that the voice Mr. Lux was hearing was a spirit that had been recognized by his own spirit, and that was why he could hear it. He said there was a bad medicine man, a witchman, somewhere nearby who was witching people. He didn't know who he was, but he pointed to a face in the fire. Lapsing into English, Blue Horse said: "I don't know, but I think if I went to some other houses around here, I'd probably find out they knew someone was going about witching people, because he would be witching them as well."

He told Mr. Lux that something was blocking his stomach where it joined the intestines, and that was why his insides hurt so much, and he also told him that while he and his wife had been speaking and talking of their ills, a piece of charcoal had moved in the fire and rolled in their direction; this, he said, was a sign that all would be well. Then he explained that the short-version Enemy Way ceremony he was about to perform was powerful. It would not only make Mr. Lux better, but would protect him so that he would stay well.

But first Blue Horse doctored to them with his pipe, praying and sucking until he had pulled out several bits of bad stuff, first from Mr. Lux and then from his wife. Only after this did he begin the Enemy Way, and taking the knotted yucca leaves he applied them one at a time to the parts of Mr. Lux's body that hurt. As he applied each one he blew his whistle, and then slowly pulled on the loose end of the yucca, unraveling the knot and so symbolically removing both the pain and the problem. As he unknotted each yucca leaf, he placed it carefully on the floor by the northeast corner of the fire until the leaves formed a neat row. Then he instructed me to get some hot ash and put it on a plate which he held out to me.

This quickly turned into a disaster. I had only my fingers for collecting the ash from around the red-hot charcoals and they quickly became burned. It didn't help that the plate Blue Horse gave me was a paper plate, and when I put the red-hot ashes on it the plate caught fire. I blew out the flames and, of course, the ash flew everywhere, so I had to start again with my already-scorched fingers. Eventually, I stopped the plate from incinerating by spitting on my fingers and rubbing spit around the burning portions to put them out. Why Blue Horse didn't bring a proper plate with him, or why it didn't occur to me to borrow one from Mrs. Lux, I have no idea.

After this, the paper plate with the ash on it was placed on the floor, and then Blue Horse took Mr. and Mrs. Lux outside into the night to pray. While he was doing this, I went outside to burn the bad stuff he'd taken out of the old people. When I came back I found myself alone with May, and took the opportunity to ask why her parents-in-law had not used a Laguna medicine man to help them overcome their illnesses? Her reply was instructive.

"There are medicine men among the Laguna, but they are not very conversant with the ceremonies these days," she explained. "So, when people need help, they go to the Navajo, who still know how to do these things properly."

It is true that other tribes frequently call in Navajo medicine men, because they recognize them as the last of those who know thoroughly the ancient ceremonies. The reason the Laguna medicine men are no longer fully conversant with their ancient art—if May was correct in what she said—is the same reason that now bedevils even the Navajo: fewer and fewer young men are able to become medicine men and learn the ceremonies, because they have to work for a living, and so they drift into the white man's world of work, and the ancient ways are forgotten.

Among the prophets who appeared among the Indian peoples during their tortured disintegration in the 19th Century was a man called Smohalla. The name means Dreamer, and he was born in what is now the eastern part of Washington State in the area of the Columbia River. Smohalla tried to lead Indians away from the white man's world, warning them that it could lead only to their destruction and the destruction of their way of life. Specifically, he used these words: "My young men shall never work, for those who work have no time to dream, and it is only through dreams that men may grow wise." The truth of this prophecy is to be seen today throughout the American Indian world, where young men must work, and so they have no time to dream; and are therefore unable to grow wise in the traditional ways of their peoples.

It doesn't help that the ancient languages like Keres, as well as several other pueblo languages, and Navajo, are all under siege from English and fewer young people are able to speak them well, or even at all. While Navajo remains for the moment relatively strong, the loss of their language by most tribes is fatal to ancient medicine and healing; as well as to the complex and highly secretive religious ceremonies carried out among Pueblo peoples. Because language and culture evolve to express each other, it is impossible to say the correct words, or to perform the correct rituals, except in their original language. Only the original language can convey the real meaning of the word, making it impossible to conduct ceremonies in English because there is no correct translation; which was the main reason Blue Horse was reluctant to use English when conducting a ceremony. This loss of language, and its impact on ceremonial may be why, recently, some Pueblos have started to cooperate more with specialist linguists, who can help them preserve their languages and teach them to their children.

After a while Mr. and Mrs. Lux and Blue Horse came back inside, and Blue Horse sent for more charcoal. This time, when he looked into the charcoal, Blue Horse saw a feather, and I could see it too. It was an eagle feather, oriented east to west, which Blue Horse said was a good sign and meant that all would be well. He wanted to doctor to May, but first he needed more fresh charcoal, and when we got it there was a really bad object lying right on top. It looked like a massive bone, and after Blue Horse had sucked some bad stuff from May, he got me to pick this "bone" from the fire. Again, I had only my fingers, which were by now quite badly burned, but I managed to pick it out and put it in a little metal saucepan I'd finally had the sense to ask for from Mrs. Lux's kitchen.

After he'd taken the bad stuff out of May, Blue Horse said he and I should go out together and burn it, and he gave me a stone spear point for protection. After we'd burned the bad stuff, Blue Horse decided to destroy the big piece of charcoal which he said represented a big curse. I'm not sure how he destroyed it, because he took it away and I didn't see what he did.

But he may have done something special, because in a long prayer, during which he condemned the curse, he cast its evil to the outer regions of the universe.

"There it is!" he shouted excitedly, as he finished praying, and pointed high into the night sky, where a marble sized full moon was almost directly overhead, bathing everything in a stark, white, light. "There it is! You can see it rising and disappearing!" he yelled. To be honest, I couldn't see anything but, on the other hand, I hadn't the slightest idea what I was supposed to be looking for.

With this the proceedings were pretty well over, and we went back inside. Blue Horse threw some more cedar on the coals and made a general blessing of the house and the family, wafting the scented smoke over everyone with his eagle feather. May's husband joined us and gave Blue Horse a large bag of cedar fronds as a present, which is a very good present to give a medicine man.

X

I was due at a peyote meeting at Ronny's mother's house, so I drove over to her hogan. But where it is I cannot say, because there is no name for this place in English, only in Navajo. Though I know the name in Navajo, I don't know how to write it in Navajo and neither does anyone else, because while they all speak their own language, no one I know can read or write it, having been schooled only in English. This is not uncommon in colonial situations, such as the one that exists between the Navajo and the United States, where conquered peoples are taught to read and write only in the language of the conqueror.

Whatever the name of the place, Betty lives on top of a small hill, on a nice spread of land in a hogan made of modern materials with a concrete, not an earth, floor. The view is spectacular and the sage here grows like the sea; deep and green, and stretching to the ends of the earth. To behold it is a joy, but to smell that sweet sage in the dew of early morning, or after a shower of rain, is to know the scent of heaven. Scattered among the measureless windblown waves of this sea are clumps of junipers, whose dark-green branches and blackened trunks, stand out like islands. In between there are patches of bare red earth, and above a sky of flawless blue in which blazes bright and merciless, the white-hot lantern of the Navajo sun.

Housing out here is rarely of the best, and the people living in it are seldom well off. But most of them would rather be here, enjoying a freedom you can't buy in London or New York no matter how much money you have, than living in a multimillion-dollar apartment where all you can see is the wall of the building next door. On the reservation, you may have to climb up to mend your own roof from time to time, but the view takes in half the world.

I didn't know what the meeting was for and I was expecting to be told the usual, "It's for so-and-so's mom, who hasn't been well recently", or "It's for a baby who's in hospital," or something like that. I almost always get less than half the story, and it's not that people don't want me to know; it's the old problem that because they know, they assume I know. Usually I don't know, but it's difficult to ask questions because even with people like me whom they know, Navajos can interpret as unwarranted prying the kind of questions white folks ask to show concern. Therefore, I find it best not to ask, even though I would often dearly like to.

This time I was lucky enough to run into Gloria, one of Ronny's sisters, and she told me the meeting was being held for Donna, the woman whose husband committed suicide a while ago.[46] The family was having trouble with the dead man's ghost, which kept coming back to haunt them.

Gloria explained: "Blue Horse cedared and told her that her husband kept coming back because he's worried about the children.[47] He's sorry he left them and wants to know if they're all right. Donna never cried about her husband and she didn't let the kids cry either, which I think was bad for them all, because the husband couldn't see from the spirit world that they cared about him. He was an alcoholic, but he always made sure his children had clothes and food, and he did care about them."

Gloria reminded me that Donna was two months pregnant with her eighth child when her husband hanged himself. She told me: "Blue Horse said that Donna's husband can't get back to the spirit world where he needs to be, because he's so worried about his children, he never even saw the last one, and it's the worry that's holding him here. Blue Horse thinks that if he can get Donna and all the children into the tepee, the ghost—*ch'įįdii*—will be able to see them there. Then they're going to pray to the medicine, and get it to show him that his children are fine and doing well

---

46 See above, Chapter Five.
47 I was absent when this cedar was held, but I no longer remember why.

at school. Then he can let go and return to the spirit world to take his proper place."

At no time did Gloria, or anyone else, ever mention the name of Donna's husband and because no one ever spoke it, I had so far not discovered it. The reason his name could not be spoken, was that while his ghost was still at large, if it heard its name it might attach itself to the speaker; an event greatly to be feared. So, the purpose of the meeting was to help the ghost of Donna's husband find its way home to the spirit world, so both he and his family could find peace.

A big tepee had been put up near Betty's hogan, and as the time for the ceremony drew near, Donna and all the children came inside and sat down. The ceremony had not long begun, with prayers and a smoke, before the youngest children began to fall asleep; tucked up in warm blankets and kept snug between their mother and various aunts. When the singing began, I declined twice when the drum came round and passed the staff to my left.

I should explain that in a medicine meeting everyone gets the chance to sing their medicine songs. A special staff is passed from person to person around the circle, and those who want to sing hold on to the staff, sit up on their knees, and the drummer sits next to them and accompanies the singer. Each person sings four medicine songs, accompanying themselves with a gourd rattle that comes with the staff, and when they have finished, the staff and the rattle are passed to the next person on the left. That person can choose to sing or not, and then the staff is passed to the next person on the left, and so on.

In the opening rounds of a meeting people will often pass the staff without singing, because they are saving their voices for the more demanding after midnight rounds. In my case—in the interests of full disclosure—I usually pass the staff because I'm an awful, tuneless, singer. Ok, there are special occasions when I do sing in the tepee but, usually, rather than embarrass myself—and probably everyone else—I prefer to keep quiet. Instead, I confine my "singing" to the sweat lodge, where I can hide in the deep darkness, and the tiny space of the sweat distorts voices enough that I don't sound too bad; or, at least, not so bad as usual.[48]

The staff had been round twice, I'm sure of that, and I'd taken some peyote medicine, although I didn't think I'd taken much, when the tepee started changing. I don't mean changing shape, although it was, and growing taller and narrower; I mean it was changing its position vis-a-vis the rest of the universe. No longer was it fixed between earth and sky, or rooted to our planet, or even floating in space somewhere between the stars and galaxies. Instead, the tepee had become a universe of its own, containing all there was, is, or ever will be, while outside there was nothing; absolutely nothing. We were traveling through the void. Voyagers within the universal tepee, journeying through the emptiness of nothingness, towards a new birth and creation.

I looked up the length of the smoke blackened tepee poles, to where they disappeared through the top of the smoke blackened canvas, before spreading out like fingers reaching for the sky, the stars and everything; and realized this was impossible, as there was nothing beyond. The night did not exist, for it had not yet been created. The poles, if they existed beyond the top of the canvas, beyond the flickering light of the fire, protruded into nothingness. Into an all-encompassing uncreated, unbeing; and I wondered if I could slide out along one of the poles, to a vastation that lay beyond: somewhere, in the nowhere of nothing.

While I was thinking this, I was listening to the pulsating beat of the water drum, and the regular high-pitched overtones from the *chink-chink-chink* of the gourd rattle. I couldn't hear the singer, only the beat of the drum and the rhythm of the rattle; then I could hear only the rattle, and then the rattle became discordant. It was if there were two rattles chinking away, but out of time with each other. When I opened my eyes and looked up to see what was happening, it was to see a young British soldier sitting down beside me. It wasn't two rattles I was hearing, the second one was the half-undone zip of his camouflage jacket jingling as he took his seat on the earth beside me. I recognized him immediately as a soldier I'd come

---

48 This may be an illusion on my part.

face-to-face with during a savage gun battle in Londonderry, at the height of the troubles in Northern Ireland.

I'd been trying to make my way up to the rebel held Bogside area of the town, but the fighting was so fierce that day the British Army mounted light machine guns in the street. I didn't know the city well, hardly at all, and with bullets bouncing off the walls all around me, I slipped into an alley in the hope of somehow finding my way through. Instead, I quickly ran into this young soldier, who was all by himself, manning a lonely lookout with a good view of rebel held positions.

Reassured by my English accent, he felt able to vent his bitter resentment of how the British authorities were covering up the number of casualties the British Army was inflicting on the Irish Republican Army: so as not to upset the nationalists too much, he believed. He had himself killed two IRA men that morning, he told me. One armed with a rifle, who was trying to cross a patch of empty ground about two hundred yards in front of us, and another who'd sneaked up behind him with a home-made grenade. Through a blasted-out window behind us, he showed me a shed with a gently sloping tin roof about four feet below where we stood. The boy had been sneaking across the roof to throw the bomb at him, but he saw him, shot him, and the powerful impact of the British Army SLR (Self-Loading Rifle 7.62) at such close range, flexed the tin roof so violently it catapulted the boy into the air and into the alley below, where his home-made grenade exploded under him.

"So I know I got him," the soldier finished grimly. "And the other one, and I killed one last week, but the government wants to keep quiet about it." It was a common complaint by British soldiers in Ulster at the time, that their superb marksmanship was ignored for political reasons, by the very government that was putting their lives in danger.

Now he was sitting beside me, so I asked him what he wanted, and he explained that I was the last person he'd talked to before being killed later that day by another bomb.[49] It troubled him that he'd been unable to make

---

[49] Readers should understand that from this point on I cannot vouch for anything regarding this soldier. What happened on the day I met him is fact, the rest is vision, and whether true or not I have no way of checking.

his report, no matter that his grudging political masters would ignore it. "I have to make my report to someone or I can't go home," he explained.

I said that I couldn't help with his report, but we were having a meeting to help people get home, and perhaps that would help. But, after a while, I became aware that I was talking to myself, and saying the same thing over and over. At least, I think I was talking to myself, because when I looked again the soldier wasn't there. I may not have been talking at all, I may only have thought I was talking: it's difficult to know. Then the scene shifted, and the fire and all the people sitting round it tipped up on end. It was as if I was looking at a wall, with the fire in the middle and all the people sat around it, all miraculously suspended in the air. I seemed to be sitting firmly on the ground, but it occurred to me later, that I would have had the same view if I'd been lifted into the air and was looking down.

Smoke from the fire surrounded me and I was coughing and choking and making a lot of noise. It took a while to realize this smoke was not wood smoke but battle smoke; and the noise was not me coughing and choking but the sound of combat. Then, through the smoke, I saw my grandfather walking towards me wearing his old-fashioned British Army uniform from World War I. He was carrying an old-fashioned bolt action rifle with an old-fashioned bayonet with a seventeen-inch blade, and he was covered in blood from his wounds. Despite his wounds, he walked steadily on through the mud towards the German trenches in France. The mud was red like Navajo mud; red and slick and sticky. But unlike Navajo mud, this mud was stained red from the blood of tens of thousands of dead and dying young soldiers.

"Granddad!" I shouted, as he walked by me, looking neither to left nor right, and my voice was the voice of the child I'd been when I last saw him. "Granddad! Granddad!" But he took no notice and continued to walk steadily forward. "Grandad! I've got your watch. I still have it. I've kept it safe for you!" [50] At this he turned his head, and for a moment he looked at

---

[50] My grandfather's watch was one of only two items I retained after destroying all my possessions. The other was the little silver box containing my children's photographs. See Chapter Seven above.

me and smiled. Then he turned once more to the front and, walking on, disappeared into the smoke.

I sat for a long time, not thinking of anything much as our tepee universe continued its journey through the void until, after what seemed an age, I became aware that a subtle change was taking place. Outside, the first faint light of dawn was breaking in the east. The void was filled, a birth had taken place; and the dawn came up as it had on the first morning on the first day of creation.

Later, when the meeting was over and we were having breakfast, I asked Blue Horse about my visions—if visions they were; for I am never sure if what I experience with the medicine is not, in fact, reality. A different reality, even a separate reality, but a reality nonetheless. I told him what I had seen and, in particular, I asked him about my grandfather. He thought for a while before asking, "Why did your grandfather smile at you?"

I was shocked by his question. "Why would a grandfather not smile at his grandson?" I wanted to know.

"He had no grandchildren," Blue Horse pointed out. "He was seventeen, eighteen years old, maybe. Why would he smile at a grandson he didn't have?"

I was flummoxed. I had no idea. It had never occurred to me. I wished I hadn't asked. Was Blue Horse suggesting it was all a fantasy? A dream? A baseless imagining? Something that couldn't have happened, that could have had no reality because of the obvious flaw he'd pointed out? Even while I considered all this, Blue Horse plowed relentlessly on. "Why did he give you his watch when he died?" He demanded.

"He wasn't a rich man, not well off at all," I told him. "He never owned a car or even learned to drive. I suppose it was the only thing he had to give me."

Blue Horse shook his head. "No. It was to make the prophecy come true."

"What prophecy?"

"You saw two soldiers. The first was tryin' to get home. His spirit been hangin' around you all these years, because you were the last person he saw while he was alive, so he was waitin' for you to help him. This was the first chance he had, when we held this meetin' to help spirits get home. So, he came to you, made his report to you, and you told him what the meeting was for, and then he was able to go home at last. See? That's why when you look up he isn't there. He's gone home. But your grandfather didn't wanna go home to the spirit world. He was alive, and he wanted to keep livin'. He saw you on the battlefield, and when you tell him who you are he smiled; he knew if he had a grandson he was gonna survive! But to make it all work he gotta give you his watch when he dies. Because he hears you tell him, 'I've got your watch. I keep it safe for you'. If you don't have his watch, how you gonna keep it safe for him? And if what he heard when he saw you wasn't true, maybe he's not gonna survive the battle."

With the fatigue of a night without sleep, it took time for all this to sink in. If the tepee really had become a universe of its own, where maybe things did happen differently, with different times, different outcomes, different everything; perhaps I was right when I thought there was nothing outside the tepee but the void, and everything had still to be created: and when it was created, perhaps it was created differently.

"Sure," said Blue Horse, when I asked him about this. "If you know about something that happen in the future, and you do something to make sure it don't happen, then all that time you lived didn't happen either, and you got to go back where you started. Your grandfather didn't wanna go back to that battle and start all over again, so he give you his watch when he die to make sure everything work out as it should. Then everythin' be alright."

His whole attitude was one of forbearance: as if this was so obvious he could scarcely believe he had to vocalize it.

"You mean, if he hadn't given me his watch, he might have had to go back to 1916 and maybe get be killed, and then I would never have been born?" It was a staggering thought.

"That's how it works," said Blue Horse, who by now was far more interested in the coffee and donuts being served than he was in me.

"And I wouldn't be here talking to you, and none of what I've lived through would ever have happened?"

"Not to you," he said.

"But," I protested. "My grandfather worked on the railway. He didn't know things like that."

"Sounds like he did," Blue Horse replied, growing bored and sticking a large chocolate donut in his mouth, an action that brought conversation to an end for some minutes while he chewed his way through it. When I thought about it, granddad was perhaps one of the few railway men who went to work with a copy of Marcus Aurelius' *Meditations*[51] stuffed in his pocket. So, perhaps, he did know a thing or two.

While I was still digesting all this, and Blue Horse was ingesting more donuts, Baa arrived having driven overnight from Oklahoma with her sister Nancy Kapatop, and Nancy's thirteen-year-old granddaughter Nelsie, who turned out to be the great-great-great granddaughter of Geronimo, the most famous of all Apache Indian leaders.

Baa seemed unsteady on her feet. She has diabetes, and I think the diabetes may have damaged the nerves in her feet, but otherwise she was in good spirits. After breakfast, I got ready to take Blue Horse back to his house, only to find he'd already left, so I climbed into my car and followed him home.

I arrived to find a sweat was being prepared. It is unusual for us to have a sweat after a medicine meeting, if only because everyone is too tired after a night without sleep. I certainly needed some sleep, and as I was still struggling intensely with the visions and Blue Horse's explanation of them, I did not want to go into the sweat lodge. But it turned out the sweat was for prayers and healing for a friend of Andrew Yellowhair, who was the cedar chief in our medicine meeting. His friend was seriously ill in hospital with cancer that had spread to his kidneys so, of course, as soon as I knew this, I said I'd take part.

While we were getting the sweat ready, I found the body of a stray kitten that Blue Horse had been caring for. It was badly mutilated, although Baa and

---

51 Marcus Aurelius Antoninus Augustus, Emperor of Rome 161 – 180AD, wrote a stunningly brilliant book of philosophy today known as *Meditations*. One of the few works read continuously for almost 2,000 years, you can still buy it online or in any good book shop. For many years during my travels, I always kept a copy with me, and it was only by chance, shortly before she died, that my mother told me that my grandfather, too, had always carried a copy with him.

her sister Nancy said it had been alive and well only an hour earlier. The kitten was lying outside a shed on the edge of the paddock, and it had been stamped to death by someone wearing heavy boots; which struck me as not only brutal, but a strangely violent way to kill a kitten. Stray animals, particularly cats and dogs, turn up and hang around reservation homes all the time, and they often die unexpectedly of causes ranging from disease to hungry coyotes, so I didn't want to read too much into it. But it did give me a bad feeling, and with everything else going on, I wondered if the kitten might be a warning of some kind? But I told myself not to be so stupid. First, I was worrying about witchmen counter-whistling us; then about people following us; then it was witches cooking up snowstorms, and now a dead kitten had morphed in my mind into some kind of warning. I knew that a couple of years ago I would never have given any of these incidents a second's serious thought. So, I told myself I was overtired, and everything would look better after a sweat and a few hours' sleep.

Had I known what was about to happen, I'd have taken the slaughter of that kitten far more seriously, and remembered more clearly Blue Horse's explicit warning that the witchmen were preparing to strike at me. I still didn't take this warning seriously, and still didn't think spells and curses could hurt me, and it still hadn't occurred to me that as an adopted member of his family, the strike might be directed at any member of the Blue Horse family. Like drug dealers, if witchmen can't get you, they'll get someone close to you; your girlfriend, your wife, your mother, your children: it's all the same to them.

When the sweat was ready we men—Andrew Yellowhair, Andrew's teenage son Malcolm, Blue Horse, and I—went into the sweat lodge, leaving Baa, Nancy, and Nelsie inside the house. Traditionally, Navajo men and women sweated separately, and while these days the sexes do sweat together on occasion, Nancy was of the old tradition and would not sweat with men, which meant the other women couldn't either.

It so happened that Blue Horse had recently enclosed his sweat lodge inside a large shed, so that it could be used more comfortably in all weathers. Even without this enclosure, once inside a sweat lodge where people are singing and praying and drumming, you can hear nothing of what's going on outside. The sweat lodge ceremony normally consists of four rounds of prayer and song, although it can run to six. These rounds are physically demanding, because steam is produced by pouring cold water onto volcanic rocks that have been heated until they glow red hot. This creates extremely high temperatures inside the small dome of the sweat lodge. So high that in summer I've often come out of the sweat to find the daytime temperature is in excess of 100 degrees Fahrenheit, and been forced to wrap up against the "cold".

Each round of a sweat is interspersed with breaks, during which the participants lay around outside the sweat lodge recovering and drinking water and soft drinks. Blue Horse said we would do only two rounds today. Then changed his mind once we were inside and said there would be four. Somehow, it seemed too many, and I had a strange compulsion to get back to the house; whether it was fatigue, or perhaps something else, is difficult to say.

When we emerged from the sweat lodge after the first round, everyone except me fell asleep for about forty-five minutes. I couldn't sleep at all; I felt edgy and wanted to stay alert. Then, before we went back for the second round, it was decided that to save time, we would skip the break after the second round and go straight into the third. We hadn't been going long, and Blue Horse was drumming while I was singing, when Andrew's son Malcolm began to show signs of distress in the intense heat. Concerned for the boy, Blue Horse ordered a short break, and this was fortunate indeed, because we hadn't been out of the sweat more than a few minutes when we heard a woman screaming at the top of her voice. It was difficult to make out what was happening until Blue Horse opened a window in the shed, and then I heard Nancy screaming: "My sister's being attacked! My sister's being attacked!"

It took a second to sink in that this was real—and then I was through the door of the shed and running up the hill towards the house; barefoot and wearing only a tiny pair of blue shorts, but I was moving like lightning. It seems strange to think that I am years from my peak as an athlete, and yet I can still move fast if I need to. I went racing up the hill towards the house, getting faster at each pace, until I was moving at top speed. Then, somehow, I went up a gear and went faster still; I can't explain how it happens, but all good runners will know what I mean.

Baa's sister Nancy was standing outside the open door of the house screaming, so at first I thought Baa was being attacked by a man who'd forced his way inside. I aimed straight for the door, but Nancy began pointing and shouting: "Round the back! Round the back!" I have no recollection of weaving my way around, or through, the several cars parked beside the house, but I do recall turning the far wall and being surprised to find no sign of Baa. So, I kept going full blast straight ahead, aware now that although the thin air at this altitude of more than six thousand feet was lacerating my lungs like a razor, I could keep the pace up for some time.

It is so hot inside a sweat that I never wear my glasses or contact lenses, and as I hadn't had time to grab my glasses, I couldn't see very well. But after only a few moments more of hard running, I saw Baa lying about fifty yards ahead of me among the scrub and junipers. She was on her side and screaming for help, but I could see no sign of her attacker. Knowing the other men must be coming up behind me, I decided not to stop, but to keep going and catch her attacker and bring him back. But as I drew closer, I saw that Baa was not alone; what looked like a big, dirty, brown rug was heaving up and down beside her.

Baa was screaming in Navajo: "Get it off me! Get it off me!" When I came alongside her, I was able to see that the dirty brown rug was a huge ram that was butting her as she lay on the ground.

Rams are big, aggressive, dangerous animals, and people are killed and seriously injured by them every year. But I was confused because this animal had no horns—some rams do not—and not knowing it was a ram, and an unusually big one at that, I dragged it off Baa thinking it was a sheep that would run away; so, I was astonished when it came back and tried to butt her some more. I punched it in the face and kneed it in the ribs and eventually managed to beat it off, but it retreated only ten feet, then turned and started back again. I beat it off again, and then Malcolm appeared with a broom and whacked it on the backside. This seemed to make little difference, so I took the broom and hit the ram in the face, going for its eyes. That made it back off, but then the aluminum broom handle bent and became useless. The ram retreated a little under my assault, but remained aggressive and showed no signs of going away; and all this time Baa was screaming in agony, lying on the ground half in and half out of a sage bush.

If I'd known anything about the behavior of rams, none of the above would have surprised me, but I didn't. What I did know was that Malcolm's dad Andrew had been a champion bull rider, and that Malcolm was a high-school rodeo champion. So, I reckoned Malcolm probably knew how to deal with animals, and so I told him to keep the animal off me while I attended to Baa. I certainly picked the right young man for the job! When I next looked up again, Malcolm had upended the ram, turned it on its back, and was holding one of its forelegs in the air, while pressing his foot on its windpipe to control it. The immediate danger was over.

Baa was still screaming in pain, but she was able to tell me that her right leg was in agony all the way down. I reckoned it was probably broken and tried to keep her still, but she continued to writhe around in agony, something that was bound to make her injuries worse. By now other people were starting to arrive. Nelsie came running up, and because Malcolm was calling for a rope to tie the ram, I sent the girl to find one. While she was doing that, Blue Horse came puffing up to say he'd called for an ambulance. By the time Nelsie came back, Blue Horse, Nancy, and Andrew were there to comfort Baa, so I took the rope over to Malcolm and gave him a hand tying the ram.

Malcolm warned me, "It's a really strong animal. Tie it really tight." So, while he held the ram still, I did a square lashing on its legs and finished with a round turn and two half-hitches, a knot strong enough to hold a battleship. Alerted by the noise, the neighbors who owned the ram began to appear, and Nancy rather unhelpfully began screaming at them about letting their animals stray; so, I sent her and Nelsie to the end of the driveway to flag down the ambulance when it arrived. Nelsie, by the way, remained calm throughout this ordeal. The neighbors seemed far more concerned for their ram than anything else, particularly the injured Baa, and loaded the animal into a pickup and drove it away without a backward glance.

With hindsight, we all agreed we should have killed the ram on the spot. But, at the time, the thought of Malcolm cutting the throat of a struggling, bellowing, ram only ten feet from where I was trying to keep Baa calm, was not attractive. The ambulance eventually came and took Baa to hospital, and shortly afterward I drove Blue Horse to see her. Andrew Yellowhair and his wife Martha came to join us as we waited for Baa, who'd been taken to the emergency room.

As we sat waiting, Andrew told me: "My son said to me, 'Man, that Charles can run. I've never seen a man run that fast. I couldn't keep up with him'."

It was a small crumb of comfort during an otherwise god-awful day, to think I had outpaced a fit sixteen-year-old rodeo rider, even if I had burned my lungs a bit while doing it. I'd been running competitively since I was twelve, but after a lifetime of enjoying running, I'd recently started to find it tedious and ridiculously hard work, and I'd stopped doing it. I took this as a timely reminder to get running and get fit again.[52]

At the hospital Baa was found to have a badly broken left leg just below the knee, not the right leg, as she'd said. For a sixty-six year old diabetic, this was not good news, and I was afraid that if her leg failed to respond to treatment, it could lead to an amputation. Despite the attack on Baa, the neighbors allowed their sheep and this ram to go free and come over a couple more times on to Baa and Blue Horse's property. At least, they did until I fired a few rounds at the animals from a Winchester, after which the intrusions stopped. Despite the great physical harm done to Baa, these people never once offered an apology, or showed the least concern for her.

Later, Nancy told me what had happened while we men were in the sweat. She said that she, Nelsie, and Baa were in the house when they saw a small flock of sheep wandering by the house. Worried that they might drop dung on the tepee ground, Baa went outside and herded them away.

---

52 I tried, and broke my ankle so badly I was never able to run again.

Shortly after this the sheep came back, and Baa had gone out again to shoo them off. At this Nancy said to Nelsie: "Come on, let's go out and watch your grandmother herd sheep, then you'll know how to do it." That was when the ram attacked Baa.

It was a good thing Nancy was there, because from where we were in the sweat, we would never have heard Baa screaming from behind the house. She could have been there for two hours while we sweated, under attack from a three-hundred-pound animal. Andrew told me it was one of the biggest rams he'd ever seen, and in such circumstances she could easily have suffered a fatal heart attack. At three hundred pounds that ram was half as heavy again as a modern world heavyweight boxing champion. Can you imagine being butted again and again by an animal as powerful as that? It might sound funny to city dwellers that someone could be attacked by a ram, but there was nothing funny about it; and we were only too aware that Baa was lucky to be alive.

As we discussed events, and waited to find out what the doctors thought of Baa's injuries, Blue Horse and Andrew, who is a medicine man in his own right, agreed that the attack was caused by witchcraft and intended to kill. Whether aimed specifically against me or Blue Horse, or who exactly they couldn't be sure, because it could have been any of us.

"We should have killed that ram," Andrew said. "It's still thinking about its attack on Baa. It's still thinking bad thoughts about her, and while it's thinking those bad thoughts it can still damage her and slow her recovery."

We briefly discussed going over to the neighbors and shooting the ram in its pen. But decided that as the authorities were already involved, in the form of the Navajo Rangers who deal with livestock incidents, it was probably wiser not to.

"Someone was definitely trying to kill you," Andrew said, speaking to both me and Blue Horse, "and that was powerful witchcraft they used."

Then we began thinking of all the things that had happened to defeat this objective. Andrew pointed out how, if his son had not been overcome by the heat, we would not have cut the round short and exited the sweat; in which case we would never have heard Nancy screaming. I asked how often Nancy came to visit her sister, and Blue Horse said he could hardly remember the last time, it was so long ago.

"And if Nancy had not been there to see what happened, Baa could have been lying there being attacked by that animal for hours," I said. "I think she would have been killed."

"It's not luck," Blue Horse said. "We have prayers: our prayers are strong. My wife brings her sister to stay. Young Malcom gets sick and we come out of the sweat. Charles runs fast like he's lightning, we get her to hospital and she's OK. This ain't luck. Their witching is strong, man, real strong; but we're stronger. They meant to kill, but our prayers, our songs, our good hearts, in the tepee last night and in the sweat today; that's enough to turn their evil aside. It struck, man, but we done enough to stop the worst."

A few days later, after visiting Baa in the hospital, I arrived back at the house just in time to meet a ranger who'd been taking statements about the ram's attack on Baa. The Navajo rangers are responsible for enforcement involving any livestock issues and he said the ram was now penned, as were the other sheep, but he was having trouble finding Andrew Yellowhair to take a statement. Unfortunately, Blue Horse had sent the ranger to the wrong address.

It appeared it would be a civil matter, because unless it could be proven that the ram had been released deliberately to hurt someone, there could be no criminal case. Of course, it would be impossible to prove the animal was released deliberately to harm someone, although I had my suspicions. It didn't help that the ranger—unlike most of his colleagues—turned out to be one of the laziest and most useless human beings I've ever encountered. His main motivation was to do as little as possible and he eventually accused us of making up the entire incident, said he would like to shoot me if he got the chance, and claimed that Baa's broken leg had nothing to do with the ram. When I said I'd send him photographs we'd taken of the ram, he deliberately gave me the wrong e-mail address so that he wouldn't have to bother with them. I doubt he ever made the official report he was supposed to make, but if he did, nothing ever came of it.

* * *

With Baa in hospital for an extended stay, the next problem was how to get Nancy and Nelsie back to Oklahoma. Baa had been in Oklahoma visiting her sister, and had driven her and Nelsie back to Arizona for a short stay. She was due to drive them back again, but that was now impossible and they had no transport of their own. One difficulty I've never overcome is how to mentally assess distance in the United States. Having spent most of my life on an island, it's difficult to think in distances of more than about two hundred miles, and no amount of time spent in North America seems to correct this fault. Knowing Oklahoma was somewhere over the hills to the east (which it is, sort of), I volunteered to drive them home.

This turned out to be a fifteen-hundred-mile round trip—approximately the same as driving from New Hampshire to Miami or from London to Moscow—and it took days to get there and back. But I never regretted it. Partly because Nancy and Nelsie were good company, but also because, to while away the journey, Nancy told me one of the most fascinating stories I've ever heard about Navajo life. It was about how, when she was a young girl, she had come close to being sold to become the wife of a rich man. The practice of families selling their daughters as brides was once the norm among the Navajo, although today most people, including a lot of Navajos, imagine this practice died out long ago. But Nancy told me she was almost sold twice in the 1960s, when she was about thirteen or fourteen years old. She escaped in the end, only because her mother would not permit it.

It's difficult to be sure when the practice of buying young girls as brides—or selling them, depending on your point of view—actually ceased. It was widespread in the 1920s and 1930s, and when I first came to the Southwest it was still possible to meet old Navajo ladies who remembered the practice well, although I never discovered if any of them had been bought as brides. It appears to have remained relatively common until after the Second World War, but in the 1950s the practice went into a steep decline. This may have had to do with young Navajo servicemen and women returning from the war with fresh ideas from the world outside the reservation but, whatever the reason, by the 1960s it was on its last legs. And, as Nancy's story makes clear, no longer acceptable to a younger generation.

The price for a bride was traditionally paid in horses or sheep. Prices varied, but six to eight good horses, or ten to twenty sheep, was reckoned a fair price for a well brought up and accomplished girl of fourteen or fifteen. Even today, traditional Navajo families may insist on a gift of sheep or horses prior to a wedding, although this is only a vestige of what was once an age-old practice.

Actually, to use terms like "bought" or "sold" is to misunderstand Navajo customs. What was happening, was that a payment known to anthropologists as a "bride price" was being given as compensation to the girl's family for losing their daughter. At one time bride price payments were practically universal, and they persist in many parts of the world today, notably in Thailand and parts of Africa and China. Nor should readers imagine this practice was unknown in the United States and Europe. Similar payments were common in American and European society well into the twentieth century, and were known as dowry. A dowry is the reverse of bride price, being a gift of wealth given by the bride's family to the groom's family for their daughter's upkeep. Regardless of who gives what to whom, the important thing from an anthropological point of view is that Navajos, Chinese, Asians, Europeans, Americans, and tribes in Africa, are united in once having shared an almost universal practice of an exchange of wealth between families to cement a wedding agreement.

As families are generally reluctant to give away large slices of their wealth to their in-laws, among European and American families it was usual on the death of the wife or the husband—or in more modern times a divorce—for the dowry to revert to the bride and her family. And this is one major difference between the Navajo bride price and a Western dowry: the Navajo husband's family will not get their horses and sheep back, no matter how badly things turn out.

Old ladies I met among the Navajo were not at all averse to the practice of bride price, and their reasons are worth recording. First, they told me, when they were young there was a big disparity between the number of men and women on the reservation. How big a disparity is uncertain, but big enough that a substantial number of Navajo girls had little chance of finding a husband.

"So, if a man came for you with horses, you went," I remember one of these women telling me. "Because if you didn't, you probably wouldn't get another chance."

Another factor to remember is that the gift reassured the bride's family that if the groom's family could pay the price, the groom's family must be hard workers. This was doubly important in a Navajo context, because the Navajo are matrilocal. That is to say, husbands move to live with the family of the bride, and the bride's family needed men who knew how to work the land.

Having set the scene, I'll let Nancy tell her story, set at a time in the 1960s when the tribe was rapidly transitioning away from ancient traditions, and into the modern world. She began by explaining the way she and her family lived at that time:

"We all lived in a hogan, me, my mother, my brothers and sisters and my aunt, and she had a boy as well; and it was not far from where Blue Horse lives with Baa now," she began.

"One night, when I was about thirteen years old, I went with some older girls to see a movie at the chapter house.[53] In those days they put on movies at the chapter house because people couldn't get into town because they had no vehicles. After the movie was over we started to walk home, when some boys came with a car and wanted us to go to Gallup with them. The other girls were older than me, about seventeen or eighteen, and they wanted to go, but I said, 'No, I have to go home.' So, they drove off and left me to walk home in the dark by myself. I was nearly home, down in the dip where the canyon is, when I heard a voice behind me. It was Tony, a boy who lived near us, and he asked what I was doing out by myself in the dark. I told him, and he said, 'You shouldn't be alone out here in the dark. I'll walk home with you,' which he did.

---

53 A chapter house is a local administrative and community center, of which there are many on the reservation.

"I thought nothing of it, but the next day, Tony's parents came over to see my mother, which they'd never done before. She gave them something to eat, and they all sat on the floor of the hogan and talked for a while, until my mother asked them straight out why they had come. Then Tony's father said, 'Your daughter must marry my son.'

"When my mother asked why, he said it was because we'd been out together in the dark. They thought we'd been up to something we shouldn't, you see, which we hadn't. Tony was a nice boy, and I liked him, but I didn't want to marry him.

"Tony's people were well off and had plenty of cattle and sheep, and they would have given sheep for me. The price was usually between ten and twenty sheep. My mother refused, but they weren't satisfied and came back more than once. But still my mother refused. They were very angry about it, but there was nothing they could do, because my mother said no and wouldn't change her mind.[54]

"A few months later—I'm not sure if I was still thirteen or had turned fourteen by then—an old man came to our hogan. I say old, he looked old to me, but he was probably about fifty years old. He was known to be very rich, and he wore magnificent turquoise jewelry; it was huge, some of the biggest jewelry I've ever seen. He told my mother he wanted me for his wife. He said that although he was rich, he was all alone and wanted a wife to share his home. I don't know how much he offered, but it was probably in horses, as he was a rich man, and he had land as well as cattle, sheep, and horses. About five or six good horses would usually do, although it could be more.

"Again, my mother refused, and this man became very angry and told her, 'You won't live for another six months, and she'll follow after you, unless you give her to me'. He was a rich and powerful man, and no one would doubt his word. But still my mother refused, and he went away very angry and swearing vengeance on us. I think I must have been

---

54 Such decisions rested entirely with the female side of the family, the mothers and grandmothers. The male side of the family, fathers and grandfathers, were not consulted and had no say in such matters.

very frightened of him, but if my mother had agreed, I would have had to go. I'd have had no choice, because girls did as their mothers told them in those days. I don't know what my duties would have been as a wife, except for the obvious sexual ones. Probably, I would have been little better off than a slave and expected to do whatever I was told. There would have been no need for a wedding ceremony. He would have handed over the horses, and I would have gone with him as his wife, and that would have been that.

"I suppose people today would ask, 'What would have happened if the white authorities had found out about it?' The answer is nothing, because they never would have found out. Even if they had, there was nothing they could have done, because it was happening among Navajos on the reservation. In those days, white people didn't come on to the reservation—you never saw them driving around like they do now; they stayed on Route 66.[55] What if the Navajo police had found out? Nothing. It was a contract between two families, and even if they'd known about it, the police wouldn't have interfered because many of them had acquired wives in the same way. No matter how much I objected, I couldn't have gone against my mother if she'd insisted I had to do it, that was the way it was in those days. The only thing I could have done was tell my brothers that I didn't want to go, and they probably would have moved me off the reservation to Gallup, so he wouldn't be able to have me. But that's the only way I could have escaped from it.

"One night, sometime after this man had made those threats against us, I was coming back through the canyon in the dark. In those days we had to collect our water in five-gallon containers from the stream that comes out of the wall of the canyon, and we women carried one in each hand: that's more than eighty pounds of water, more than forty pounds in each hand. Well, I heard this noise, it was someone chanting and shaking a rattle. I looked in the bushes and saw it was the rich man, and I knew he was making bad medicine against us.

---

55 Now I-40.

"Sometime later, but within the six-month period he'd warned us about, it was raining heavily and my mother was crossing Route 66. Even with the rain and so on, I don't know how she failed to see that truck, but she didn't, and it hit her and she was killed.[56] After that, I left the reservation and went to Gallup, and so his bad medicine against me was left behind on the reservation.

"Do I think things girls still get sold like that today? I couldn't say for sure. Obviously, it doesn't happen much anymore, but there are places on the reservation that are isolated enough that a young girl could be sold like that. Who'd know if it was an agreement between two families? There's no way anyone would know unless the girl complained, and it's not likely she would go against her mother and her family, especially not after horses and sheep have been given. In any case, you shouldn't assume the girls were always unwilling. Many of them were only too happy to get away from their families and get a rich man for a husband. Even if he's a lot older, if he treats you right and gives you presents, there's no reason why you'd want to complain, especially not after you've had your first child."

Nancy told me this and many other stories as we were driving along through the night, and in this way we passed the night driving from Arizona to Anadarko, Oklahoma, where we arrived shortly after dawn.

The next day, after we'd recovered from the journey, we visited nearby Fort Sill, where the last Comanche war chief Quanah Parker is buried. It was Quanah who brought the peyote medicine ceremony from Mexico, and it was from the Comanche that the medicine ceremony and the peyote religion spread to the other tribes, including the Navajo. Also buried at Fort Sill is Geronimo, and it was a rare honor to visit his grave in the company of his grand-child Nelsie.

∗ ∗ ∗

---

56 At the time Route 66 was a two-lane highway with one lane in each direction and not much wider than a suburban street. It took only a few seconds for a pedestrian to cross, which makes the death of Nancy's mother more difficult to understand, but easier for Navajos to attribute to witchcraft.

Shortly after returning from Anadarko, I found myself in a lively discussion with Blue Horse and Lydia, another of Baa's daughters, about horses, sheep, marriage and tradition. Blue Horse and Lydia both agreed that the practice of buying young brides with horses and sheep had continued into the 1950s, but had died out during the 1960s; which squared pretty exactly with what Nancy Kapatop had said. Blue Horse said he thought twelve good horses and some money would be needed for a wedding. Lydia said she'd heard all sorts of amounts, but both agreed it was for the mother and grandmother to decide whether the girl should go as a bride, and what the price should be.

"The woman gives birth, so it's up to the mother and grandmother to decide, because it's their daughter," Lydia told me. "Men keep out of it. It's nothing to do with them, the fathers, the brothers. They keep out. Maybe you offer six horses, and the mother says, 'My daughter's expensive. She's been brought up right. She's going to be real good for you—look after your home, have children for you. You need to offer more'. So, you give twelve horses and some money, and then it's all right."

Blue Horse added, "But then you don't take her to your place. You have to go and live with the in-laws, and they give you tests to do. You have to chop wood. Butcher a sheep. Maybe break in a horse for them. You have to show you can do the things a man can do. If you fail, they send you away, and the marriage is off."

"Do you get your horses back?" I asked.

"No!" Blue Horse almost shouted for emphasis. "You failed, so you don't get nothin' back. You go away, learn the proper skills, and try again somewhere else. Some families with pretty daughters probably got a lot of horses that way, I don't know. But if you pass the tests, then you build a house on her family's land and live there with her. It had to be a hogan you built; a trailer like they have now wouldn't do. You had to show you could build a home."

With Nancy's story in mind about the rich older man who'd come to buy her when she was a teenager, I asked what they thought would have happened if a rich older man who already had a home, horses, land, and sheep had come for a girl. Would a rich man have to pass these tests, or would he just take the girl home with him?

Blue Horse said that even a rich man would still have to go and live with his in-laws for a while to make himself acceptable, and probably have to perform at least some of the tasks listed above. Only once his in-laws were sure he would make a suitable husband would they allow him to take their daughter away from them. I said this sounded like a sensible insurance policy to protect a girl from marrying the wrong man, and they agreed.

"These are our traditions going way, way, back, long time ago," Blue Horse said. "Even today, a traditional family will want to see a male in-law can do the things a man should do. The family can still insist on horses or sheep as part of the deal, and don't expect to get 'em back."

Both Blue Horse and Lydia agreed that brides were no longer acquired in the old way, adding mysteriously, as had Nancy, "so far as anyone knows." Like Nancy, they thought it was possible such a thing could still happen in the more isolated places on the reservation, but they were far from sure if it did.

Later, after coffee, Blue Horse and I went outside to chop wood for the stove. We were alone in the yard discussing poor Baa's injuries, when Blue Horse unexpectedly asked if I was carrying the gun with the ash-tipped bullets he'd recommended; and I had to admit that I was not.

"They got my wife," he said. "I feel bad I couldn't protect her."

There was no doubt, he said, that the attack was the result of witchcraft. So, I had to ask if I was the cause of the trouble; if the witchcraft had been aimed at me, but had struck Baa instead? It was a difficult question to answer and, in fact, Blue Horse did not answer it. Preferring to speak in a roundabout fashion, he said neither "yes" nor "no", but indicated that if I learned more about such matters—as he wanted me to—such questions would resolve themselves.

But I was reluctant to take the path he was urging me along, that would lead me deeper into Navajo medicine and learning. I was already finding it difficult to separate my life as a white man from my life as a Navajo medicine man's apprentice. In the parallel world I inhabited between western civilization and the Navajo, it was becoming increasingly difficult to interpret events such as the attack on Baa as anything other than evidence of witchcraft. This, despite the fact that I knew that not so long ago I would never have entertained such a thought. I might have nodded politely when Navajos said it was witchcraft, but privately I would never have believed such a thing. Now, it was becoming increasingly difficult not to believe it, because I saw so much evidence of witchcraft all around me. I knew this was a danger sign; a sure sign of losing objectivity and independence; and if I lost that, how could anybody have confidence in me? How could anyone be sure I was telling the truth about events that had taken place before my eyes?

On the other hand, what if the Navajos were right? What if our western society's modern rejection of witches and witchcraft was wrong? After all, I'd seen enough evidence that witches and witchcraft are real, and I had to admit I'd seen Blue Horse perform many remarkable feats. So many, that it was becoming difficult to think anything other than that he possessed powers outside the ordinary. And if Blue Horse possessed such powers, why not the witchmen? And then there was Baa.

"They didn't manage to kill her," I pointed out. It was meant as a comfort, but when I thought of the serious injuries she'd suffered it was no comfort at all. Also, whether this particular piece of witchcraft was aimed at me, or at Baa, or anyone else in the family, or whether it was real or not, it meant I could not leave. In truth, I'd been contemplating calling an end to my exploration of Blue Horse's world for some time. My field diaries ran to hundreds of thousands of words, and I had more than enough to write several books like this one. I didn't need to stay, and I didn't want to enter the deeper and more difficult levels of Navajo magic and sorcery that Blue Horse was inviting me into.

But after the attack by the ram, I felt that whatever I might think of witchcraft; the important thing was that the Navajos believed it. And if they believed they were under attack from witchmen, I could not abandon them in this crisis. So, I explained to Blue Horse that I wouldn't walk away and leave him, Baa, Fox and the rest of the family, to face dangers that it may have been my fault to have brought upon them. His answer astonished me.

"You can go if you want," he replied nonchalantly, making it sound as if it really didn't matter one way of the other.

"Don't you want me to help you?" I blurted out. "I'm your apprentice after all!"

"Before you can be of any use you have to learn more, and you can't learn more because you don't believe," he said. "You have to believe in what I teach you. You have to shut your eyes and walk forward when I tell you, even if it means walking over the highest cliff in the world. You have to believe you can do that, you have to believe in our ways; that our ways and traditions will hold you up and you won't fall, or you can't learn anything. And you can't, because you don't believe. You're a man who doesn't believe in his heart what I show him and teach him, so there's nothin' more I can teach you," Blue Horse finished, and he never sounded more serious.

"But you've taught me so much," I protested, and at this he laughed out loud.

"A little child thinks the yard at the back of his house is the world," he scoffed. "He knows the yard, so he thinks he knows everythin'. But if his parents don't look after him he'll die, because he doesn't even know how to feed himself. You don't even know the yard, you just think you do. Me, I've been a medicine man for more than forty years and I hardly know nothin'. There's old medicine men up there in the hills that know a thing or two and maybe, one day, I'll know somethin' too; but right now, I know nearly nothin', and you don't know nothin' at all. Go and write your books for the bilagaana people, and probably they'll think you're very clever, and me too, probably; not that I care. But I'm tellin' you, what you know is less than one grain of sand in this desert, and me ..." He paused for a moment to bend down and take a pinch of the desert floor between his right thumb and finger. Then he threw the sand grains to the wind and held out his hand to show me the few tiny grains of sand still stuck to the sweat of his fingers.

"Me, if I knew even this much of all this—and he pointed to the trackless desert—then I'd be wise. But I don't." And he rubbed his hands together to remove the last clinging grains. "If you gonna learn anythin', you first gotta learn that you know nothin'. Nothin' at all."

"You mean that Navajo learning is bigger than this desert?" I asked, I wasn't sure I was following him.

"It was. In the old days it was; much bigger. In those days our medicine men knew everythin' in the world there was to know," he assured me, then he laughed again. "And in the stars too, probably. Now, today, I don't know; I only know what I know."

Before I could say anything more, he began to enumerate the changes that had come over me since I became his apprentice and started to use the medicine.

"Your life's different now," he reminded me. "You used to live in England; now you don't. You used to work in an office; now you don't. You hated every day; now you don't. You were unhappy; now you're not. You didn't know what to do, or where to go, then you stayed here and that was good; and all this because of the medicine. Because you take the medicine, you listen to the medicine, you believe in the medicine, and so it changed your life. You know that's true."

"Yes," I replied honestly. "It is true."

"You believe that, but you don't want to believe in the rest of it?" He asked pointedly. "Does that make sense? There's a long way to go, Charles. You're gettin' there, but there's a long way to go. Many things I got to teach you, many things you got to learn, but you got the main one."

"What's that?"

"You respect the medicine, and it likes you. That's where it all begins."

"What should I do?" I asked.

"Don't ask me, ask the medicine. It'll know what to do." he said, reassuringly.

The sun was going down in a fiery sunset, so startlingly lurid it looked as if the whole of the western sky was one huge red and orange inferno, and in its dying moments it cast long black shadows over the pale desert sand. A small bird perched on a cactus and pecked at some succulent morsel and then flew away. A deer appeared for a moment in a patch of junipers, then disappeared without a sound among the lengthening shadows. Above us the first stars were coming out, one by one, and I knew it was time to choose.

"When?" I asked. "When can I do this?"

Gently he placed a hand on my shoulder and, turning me around, began to walk me slowly back toward the house.

"Tomorrow," he said. "We can talk about it tomorrow."

The End